Joan Crawford
in Film Noir

Joan Crawford in Film Noir

The Actress as Auteur

DAVID MEUEL

McFarland & Company, Inc., Publishers
Jefferson, North Carolina

ISBN (print) 978-1-4766-9147-3
ISBN (ebook) 978-1-4766-5252-8

LIBRARY OF CONGRESS AND BRITISH LIBRARY
CATALOGUING DATA ARE AVAILABLE

Library of Congress Control Number 2024004649

Front cover image: Joan Crawford in *Mildred Pierce*, 1945
(Warner Bros. Pictures/Photofest)

Printed in the United States of America

McFarland & Company, Inc., Publishers
Box 611, Jefferson, North Carolina 28640
www.mcfarlandpub.com

Once again,
to Kathryn

And this time,
to Peter and Ann, Mary and Craig,
and Betty and Michael

Acknowledgments

Although a book may only have one credited author, numerous people help in many ways to move a project from concept to completion, and I would like to thank several people in my life for their cogent insights on film, excellent listening skills, patience, and support as this book has taken shape. Specifically, these are Jimmy Meuel, Annette Hulbert, Elliot Lavine, Bonnie Rattner, Bob and Melanie Ferrando, Jim Daniels, Peter Nelson, Natalie Varney, and Paul Bendix.

I would also like to acknowledge a great debt to the work of the scores of film critics and scholars whose various books, articles, and interviews have been indispensable to this project. Their names are all listed in this book's bibliography.

Finally, I would like to extend a very special thanks to my long-time friend Mary Scott ("Scotty") Martinson for devoting both her expertise and many hours of her time to editing the manuscript. This is the sixth book of mine that she has edited, and her work is, as it always has been, highly valued and greatly appreciated.

Table of Contents

Author's Note

Today, it is almost impossible to write about Joan Crawford in any depth without addressing the highly negative public perception of her that continues to persist decades after her death. Central to this perception, of course, are *Mommie Dearest*, the best-selling 1978 memoir by Crawford's adopted daughter Christina and the 1981 film based on it starring an over-the-top, scenery-chewing Faye Dunaway as Crawford. Together, the book and the film present a deeply disturbing and, I believe, highly distorted monster-like image of the actress, one which quickly entered, and continues to linger in, the public imagination. Also contributing to this perception are several sensationalized and poorly researched Crawford biographies. Largely for marketing purposes, these books have further marred the actress's legacy by focusing disproportionately (and often inaccurately) on the lurid parts of her life, often with nothing more substantial to support their claims than recycled Hollywood gossip. Altogether, these developments have helped to turn her, in many quarters, into a widely ridiculed and reviled camp figure. In fact, "No wire hangers!," the line screeched by Faye Dunaway's deranged Crawford at a terrified Christina in the film version of *Mommie Dearest*, may be the best-known and most widely used quote ever attributed to Crawford.

This tragedy has had many ramifications. The saddest of these, of course, is the destruction of Crawford's personal reputation. As a human being, the real Crawford may not have been all that she wanted the world to see her as, but she certainly wasn't the monstrous figure many people now assume she was. A second consequence is less apparent but, I believe, just as destructive to the actress's professional legacy. Widespread modern perceptions of her have led many filmgoers to see her work—which is often highly emotional and deeply personal—through an absurdist high-camp lens. People watch the actress on screen and can't help also seeing Crawford, the camp punchline. As a result, their viewing experience is greatly tainted and diminished.

My hope is that, the more completely classic film enthusiasts can put aside the image-bashing that has, for decades, distracted many of them from seeing Crawford's real, and quite substantial, professional achievements more clearly and fully, the better they will understand and appreciate her contributions both to her films in particular and to film overall. These are, perhaps more than any other aspects of her life, what make her a subject worthy of continuing study.

My wish is that everyone who chooses to read this book will approach it in this spirit.

Preface

Although I had known about Joan Crawford since I was a teenager in the 1960s, I only really began to discover her as an actress in 2010. This was, coincidentally, the same year that I began to look more closely at film noir, the cinema's enormously influential and much celebrated dark art.

The trigger event came on October 21, 2010, when I first saw Crawford in one of her great noir triumphs, 1952's *Sudden Fear*. Fortunately, I was watching an excellent print shown on the big screen in a revival theater, and I was, to put it mildly, stunned. This was a remarkable film, and Joan Crawford—the same Joan Crawford who had long before become a camp joke to many people—had delivered an astounding performance in it. Almost immediately, I began to see more of her films, revisit films I had seen but had probably dismissed too quickly, check out her television acting appearances, read books and articles on her, and watch interviews with her and documentaries about her.

What emerged from this decade-plus deep dive into Crawford was a transformation in my thinking about her and her work.

Most of what I learned is not news to those familiar with Crawford and her films. For example, she wasn't simply the glamorous, glitzy movie star people often typecast her as. She was also an accomplished, deeply committed actress capable of giving consistently good and occasionally great performances. In addition, she was an intelligent, highly professional business woman who consistently made shrewd, thoughtful career choices. Perhaps the best proof of her talent, commitment, and business savvy could very well be the most obvious: her longevity. Her career spanned forty-seven years, which was (as it continues to be) exceptional for a female star in Hollywood.

The more deeply I delved into Crawford's career, the more captivated I also became with one enormously important part of it: her work in, and substantial contribution to, classic-era film noir, which was pervasive in Hollywood throughout the 1940s and 1950s. Although rarely discussed in its totality, this is certainly one of her most impressive and far-reaching career achievements and a subject worthy of close, book-length examination.

Between 1941 and 1958, Crawford starred in a dozen films and a pair of television dramas that more than qualify as noirs or are, at the very least, deeply "noirish" in content and style. Several of these films contain what may very well be her best acting work. For her performances in three of them, she received Best Actress Academy Award nominations, one of which led to her Oscar win in 1946 for her work in *Mildred Pierce.* In several other of these films, her work, although passed over by Academy voters, was at least as good. And in all of these films, her personal stamp is also very much in evidence. These aren't conventional noirs, they are Joan Crawford noirs: highly distinctive films that, because of their distinctiveness, actually extended the boundaries of noir content and brought added depth and dimension to the noir style.

The way Crawford usually accomplished this is also very telling. Unlike most other actors and actresses who regularly adapted to the needs of particular film projects and directors, Crawford approached every film, first and foremost, as a Joan Crawford vehicle. For the first decade and a half of her career, she had worked tirelessly both to improve as an actress *and* to learn about every other facet of film production from the selection of content to screenwriting, directing, cinematography, lighting, and set and costume design. As she moved into her noir period, she also began to exert greater control over these and other production functions in her films, at times effectively operating as a de facto producer. This was extremely rare for a Hollywood actress during that time. In most cases, too, it brought considerable value to individual projects, resulting in higher quality films than would otherwise have been the case.

Not all of Crawford's noir and noir-tinged efforts released between 1941 and 1958 are among her best work. A few, in fact, are far from it and unwittingly helped to establish her as a camp figure in her later years and after her death. The majority, though, are well worth the time and attention of anyone interested in her work, film noir, or both.

By looking at these films as a collective and relatively cohesive body of work, and by delving deeply into most of them, we can get a much better understanding of what she aspired to achieve in her art, how—when the circumstances were right—she could deliver superb results, how she helped extend the boundaries of noir, and why the best of her efforts speak to us across the decades with such intensity and authority.

This is a fascinating and, I believe, quite significant story that needs to be told in this way.

◆ ◆ ◆

A final note: I want to emphasize that this book is *not* a biography of Crawford and should not be viewed as such. Although it often includes biographical details drawn from numerous sources to provide context and occasionally to bolster arguments, this book was conceived and developed mainly to be a critical evaluation of Crawford's work in, and contribution to, classic-era film noir.

There is, of course, certainly a need for additional research on, and perhaps a more definitive biography of, the actress's life. But the focus here—one that is mainly on the films themselves—is quite different.

Introduction

From Cinderella
to Cinema's Dark Art

As the year 1941 began, actress Joan Crawford, who for years had been one of Hollywood's most popular and bankable stars, was sensing a career reckoning ahead. She was only in her mid-thirties, but she had already been a fixture in Hollywood, and at the iconic Metro-Goldwin-Mayer (MGM) studio, for sixteen years. Now, her films weren't doing as well at the box office as they had been; her contemporaries and longtime rivals for the studio's plum roles, Norma Shearer and Greta Garbo, were both eyeing retirement; and murmurs were swirling about that Crawford, too, might be past her prime.

All this must have seemed quite disturbing to the intensely ambitious actress, who, for most of her sixteen years at MGM, had lived what millions of her ardent, mostly female fans had long assumed was a classic Cinderella story.

Born into an impoverished, dysfunctional family in Texas, most probably in 1906,[1] and named Lucille Le Sueur, the future Joan Crawford received limited formal education and spent much of her childhood working at menial jobs to help make ends meet. From an early age, though, Lucille had aspirations to be a dancer, worked hard at improving her skills, and eventually found work in traveling dance companies. Then, in late 1924, she was chosen from a group of chorus dancers in New York to go to Hollywood to work at newly formed and extremely well-resourced MGM. Lucille, who had never acted and had only seen six movies in her life, wanted desperately to dance, nothing else. Still, MGM was paying her seventy-five dollars a week for a full six months, higher pay and more job security than she had ever had. Harry Rapt, the MGM talent scout who had "discovered" her, was quite impressed. "I knew that she had that rare thing—personality," Rapt told a magazine

5

writer at the time. "She is beautiful, but more essential than beauty is that quality known as screen magnetism. Even before we made camera tests of her, I felt that she possessed this great asset. Her tests proved it."[2]

On January 3, 1925, at the height of Hollywood's silent film era, Lucille arrived in Los Angeles. A few days later, she signed her MGM contract and, shortly after this, realized that, if she were going to last at MGM, dancing would not be enough: she would have to learn how to act. Soon, she was given her new name, Joan Crawford, and non-speaking and bit parts in movies starring Shearer, John Gilbert, Ramon Novarro, and other top MGM players.

All seemed to be progressing nicely, but Crawford was anxious about failing and worried about someday getting a one-way train ticket back to the poverty and dysfunction she'd come from. So, when she wasn't working, she spent as much time as she could watching MGM's veteran actors, directors, cinematographers, lighting technicians, art and costume designers, and virtually every other kind of artist or artisan involved in film production. If she wanted to increase her chances of succeeding in this business, she reasoned, she would have to improve on her personal best continuously. To do this most effectively, her reasoning continued, she would have to learn as much about the business as possible.

In addition, these experiences led to insights that served her well throughout her professional life. By watching and learning, she began to see film production from a more holistic perspective than most of her acting peers did. Filmmaking, she realized, was a highly collaborative process, one in which the quality of any contributor's work could have a profound impact on the quality of any film she was acting in as well as its success, or failure, at the box office. Gradually, she became more assertive about virtually every aspect of film production that affected her from writing to costuming, to make-up, to lighting, suggesting changes she believed would be both in her interest and the film's.

By 1927, she had moved up to ingenue roles, and, in a dark thriller-romance set in the circus world called *The Unknown*, she was assigned to work with one of Hollywood's most respected character actors, Lon Chaney.

During the filming, Crawford watched Chaney's work closely and quickly developed an intense admiration for his approach. "[With him] I became aware for the first time of the difference between standing in front of a camera and acting," she later said. "Until then I had been conscious only of myself. Lon Chaney was my introduction to acting. The concentration, the complete absorption he gave to his characterization, filled me with such awe that I could scarcely speak to him."[3] Describing the dramatic conclusion of *The Unknown*, she also recalled how Chaney "was able to convey not just realism but such emotional agony that it was both shocking and fascinating."[4]

The experience made an enormous impact on the young actress. "He demanded a lot of me," she said. "Watching him gave me the desire to be a real actress."[5] She worked hard to deliver an excellent performance, effectively portraying a character who was repelled by certain aspects of the Chaney character while also being quite sympathetic towards him. The critics also took note. As one reviewer at the time, Langdon W. Post of the *New York Evening World*, wrote, "Joan Crawford is one of the screen's acknowledged artists. Certainly, her performance in this picture is a most impressive one."[6]

The following year, and after some hard behind-the-scenes lobbying on her part, Crawford was assigned her first lead role. The film was *Our Dancing Daughters*, a romantic drama about the Roaring Twenties party set. An instant hit with the public, *Our Dancing Daughters* quickly raked in six times its production costs at the box office, and, with the same lightning-like speed, Joan Crawford became a star.

The literati took notice as well. After seeing Hollywood's newest star on screen, F. Scott Fitzgerald, the novelist and astute chronicler of 1920s manners and mores, famously wrote, "Joan Crawford is doubtless the best example of the flapper, the girl you see in smart night clubs, gowned to the apex of sophistication, toying iced glasses with a remote, faintly bitter expression, dancing deliciously, laughing a great deal, with wide, hurt eyes. Young things with a talent for living."[7]

Unlike many of her silent film contemporaries, Crawford found the move to sound films to be relatively easy. She was a fresh face, was perceived as very modern (in contrast to such silent screen veterans as Mary Pickford and Lillian Gish), and had a pleasant speaking voice.

In addition, Crawford did something that was quite remarkable and, even today, rarely discussed. In a very short time, about three years, she had learned how to excel at silent film acting. When she moved to sound films, she began to apply methods she'd learned for the old medium to the new. The eventual result was a fascinating, if not unique, melding of the best technique of silent film acting with the best technique of sound film acting that often gave her performances great authenticity, depth, and emotional resonance. Just as she could excel at delivering a critical line of dialog, she could communicate complex and often conflicting feelings in split-seconds with extremely precise and very credible facial expressions and other body language. By continuing to use and refine these visual techniques throughout her long career in what has always been a mainly visual medium, Crawford was able to give her best performances a highly distinctive and emotionally rich quality.

As the U.S. moved from the high-flying 1920s to the economically depressed 1930s, Crawford's producers at MGM quickly saw that the young actress was at her most effective when the characters she played on screen mirrored her (or at least the popular image of her) real-life rags-to-riches story—the scrappy woman from humble beginnings whose grit and determination eventually lead her to success, wealth, true love, or some combination of these. Crawford, who firmly believed that audiences would strongly identify with this kind of character, fully supported efforts to develop these kinds of roles for her, and, during the 1930s, she made a number of popular films that more or less followed this formula. Audiences called them "Joan Crawford pictures." Studio head Louis B. Mayer saw her as MGM's modern-day Cinderella, the very

In the lively musical-romance *Dancing Lady* (1933), Crawford's Janie Barlow is, as was usually the case in 1930s Joan Crawford pictures, torn between at least two suitors. In this instance, she longs to be with Clark Gable's theatrical director Patch Gallagher (left) while Franchot Tone's millionaire playboy Todd Newton (right) longs to be with her (MGM/ Photofest).

relatable star who repeatedly proved to a legion of loyal female fans that, yes, even during the Great Depression, fairy tale endings were possible. And for most of the decade, this pairing of star and formula made MGM millions of dollars.

Today, a good number of these so-called Joan Crawford pictures remain quite interesting. Among this author's favorites are four released between 1931 and 1937. These include Clarence Brown's *Possessed* (a 1931 film that shares the title with another Crawford effort released in 1947 but is a completely different story), Robert Z. Leonard's *Dancing Lady* (1933), Brown's *Sadie McKee* (1934), and Frank Borzage's *Mannequin* (1937). All share the elements of the classic Cinderella story. Yet, while they all generally adhere to the formula, individual films diverge in various ways. In *Dancing Lady*, for example, her chorus-girl character is pursued by a playboy but eventually wins the heart of her true soulmate, a Broadway producer who understands and appreciates her passion to dance. In *Possessed* and *Mannequin*, each Crawford character solidifies her relationship with her Prince Charming, but only as both men face major setbacks, one politically, the other financially. Both films end with her character standing by her man and committing to help rebuild their lives together: vivid demonstrations that, as well as spunk, these heroines have character. In *Sadie McKee*, the road to happiness is even bumpier: the Crawford character loves one man who leaves her, marries another she doesn't love, divorces him, and, in the end, may be getting together with a third man who has long loved her but that she has misunderstood.

About the time of *Mannequin*, however, clear signs were emerging that the tried-and-true combination of star and formula that had been the essence of a Joan Crawford picture was beginning to lose its box office luster. Although the film made money, profits weren't nearly as impressive as they had been with previous Crawford vehicles. *Possessed*, for example, had made four times its production costs. Likewise, the relatively expensive *Dancing Lady* had made two and a half times its production costs. In addition, there was growing evidence that *Mannequin's* tepid box office performance was part of a disturbing trend. The films Crawford made immediately before and after *Mannequin*, for example, *The Bride Wore Red* (1937) and *This Shining Hour* (1938), barely made more than their production costs.

Then, on May 4, 1938, an advertisement in a film industry publication *The Hollywood Reporter* rocked the U.S. film production and distribution communities. It was written by Harry Brandt, the head of an industry group called the Theatre Owners Association, and it was titled "WAKE UP! Hollywood Producers." In the ad, Brandt listed a number of actors who he felt weren't worth the salaries they were receiving from their studios and, therefore, were drags on the entire film industry. He called them "poison at the box office,"[8] a phrase that has since entered popular culture as the slightly altered and catchier "box-office poison." Among those listed—along with such stars as Mae West, Katharine Hepburn, Greta Garbo, Marlene Dietrich, and Kay Francis—was Joan Crawford.

When queried by the press, Crawford, who had just signed a lucrative new five-year contract with MGM, laughed off the advertisement. Yet, as someone who had always been strongly focused on her own professional survival, the "poison" label must have been quite disturbing. In a memoir she wrote in the early 1960s, she recounted what a friend of hers, a silent- and early sound-film actor named William "Billy" Haines, had once told her about how it felt when his career began to slide. "It was," he said, "like walking on nothing."[9] At the time, she hadn't fully understood the chilling remark. Now, in 1938, it must have resonated to the core of this self-made woman who had once so deeply dreaded the prospect of MGM sending her back to her family with a one-way train ticket.

Something needed to be done.

To counter the "box-office poison" label, she knew she had to come

Director George Cukor meets with key cast members of *The Women* (1939). Shown standing from left to right are Cukor, Phyllis Povah, Paulette Goddard, Crawford, Rosalind Russell, Norma Shearer, and Florence Nash. In front sitting is Mary Boland (MGM/Photofest).

up with a nugget of box-office gold: a great role in a hit film. Always on the hunt for plum parts, she lobbied for the small but key supporting role of Crystal Allen, the trashy bad girl who steals a good woman's husband away from her in MGM's upcoming film adaptation of Clare Boothe Luce's hit Broadway play *The Women*. Louis Mayer objected to the idea, saying both that the role was too small for a star of Crawford's stature and that playing Crystal would hurt her carefully cultivated Cinderella screen persona. She persisted nevertheless, winning over the film's director, the highly respected George Cukor, and getting him to support her cause. Eventually, she won out, played the role to perfection, received rave notices, and helped to make *The Women* one of the big hits of 1939.

In the process, Crawford had also taken an important step forward in influencing her professional destiny. By lobbying to play Crystal Allen, she was consciously trying to break the mold, a move that would lead, she hoped, to more widespread acceptance of her, not just as a movie star, but also as a real actress who could ably tackle a range of roles and, as a result, continue to stay fresh and relevant.

Trying to build on her success in playing against type, Crawford soon accepted two new roles, both radical departures from the Cinderella persona. The first of these was Julie, a world-weary cabaret singer and prostitute in the Frank Borzage–directed *Strange Cargo* (1940), a gritty romantic drama that also aspired to religious allegory. Along with the film, she received mixed-to-unenthusiastic reviews. The second was Susan Trexel, a self-absorbed society matron whose newfound religious fervor alienates many of the people in her life, in *Susan and God* (1940) a tedious, stage-bound comedy-drama directed by Cukor. Although Crawford brought all her usual professionalism to the role, she was painfully miscast, and the film lost a significant amount of money. In the end, neither film did anything to further her career aspirations.

Soon, though, she would reunite with Cukor for a project that had intrigued her for more than a year and that she had been actively promoting for herself. This was to be a Hollywood remake of a 1938 Swedish film called *En kvinnas ansikte*, or *A Woman's Face*, and the story had, along with many dark undertones, a great lead role for an actress.

Then, as the year 1941 began—on January 23, 1941, to be exact—Crawford, Cukor, and company started production. When it premiered in late May of that year, *A Woman's Face* was a modest box-office success, but the big story for many critics who saw it was Crawford's performance. They were enthralled by how well she had captured a very dark, troubled, complex character and, with great insight, sensitivity, and skill, taken that character through a series of major life changes.

The portrayal was a triumph, with many critics and viewers discovering that this actress could do so much more than play variations of Cinderella. For the first time in her career, Crawford was the subject of serious Oscar buzz, and, while she ultimately wasn't nominated for a Best Actress Academy Award for her work in the film, she had emphatically made her case that she could deliver a world-class performance.

At the time, *A Woman's Face* didn't immediately resolve all of Crawford's career concerns. It didn't, for example, instantly lead to getting more of the high-quality roles she eagerly sought or to silencing the murmurs that she might be past her prime.

The experience of doing the film, however, did set her on a new career trajectory, one that would serve her quite well throughout most of the 1940s and 1950s. First, of course, the film had given her an opportunity to play a complex, nuanced character; follow through with a bravura performance; and, in the process, show both her industry colleagues and fans that, in addition to being a movie star, she was a serious and talented actress. Second, after continued frustration with studio-assigned roles, she had taken greater control over her professional destiny. Specifically, she had identified a property with an excellent female lead role, championed the property as the basis for a new film starring (to no one's surprise) Joan Crawford, and then driven the project forward. Without her initiative, determination, and persistence, this film would probably never have been made. Her success at both these tasks undoubtedly gave her a greater sense of professional self-worth and, in the future, would enable her to advocate more confidently and effectively for her various career interests. Finally, though she had no idea at the time, the film also served as her first foray into the dark, twisted world of what we today call film noir, a world she would regularly contribute to, continuously help reshape, and greatly benefit from for the better part of the next two decades.

Far from being past her prime, Joan Crawford was just entering it.

◆ ◆ ◆

Crawford's late–1930s and early–1940s professional ups and downs were occurring, of course, within an infinitely larger, and far more ominous, context, one in which Hollywood, the U.S., and much of the rest of the world were also facing major reckonings.

In Asia in January 1941, the military dictatorship in Japan, which, during the 1930s, had subjugated large areas of China, had just invaded French Indochina. Now, Japan's rulers were setting their sights on the Philippines and other possible Asia-Pacific targets.

In Europe, Adolf Hitler's totalitarian, antisemitic Nazi regime in

Germany—which, by late 1939, had already seized Austria, Czechoslovakia, Lithuania and Poland—had markedly stepped up its aggression. In 1940 alone, Germany's formidable war machine, in addition to delivering devastating bombing raids on England, had conquered Belgium, the Netherlands, Luxembourg, Denmark, Norway, France, Yugoslavia, and Greece. Now, it was finalizing plans to invade the vast Soviet Union.

It had been only two decades since the bitterly negotiated Treaty of Versailles had officially ended the deadliest and most destructive war ever waged, a war that had left twenty million dead and twenty-one million wounded soldiers and civilians in its wake. Now, a new worldwide conflict, one with the potential to be far deadlier and more destructive than the first, was underway. Hundreds of millions of people were already involved, and the U.S., for the moment still officially neutral, would almost certainly be called upon to play a pivotal role.

For much of the 1930s, Hollywood's major studios had partially distracted audiences from these grim and growing overseas realities by churning out light, escapist entertainments such as Fred Astaire–Ginger Rogers dance musicals, Cary Grant screwball comedies,[10] and, yes, Joan Crawford pictures. Now, these realities had become too imminent, too frightening, for more and more people to avoid by simply watching a Hollywood musical, comedy, or modern-day Cinderella story.

As all this weighed heavily on the general public, filmmakers, who wanted to reflect the darkening world landscape in their work, and studios, who wanted to remain relevant and commercially viable, responded. One result is that more and more films made during this time, especially in the traditional crime or gangster genre, began to exhibit a darker, harsher, more pessimistic tone. Screen violence (though mild by today's standards) was gradually becoming more intense, visceral, and graphic. Heroes could be weaker and more easily corruptible. Leading ladies, while still beautiful, were sometimes more manipulative and just pure evil, eventually earning themselves the unflattering label of "femme fatale," or "fatal woman." Characters were often more complex and contradictory, more nuanced psychologically, and more at the mercy of personal demons or serious character flaws. To ratchet up audience anxiety, these films were also photographed in very different ways from what audiences were used to seeing. Most were darkly lit, with scenes frequently taking place at night and on gloomy (and sometimes rainy) city streets. Shadows were prominent and usually meant to suggest menace or someone sinister. While musicals, westerns, and other kinds of films were gradually moving to color about this time, these darker, more downbeat films thrived in—in fact, seemed tailor made for—the more abstract, otherworldly, and emotionally detached film medium of black and white.

At the time, no one called these kinds of movies "film noir," or "the black film." The term didn't even exist until it was coined by the Italian-French film critic Nino Frank in 1946,[11] and it wasn't widely used until it began to appear in film criticism in the 1960s. For years, audiences simply referred to them as crime stories or melodramas. But whatever they were called in the early 1940s, there was, as many people at the time certainly sensed, something different about them, something bleaker and more foreboding than they were accustomed to, but also something that spoke to the moment, and to them, in a powerful, seductive way.

Although the soon-to-expand war in the Asia-Pacific region and Europe (and the more despairing attitudes it spawned) was certainly a driving force behind the emergence of these darker films, it was by no means the sole factor. The roots of film noir are many and varied. In literature, they go back to the "hard-boiled" school of crime fiction[12] that includes the work of Ernest Hemingway, Dashiell Hammett, Raymond Chandler, James M. Cain, Cornell Woolrich, and many, many other writers. In fact, classic film noirs have been made from Hemingway's *The Killers* (1946), Hammett's *The Maltese Falcon* (1941), Chandler's *The Big Sleep* (1946), Cain's *Double Indemnity* (1944) and *Mildred Pierce* (1945), and Woolrich's *The Black Angel* (1946). In film, the roots of noir date back to the German silent efforts of the 1920s that were heavily influenced by expressionism, the art of distorting visuals to suggest or reflect interior states of mind or to intensify mood or atmosphere.[13] Among early examples of these films are Robert Weine's *The Cabinet of Dr. Caligari* (1920), F.W. Murnau's *Nosferatu* (1922), and Fritz Lang's *Metropolis* (1927). Also in film, the U.S. gangster movies of the 1930s, which featured ample violence and terse, hard-hitting dialogue and sometimes depicted their outlaw anti-heroes as complex, somewhat sympathetic individuals, were quite influential. And, in the visual arts, the art deco movement of the 1920s and 1930s, which emphasized such features as bold geometries, intricate line art, and aerodynamic curves to create desired effects, played a major role in the "look" of many noirs.

Ironically for Hollywood within the context of noir's emergence, the dark cloud of Nazism also had a silver lining. As a direct result of Hitler's rise to power and military aggression in Europe, hundreds of Europe's most gifted film professionals, many of them Jewish and fearing for their lives, and all of them fiercely opposed to Hitler, migrated to the U.S. Among them were numerous film artists and artisans well-schooled in European expressionistic film techniques. Then, by the early and mid–1940s, a number of these people—including such directors as Fritz Lang, Robert Siodmak, Curtis Bernhardt, Anatole Litvak, and Billy Wilder—had, quite logically, established themselves as masters of noir.

Precisely, what elements define a film noir? This is a subject that film aficionados have argued about for decades. Some people are quite flexible in their definition, while others are quite rigid, insisting that a "real" noir must have all, or nearly all, the requisite components.

Briefly, a textbook noir is a film characterized by a number of content elements and presentation techniques. The main character, for example, is usually a man who, for greed, ambition, lust or a combination of these, starts down a crooked path he can't return from and must ultimately pay a stiff price, often either imprisonment or death. The impetus for his "wrong turn" is sometimes a seductive, scheming woman, the femme fatale. To help amplify the downbeat mood or feeling of the film, many distinctively noirish filmmaking style choices are made. Scenes, for example, can be darkly lit to add an ominous presence to characters and create anxiety among viewers. The use of flashbacks can reinforce the sense that a character's fate is preordained. Characters can provide voiceover narration to convey feelings of fear or anxiety they would conceal from other characters. Also, cameras can capture scenes from extremely high or low angles, conveying a sense that things are out of joint, not normal, not right, and adding to a viewer's general feelings of unease. While some classic noirs such as Wilder's *Double Indemnity* and Jacques Tourneur's *Out of the Past* (1947) satisfy even the strictest of noir purists, most noirs don't contain all or nearly all of the classic elements. Many, such as Max Ophüls's *The Reckless Moment* (1949) or Nicholas Ray's *In a Lonely Place* (1950), don't have a femme fatale, and some, such as Anthony Mann's *Railroaded!* (1947) or *Desperate* (1947), have unabashedly happy endings. In the end, deciding what is noir and what isn't may simply mean making a personal choice: if the film is sufficiently noir in tone and has enough noir elements in it to satisfy you, then it's noir; if it doesn't, it isn't.

Another subject that has often provoked spirited argument over the decades is the essential nature of noir: Is it a film genre or a filmmaking style? We can make a case for either of these designations, but, with the passing of time, more people seem to be opting for the latter. Although most noirs are crime films, the distinctive noir style has seeped into other established genres such as westerns, science-fiction and horror films, and even a few musicals. Rather than a genre, they've come to see it as a highly distinctive presentation style that can transcend specific genres.

In the title role, Peter Lorre (left) has a very unsettling effect on Margaret Tallichet's Jane (right) in Boris Ingster's eerie and quite effective _Stranger on the Third Floor_ (1940), many critics' choice as the first fully formed film noir (RKO Radio Pictures/Photofest).

Although film historians pretty much agree that the first true, fully formed film noir premiered in the 1940 and 1941 timeframe, it's interesting that there is still much disagreement on which of the noirish films that came out during this time is actually the first. A leading candidate from late 1940, for example, is Boris Ingster's _Stranger on the Third Floor_. Featuring Peter Lorre as the doomed man in the title role, some striking expressionistic sequences, the gorgeous, moody cinematography of Nicholas Musuraca, and some genuinely creepy scenes, it is filled with classic noir elements. Other possibilities, however, might be Raoul Walsh's gritty _They Drive by Night_, or even Alfred Hitchcock's moody, angst-filled _Rebecca_, which both premiered earlier in the year. Two other popular contenders from 1941 are Walsh's _High Sierra_ and John Huston's _The Maltese Falcon_. _The Maltese Falcon_ is a very slick, polished example of a hard-boiled crime novel brought to the big screen, and it features one of noir's iconic femmes fatales, Brigid O'Shaughnessy, played by the wonderful Mary Astor. But, if you prefer to be rigorously strict in your interpretation of noir, the only one of these films that really does take its flawed hero to his preordained doom is *High Sierra*.

These weren't the only films containing significant noir content released during this time, of course. One can make a strong case for several others, including William Wyler's *The Letter* from 1940, and, from 1941, H. Bruce Humberstone's *I Wake Up Screaming*, Mervyn LeRoy's *Johnny Eager*, Litvak's *Out of the Fog*, Josef von Sternberg's *The Shanghai Gesture*, and Hitchcock's *Suspicion*.

In addition—and quite significant to the subject of Joan Crawford's relationship with noir—one can also, and quite confidently, put Cukor's *A Woman's Face* on this list. Often called a straight drama or a melodrama, this film is also deeply noirish in content, tone, and style. It's not textbook noir in every respect, but it definitely contains as much noir content as *The Maltese Falcon*, *I Wake Up Screaming*, and scores of other films that are routinely categorized as noir. If we can accept *A Woman's Face* as, at the very least, noir-tinged, this means that Crawford's noir debut, which many contend occurred in *Mildred Pierce* in 1945, actually occurred in *A Woman's Face* in 1941.[14]

❖ ❖ ❖

Beginning with *A Woman's Face*, and continuing until 1956, Crawford starred in twenty films. Four of these were straight dramas, two comedies, the musical/romance *Torch Song* (1953), and the cult western *Johnny Guitar* (1954). The remaining twelve, the majority, more than qualify as noirs or are, at the very least, deeply noirish in content and style. These range from bleak, fatalistic stories such as *Mildred Pierce*, *Possessed*, *The Damned Don't Cry*, and *Queen Bee* to the noir woman-in-distress thriller *Sudden Fear*, to dramas and melodramas with significant noir content such as *A Woman's Face*, *Humoresque*, *Daisy Kenyon*, *Flamingo Road*, *This Woman Is Dangerous*, *Female on the Beach*, and *Autumn Leaves*.

Between 1953 and 1958, Crawford also starred in four half-hour television dramas. These include a pair of obscure but intriguing noir-infused efforts that first aired on the CBS anthology series[15] *General Electric Theater*: "The Road to Edinburgh" and "Strange Witness."

Because these efforts are quite distinctive, noir purists have often dismissed them as mongrelized noir, "noir-lite," or simply "women's pictures," the patronizing name given to female-centered melodramas that were a Hollywood staple from the 1930s to the 1960s.

A much more accurate and intriguing way to view them, however, may be as "aspirational noirs" that extended the boundaries of noir content and brought added depth and dimension to the noir style. Far from diluting or diminishing the cinema's dark art, they enhanced and enriched it, helping to pave the way for a wider range of female-oriented stories and perspectives in noir as well as opportunities for actresses to play roles other than noir stock-character femmes fatales or one-dimensional good girls.

In many ways, all these efforts are clearly in the noir mainstream. Depending on the specific story, example, they feature familiar noir content such as crime, personal betrayal, jealousy, madness, obsession, and fatalistic world views. In addition, they are amply supported by such standard noir stylistic elements as stark black-and-white lighting, off-kilter camera angles, flashbacks, edgy dialogue, voice-over narration, and intricate plots.

In other ways, however, they are decidedly different—not noir in the strictest, purist sense. While the vast majority of noirs center on flawed or disillusioned male protagonists presented in fairly straightforward ways, for example, Crawford's, as we might readily assume, center on the characters she plays, women who, while often flawed, are usually quite varied, complex, and nuanced.

This predominantly female perspective is one of the more fascinating aspects of a Crawford noir. First, it provides the opportunity to explore various female-centered themes few conventional noirs address. These can range from the challenges for working women to the roles and responsibilities of wives and mothers, to the limited opportunities for women to obtain power, all in a male-dominated society. Second, this perspective rejects many of the stereotypical roles that were often the only choices actresses had if they wanted to act in noirs. Crawford, for example, rarely played a femme fatale and never played a one-dimensional good girl. If anything, her films regularly subverted noir norms. Instead of the femme fatale, for example, they often featured the "homme fatale," a bad or otherwise flawed man who creates serious problems for her heroines.

Especially in an era of widespread condescension toward women in Hollywood films, it's also intriguing that this perspective, relative to most other films of the time, is somewhat less condescending. One reason for this may be that, in the development of these films, those involved—be it Crawford, her producer, and/or her director—paid more attention to getting perspectives about female experience from females. All of Crawford's noirs were directed by men, of course, because women had virtually been shut out of the directing profession at the time.[16] Most of these films, however—nine out of the twelve to be exact—were based on stories written by women, screenplays co-written by women, or both. These include *Mildred Pierce, Humoresque, Possessed, Daisy Kenyon, Flamingo Road, The Damned Don't Cry, Sudden Fear, Queen Bee,* and *Autumn Leaves.*

Overall, it may be more precise to characterize Crawford noirs or noirish efforts as hybrids that incorporate, and often synthesize, essential elements of three distinct kinds of Hollywood films. The first kind, of course, is the standard noir crime drama or melodrama. The second is the women's picture melodrama mentioned earlier. One aspect of many of these films included in some of Crawford's noirs is the need for the story's conflicted heroine to make a major choice, say, between two male suitors or between romance and responsibilities to others, that may determine the future course of her life and/or the lives of loved ones. The third is the Joan Crawford picture of the 1930s with a twist—the twist being that the Crawford character's rags-to-riches story arc is amended in a very noirish way to follow from rags to riches to ruin. The result is a kind of film filled with familiar elements from all three genres that is also utterly unique: the Joan Crawford noir melodrama.

Crawford, of course, was not alone in bringing a woman's perspective to the very male-focused noir world. Along with the various people who worked with her on her films, many others—including actresses more readily associated with noir such as Barbara Stanwyck, Ida Lupino, Joan Bennett, and Claire Trevor—were following similar paths during this time. What makes Crawford's contribution distinctive, if not altogether unique, is that, as a group, her noir efforts appear to be fairly unified in overall vision and execution. While the stories adapted for each project are different, her roles quite varied, and her filmmaking collaborators always shifting, the actress's personal imprint, her brand, if you will, is front and center in all of her films. It's little wonder that film writer Molly Haskell once called Crawford one of the very few actresses in studio-era Hollywood "who are their own genres."[17]

The "how" behind this is also quite unusual. Unlike most other actors and actresses who regularly adapted to the needs of particular film projects and directors, Crawford approached every film, first and foremost, as a Joan Crawford vehicle. Noir historian Eddie Muller has even taken this point further, calling Crawford "one of the genuine auteurs in Hollywood, especially during the peak of the film noir era."[18]

The actress as auteur—this may seem to be an odd connection to make, but there is a great deal to it. Crawford was not a film auteur in the traditional sense, not in the way we might use the term to describe directors who brought a strong, distinctive personal vision to their films such as Charlie Chaplin, John Ford, Alfred Hitchcock, or Billy Wilder. She didn't get the credit for writing, directing, or producing her films, but she did, especially during the noir era, exert great control over many of these functions in many ways. This was almost unprecedented for a Hollywood actress during this time. But the results, as we say, speak for themselves: because of who she was, what she knew about filmmaking, and how she exercised her power, she was instrumental both in establishing the essential nature and in improving the quality of many of these films.

From her very first years in Hollywood, when she was driven to improve in her craft by learning as much as she could every facet of film production, Crawford added to her knowledge. Gradually, she had more and more to say about the selection of story properties to be filmed, the selection of writers, script development, the casting of other actors, direction, costume and set design, make-up, cinematography, and virtually every other major component of the filmmaking process. "I never worked with an actor who knew so much about film," Vincent Sherman, who directed her in three films in the early 1950s, once said about her.[19] This was high praise, especially when it came from a person who had also directed such brilliant actors and astute film industry figures as Ida Lupino, Bette Davis, Humphrey Bogart, and Claude Rains.

◈ ◈ ◈

The journey through the noir years that eventually yielded these results for Crawford was not without its professional challenges. But, being the resourceful, intensely ambitious competitor that she was, she continued to pivot and do whatever was necessary to turn these challenges into opportunities for continued success.

When the good roles she had hoped to get at MGM after her fine work in A Woman's Face didn't materialize, for example, she made one of the riskiest, and shrewdest, decisions of her career. In June of 1943, she left MGM, which had been her professional home for eighteen and a half years, and signed with Warner Brothers. Her new agreement didn't offer her an enormous amount of money, but it did give her something she had long sought: a major role in the filmmaking process. She would have script approval. She would also have input, and often final say, on the selection of actors and actresses, the cinematographer, the set and costume designers, and other key contributors to her films. In addition, the agreement led to a strong, extremely productive professional relationship with Jerry Wald, a smart, perceptive Warner Brothers producer who understood Crawford extremely well and worked closely with her on most of her best mid- and late 1940s films.

Combine this arrangement with Crawford's own very forceful personality and she became a particularly formidable presence. Frequently, for instance, she demanded—and got—extensive script rewrites, the dismissals of cast members and production personnel whose work dissatisfied her, and much, much more.

All this duly noted, what Crawford and her various Warner Brothers colleagues did during the mid- and late 1940s was nothing less than remarkable. Most significantly, in films such as *Mildred Pierce, Humoresque, Possessed, Flamingo Road*, and *The Damned Don't Cry*, their work formed the lion's share of her very substantial contribution to noir.

Despite these results, the cycle repeated itself in 1951 and 1952. Again, Crawford saw prospects at her home studio drying up, and again, she took a calculated risk, leaving a secure situation to pursue an uncertain opportunity. This time, it was to make an independent film on which she would function as de facto producer as well as star. The result was *Sudden Fear*, an exceptionally well crafted and enormously successful woman-in-distress noir thriller, over which she supervised virtually every facet of production. As *Mildred Pierce* had done seven years earlier at Warner Brothers, *Sudden Fear* revitalized her career, opening doors to more projects, including several noirs and noir-tinged films, throughout the 1950s.

Also of note is the quality of Crawford's performances in several of these films, especially those from *Mildred Pierce* to *Sudden Fear*. Her work during this time brilliantly conveys the complex, often conflicting emotions of a range of characters from a neurotic mother to a schizophrenic, to a gangster's gun moll, to a successful Broadway playwright, with great clarity and conviction. For this seven-year period—the height of the classic noir era—she was as good as any actress in Hollywood. This is perhaps why she received, in addition to much critical acclaim, Best Actress Academy Award nominations for *Mildred Pierce, Possessed*, and *Sudden Fear* as well as her only Oscar win for *Mildred Pierce* (which she firmly believed had been at least partially secured by her earlier work in *A Woman's Face*). A strong case can also be made that she deserved an additional Academy Award nomination in *Humoresque*, which many people, including three of her biographers,[20] consider to be the best performance of her career.

Not all of Crawford's noir and noirish films are masterpieces, of course. A few of them, such as *This Woman Is Dangerous, Female on the Beach*, and *Queen Bee*, are far from good and unwittingly helped to establish her as a camp figure in her later years and after her death. Still, especially for a person who took the number of professional risks that she did during her noir years, her success rate is quite high and certainly impressive.

❖ ❖ ❖

    Film noir and Joan Crawford both blossomed into full bloom at about the same time and together. Perhaps more significant, the hugely influential filmmaking style and the actress who often exerted great influence and control over specific film projects shared a highly productive, symbiotic relationship between 1941 and 1958, years that map almost exactly with the period most film historians today call the classic noir cycle. Noir both invigorated her career and challenged her as an actress in ways she had never experienced before. In her own way, she challenged noir, too, playing demanding roles, both in front of and behind the camera, that ultimately expanded the possibilities of noir content, greatly enriched the noir style, and, by extension, made an enormous contribution to U.S. and world film culture.

    The twelve chapters that constitute the lion's share of this book attempt to make the case for these claims. The first eleven of these focus on the twelve films Crawford starred in between 1941 and 1956 that are clearly noir or significantly noirish in terms of both content and style. The final chapter focuses on the two little-known but quite interesting noirish television dramas from the 1950s that first aired on CBS's *General Electric Theater*. The hope is that they all fit together, much like pieces in a mosaic, to create a higher level, more all-encompassing view of Crawford's relationship with noir, a view from which readers will clearly see—in addition to the quality of her achievements in individual efforts—the breadth and depth of her overall, and still greatly under-appreciated, accomplishment.

1

"The world belongs to the devil"
A Woman's Face (1941)

It's surprising that more people don't give *A Woman's Face*, the captivating and often overlooked gem that Joan Crawford made at MGM in 1941, the attention it deserves. As well as being a fascinating transition piece in terms of her development as an actress and her desire to exert more control over her own artistic expression and professional destiny, it is intriguing both as her entrée into film noir and, in its own right, as an excellently crafted film.

Although most people with thoughts on the subject will say that Crawford's noir debut was in her 1945 triumph *Mildred Pierce*, *A Woman's Face*, usually considered a drama or a melodrama, is filled with familiar and widely accepted noir elements. The story, for example, features a morally compromised protagonist, petty criminals, a depraved murder plot that goes awry, an actual killing, a reckoning with justice, a homme fatale, a cheating wife, and even references to the evil that led to World War II, which had officially begun in Europe several months before the film's May 1941 release. While the film has a few light moments, its tone is more often dark, suspenseful, and somber. Finally, the film relies heavily on such noir-style storytelling techniques as flashbacks, darkly lit characters and scenes, and disorienting camera placements (such as very low-angle shots) to achieve various desired effects. It's not a textbook noir that includes all the classic components, but, as the saying goes, "its cup runneth over" with noir content and storytelling techniques.

In addition, *A Woman's Face* introduces several elements that give *Mildred Pierce* and many of Crawford's subsequent 1940s and 1950s noirs their "distinctly Crawford" flavor, and, in turn, helped to expand the range and possibilities of noir storytelling. Just a few of these include the complex female protagonist who undergoes a major personal change (for the better or for the worse); the homme fatale; and the negative consequences of manipulative, obsessive, or otherwise dysfunctional love relationships. Ironically, these are also some of the elements that, even today, lead audiences and critics alike to persist in seeing 1940s and 1950s films starring Joan Crawford—no matter how dark, deadly, and noirish they actually are—merely as female-centered melodramas or darker versions of 1930s Joan Crawford pictures.

A Woman's Face is also a splendidly crafted effort. Director George Cukor is firmly in control of every aspect of production. In addition to Crawford, other actors, most notably co-stars Conrad Veidt and Melvin Douglas, deliver excellent performances. Finally, other major collaborators from scriptwriters Donald Ogden Stewart and Elliot Paul to cinematographer Robert Planck more than ably carry out challenging assignments. While not flawless, the film is, overall, a fine beginning to a new and what would prove to be an extremely fruitful period in Crawford's career.

❖ ❖ ❖

As an artistic property, A Woman's Face has quite an eventful history. The original version of the story had been an early twentieth century French stage drama by the Belgian-born playwright and opera librettist Francis de Croisset (1877–1937). In 1938, it was adapted into a Swedish film directed by Gustaf Molander (1888–1973), a major Swedish filmmaker whose career credits would eventually include more than seventy films between the 1920s and the 1960s. This version, which received much critical praise and eventually international recognition at the 1938 Venice Film Festival, starred a gifted young actress Molander's studio had put under his tutelage. Her name was Ingrid Bergman.

In the fall of 1939, the Swedish version of A Woman's Face (or En kvinnas ansikte) was released in the U.S. Crawford, increasingly on the lookout for stories that featured strong female leads, saw the film, loved it, and even wrote Bergman a fan letter praising her portrayal of the story's tragically scarred, deeply embittered heroine, Anna Holm. About this time, Bergman had also come to Hollywood to star in films for producer David O. Selznick, and eventually the two actresses met. The occasion was a party Selznick was giving for the premiere of Bergman's first U.S. film, Intermezzo (1939), itself an adaptation of another earlier Molander/Bergman effort in Sweden. As they chatted, Crawford asked Bergman if it would be impertinent of her to ask MGM's Louis Mayer to secure the rights to A Woman's Face so she could star in an English language version. Bergman was touched by Crawford's solicitude and gave her blessing to the effort.[1]

The next person Crawford needed to win over was Mayer, who, two years earlier had opposed the idea of her playing the scheming Crystal Allen in *The Women* because he believed it would damage her carefully-cultivated Cinderella image. Now, as Crawford later recalled, Mayer now "balked at me playing a scarred woman who hated the world."[2]

In her campaign to win Mayer over, she again turned to the man who had helped her win the role of Crystal Allen, the director of *The Women*, George Cukor. Cukor, who admired both her work and her work ethic, agreed to help and even offered to direct a new film version if Crawford played Anna Holm. The strategy worked, and a reluctant Mayer gave his blessing as well.

At the time, Cukor (1899–1983) was about as powerful an artistic ally as anyone at MGM could have. A promising stage director on Broadway, he came to Hollywood in 1929, just as talkies were replacing silent films, and immediately began making critical and commercial hits. Although he worked at various studios from this time until the early 1980s, many of his most popular and best remembered films—such as *Dinner at Eight* (1933), *David Copperfield* (1935), *Romeo and Juliet* (1936), *The Women* (1939), *The Philadelphia Story* (1940), *Gaslight* (1944), and *Adam's Rib* (1949)—were made at MGM.

Almost from the beginning of his film career, Cukor had developed a reputation for being a woman's director because of the superb performances he was able to get from such actresses as Katharine Hepburn, Greta Garbo, Norma Shearer, Ingrid Bergman, Judy Garland, and Judy Holliday. It might be more accurate, however, to call him a consummate craftsman who worked hard on every facet of his films and asked a great deal, not only of actresses, but of everyone who contributed to them. He was, for example, able to get an amazing against-type performance from Ronald Colman in *A Double Life* (1947), which netted Colman a well-deserved Best Actor Academy Award. He also pushed other collaborators from screenwriters to cinematographers, to art and costume designers to great lengths to get the results he wanted.

Crawford, ever the perfectionist, craved working with strong, smart, driven, demanding directors who could push her hard as an actress and get the best performances possible, and the prospect of teaming with Cukor once again delighted her. She had considered him instrumental in getting the memorable against-type performance from her when she'd played Crystal Allen in *The Women*, and she hoped lightning would strike again in *A Woman's Face*.

Before Crawford could get to work on the film, however, Cukor brought in another past collaborator of his, screenwriter Donald Ogden

Stewart, to work on a new adaptation of the story. Perhaps best known today for his film versions of sophisticated comedies such as *The Philadelphia Story* and classic works such as *David Copperfield*, Stewart (1894–1980) was also quite skilled at adapting dramatic and melodramatic material. Another writer, Elliot Paul, also contributed to the script. Primarily a novelist and journalist, Paul (1891–1958) is credited with working on ten film scripts for Hollywood studios between 1941 and 1953. Perhaps his best-known film is the biopic of composer George Gershwin, *Rhapsody in Blue* (1945) starring Robert Alda.

The filming of *A Woman's Face*, which concluded in late March of 1941, was, as George Cukor–directed films usually were, a well-organized and highly professional effort. Crawford often spoke of what an excellent job he did of getting her to reduce "my emotionalism," as she once put it,[3] and deliver a highly disciplined, understated, and nuanced performance. "I say a prayer for Mr. Cukor every time I think of what *A Woman's Face* did for my career," she noted years later. "It fortified me with a measure of self-confidence I'd never had."[4] In addition, Crawford deserves full credit for her ability to see the opportunity in the story for herself and then to play a key role in getting the new version produced.

❖ ❖ ❖

The 1941 version of *A Woman's Face* is quite an intricately plotted affair.

The film begins with a close-up of an official Swedish government notice informing us of a murder trial and its defendant, an Anna Holm (Crawford). We then see a cadre of guards escorting a mysterious woman into a courtroom, a broad-rim hat partially concealing her face. Several witnesses are summoned, told they will be asked to provide their accounts of actions that led to this murder, and asked to swear an oath.

As each of these witnesses shares his or her account and Anna shares hers, her story, and the story of her relationships with Torsten Barring (Conrad Veidt), the charismatic, unscrupulous member of an extremely rich Swedish family; Gustaf Segert (Melvyn Douglas), a renowned plastic surgeon; and others are revealed in flashbacks.

When Anna and Torsten first meet, he notices the severe disfigurement on one side of Anna's otherwise beautiful face. Rather being repulsed by the sight of it as others usually are, he is fascinated both by it and by her hard, bitter attitude toward the world, an attitude he knows the scar has helped cause. She is amazed that someone like him could find someone like her attractive. Soon, they become lovers.

Conrad Veidt's suave and seductive Torsten Barring (left) befriends Crawford's Anna Holm in an early scene in George Cukor's *A Woman's Face*
(1941). In this film, Veidt, often photographed in varying shades of noirish
shadow, is the quintessence of the noir homme fatale, a character type that
will again appear in several more of Crawford's 1940s and 1950s efforts
(MGM/Photofest).

In the meantime, Anna, a disreputable person who leads a gang of
blackmailers, has come into possession of love letters between a cheating wife, Vera Segert (Osa Massen), and one of her amours, and goes to
Vera's house to extract payment for the letters' return. Unexpectedly,
though, Vera's husband, Gustaf, returns and Anna is injured trying to
escape. Gustaf, a plastic surgeon and an unusually kind and consider-
ate man, is also fascinated by Anna's scar and, rather than having her
arrested for what he assumes is an aborted home burglary, offers to
operate on her to restore the side of her face. She agrees and undergoes
twelve painful operations. Finally, after many months, the final bandages are removed, and she sees that the operations have proven successful: the scar has vanished, and her face, for the first time since she
was a child, is beautiful on both sides.

She returns to Torsten, who was unaware of the surgery, and he is now stunned and delighted at seeing her new face. Knowing about her illegal activities and her reputation for ruthlessness, he also tries to enlist her in a scheme of his own. His very old, very rich uncle, Consul Magnus Barring (Albert Bassermann), has bequeathed the entire family fortune to his four-year-old grandson, Lars-Erik (Richard Nichols). If the boy dies, however, Torsten would inherit the fortune, and, if Anna were to help Torsten by killing the boy, she would be well compensated. Anna is uneasy about this, but Torsten, who continues to hold a seductive power over her, compels her to agree. His uncle has asked him to hire a new governess for Lars-Erik, he says, and he would like Anna to accept the position and go to live at the family estate, Barring Hall, which is in the Swedish mountains, across a powerful river from the metal works responsible for the family's riches.

Under the name Ingrid Paulsen, Anna arrives at Barring Hall and begins her duties as Lars-Erik's governess. Although she clashes a bit with the jealous housekeeper Emma (Marjorie Main), Anna takes a liking to both the kindly consul and the friendly, good-natured Lars-Erik.

Soon, it is the consul's birthday, and among the many people who descend on Barring Hall for a big celebration are Torsten and, for Anna, an unexpected guest, Gustaf. Privately, she tells Gustaf that she has reformed from her criminal ways and that the name change is part of an effort to make a fresh start in her life. Gustaf agrees to keep her secret safe.

The next day, however, Anna accidentally leaves Lars-Erik under a sun lamp for too long. The boy is not seriously harmed, but, realizing that he could have been, she is quite upset. Observing this, Torsten sees that Anna is weakening in her resolve to go through with his plan and demands that she kill the boy the following day.

The next day, Anna takes Lars-Erik for a ride in the aerial cable tram that crosses the river between Barring Hall and the metal works. The experience excites the boy, who hops all about the small tram car. Anna is profoundly distressed. All she'd need to do now, she appears to be thinking, is give him a little nudge here or push there and he would fall to his death in the river. At one point she even puts her hand on the latch that secures the tram car gate and, for a tense moment, toys with it, realizing that she could open the gate, Lars-Erik could fall out, and she could credibly claim later that the gate wasn't properly latched to begin with. Then, she relents, taking her hand away from the latch and sitting with Lars-Erik until the tram reaches the end of the ride and safety.

Watching this brief drama from two different vantage points on the scene are Gustaf and Torsten. Gustaf, who senses that something is not right, is relieved that nothing tragic has occurred. Torsten, on the other hand, is furious.

That night, two customary events are scheduled at Barring Hall. First, the consul will open his birthday gifts and then the Barrings and their guests will go for a sleigh ride.

Before these events, Torsten and Anna meet privately in the hall's dark, shadowy attic. Torsten tells her of his immense disappointment in her and says that by, ridding her of her disfigurement, Gustaf has robbed her of her hardness and strength. He then talks about the great things he could do if he only had the money and, of course, the power that can come with it—great things, he implies, similar to what Hitler and other totalitarian leaders are doing in 1941. His words horrify Anna.

After the consul's other presents are opened but before the sleigh ride, Anna gives the consul her present, a pocket chessboard, which he thanks her for and passes to Emma for safekeeping.

As Anna leaves for the sleigh ride, she sees Torsten speeding away in a sleigh wildly lashing the horses. Lars-Erik is with him. Immediately knowing what Torsten has in mind, she enlists Gustaf to jump into another sleigh with her and follow in pursuit. Knowing that Torsten won't stop and that she must take extreme measures to save Lars-Erik, she pulls a gun from her purse and shoots and kills Torsten. His body falls out of the sleigh, into the river far below, and then over a raging waterfall. The horse pulling the sleigh slows down, and Lars-Erik is saved.

Describing these events in the courtroom, Consul Barring, one of the witnesses, says that he believes that Anna is innocent, that she was driven by a desire to save the Lars-Erik and not by a premeditated plan to kill Torsten. The judges, however, are not convinced.

Anna protests, saying that she had left a letter inside the pocket chess set she'd given the consul as a birthday present that will prove that she was not planning to kill Torsten. Emma, the housekeeper, admits to taking the letter out of the chess set and then keeping it, assuming Anna has written it to curry favor with the consul. Emma adds that, because she staunchly believes in never reading other people's mail, she does not actually know the contents of the letter. She then gives it to the consul, who opens it and reads it aloud, quickly revealing to everyone present that the letter is both a confession and a suicide note. Rather than being a part of any effort that might harm Lars-Erik, Anna was planning to warn the consul and then take her own life.

As the judges deliberate and an acquittal appears to be inevitable, Gustaf and Anna sit in a room adjacent to the court to wait for the verdict. Alone at last, the two express romantic feelings for each other. It is now clear that, once Gustaf, who has learned of Vera's adultery and initiated divorce proceedings, is free, he and Anna will marry. After a few minutes, they are both asked back to the court to hear the judges' verdict.

◆　◆　◆

Although the 1938 Swedish version of *A Woman's Face* is a good film, most people familiar with both this and the 1941 Cukor-Crawford version prefer the latter. To support their positions, they usually then focus on Cukor's skill as a director, Crawford's breakthrough performance, and sometimes the fine co-starring turns by Conrad Veidt as Torsten and Melvin Douglas as Gustaf.

There is, however, another, and quite significant, factor at work here: the screenplay by Donald Ogden Stewart and Elliot Paul. In their adaptation of the story (which likely received inputs from Cukor), they make numerous changes to both the theatrical and earlier film versions. Several of these changes, such as combining elements of two key characters into one, which results in Gustaf, simply make for more economical and effective storytelling. Three major changes, however, make a big difference both in the U.S. version's darker tone to an already dark story and to the more suspenseful way that events are revealed. In the process, they also move the story much closer to the noir style.

Two of these changes are especially significant in terms of the way the story is structured and we learn about events. They are the additions of the killing of Torsten and the trial of the accused murderer, Anna. With the trial as a framing device, most of the story is now told in noir-style flashbacks with different characters presenting their accounts of the events leading up to the killing. Central to these accounts, of course, is the personal journey of Anna, who for much of the film is seen only as a mysterious, partially hidden presence in the courtroom. It's intriguing, too, that for most of the trial the name of the murdered person is not revealed. It could, of course, be Torsten, who isn't present as a witness. It could be Lars-Erik, who isn't present, either. It could also be someone else altogether. We don't know the identity for certain until fairly late in the film's running time, and this, of course, makes for a more suspenseful and satisfying viewing experience.

Curiously, the additions of the murder of the homme fatale, the reckoning with the justice system, and the flashback story structure are all strikingly similar to the noir-style additions made to the novel *Mildred Pierce* when it was brought to the screen four years later with Crawford in the title role. Although many film aficionados quickly point to these elements to help affirm *Mildred Pierce's* noir credentials, it is odd that few connect almost identical elements in *A Woman's Face* with noir.

The third noirish change to *A Woman's Face* was to update the story to 1941 and, in one scene especially, to emphasize the chilling message that, with Europe now deeply embroiled in World War II, this was truly a time when conventional civility has broken down and the forces of darkness were emphatically on the march. The scene is Anna and Torsten's meeting in Barring Hall's attic after Anna has squandered the chance to kill Lars-Erik when the two were in the tram car earlier that day. It is fascinating in terms of what it reveals about Torsten, who tells Anna how disappointed he is in her since Gustaf has removed the scar from her face. Once so cold, hard, and detached—qualities he equates with strength and greatness—she has become kinder, more empathetic, more connected with other people—qualities he despises. He continues:

> TORSTEN: I could kill that doctor.
>
> ANNA: Why him?
>
> TORSTEN: Because he has changed my partner into a dove, a tame cooing dove, soft and weak and full of love for her fellow men: the old and the weak and the unimportant. (sarcastically) You should love your fellow man—you? Your fellow man loved you, didn't he? People held out their arms to you and offered you love and life and laughter and everything a woman wants, didn't they?
>
> ANNA: Oh, you know they didn't....
>
> TORSTEN: [But] I saw the real Anna, the hard shining brightness of you. There have been women like you before. They became conquerors, queens, empresses.
>
> ANNA: Oh, Torsten, this is 1941.
>
> TORSTEN: (again, sarcastically) Oh, I apologize. I forgot. This is 1941, yes! The spirit of love has triumphed, yes! God's in His heaven, yes! No, no, Anna, the times are ripe. And I could be, I could be greater than any Barring had ever been, or ever will be. You thought that I was concerned about my debts, that I wanted money so that I too could live safely and comfortably like the other tame pigeons.... Oh no, you didn't know me, Anna. Nobody knows me. I played the charming, good-natured fool because I was also waiting. I was waiting to find someone like you who had also been cheated. Yes, Anna, God cheated you when He gave you that scar. He cheated me when that little boy was born to take away from me what was mine by right because, Anna, I could use this power. What others have done in other countries, I can do here. Because, Anna, the world belongs to the devil, and I know how to serve him, if I can only get the power. The power!

As Anna learns here, Torsten is much more than an amoral schemer intent on obtaining the family fortune: he is a megalomaniac with visions of becoming Sweden's Hitler. She is both understandably appalled by him and filled with self-loathing for even considering to collaborate in his scheme to kill Lars-Erik. Clearly, this interaction leads to her decision to write the letter to the consul exposing Torsten's scheme and then to take her own life (most likely with the gun she eventually uses to kill Torsten).

The reality of World War II is an element in many noir films, especially those released in the late 1940s and early and mid–1950s. Because the vast majority of noir films were made in these post-war years, noir viewers have had much more exposure to the stories that focused on the after-effects of the war, especially on returning veterans and those close to them. Familiar storylines might be about vets who struggle with PTSD (post-traumatic stress disorder), the transition back into civilian life, the need to avenge a wrong done to them during the war, or other challenges.

In contrast, most wartime noir and noirish films stuck to their pulp fiction sources and ignored the war's reality. A few, however, commented on this reality in quite intriguing ways. One very interesting example is Alfred Hitchcock's great film, *Shadow of a Doubt* (1943). Set in the idyllic small town of Santa Rosa, California, and focusing on a happy, wholesome, loving family, the story examines how pure evil in the person of Uncle Charlie (Joseph Cotten) can insert itself into any situation and wreak havoc. In the film, the war is never mentioned, but we briefly see servicemen (probably on leave) as well as signs urging people to buy war bonds. These small, seemingly extraneous additions could very well have been Hitchcock's sly, subtle way of suggesting that real-life Uncle Charlies exist throughout the world, that some of them take over entire nations, and that, at the moment, these Uncle Charlies present a clear and present danger to the rest of humanity. Not only can evil strike anywhere, the message seems to be, but it can also strike everywhere.

In *A Woman's Face*, a similar message is communicated. When Torsten tells Anna of his craving for power as well as money, the larger, extremely dangerous world situation is brought front and center, and the troubles of Anna and others are set against a much larger and more perilous backdrop. A major multi-national war is now being waged, pure evil like the kind Torsten exemplifies is one of its main drivers, and millions of people will suffer because of it. Again, the evildoing shown in the story becomes a metaphor for, and reminder of, the very large-scale evildoing that's occurring elsewhere in the world. Unlike the war-related storylines of the post-war noirs that focus on recovery and moving on from the conflict, these war-time films focus on a major reason for the conflict—on the cause rather than the effects. It's a fascinating and quite insightful perspective on World War II, one which later noirs usually don't include because the war had ended by the time they were released and audiences, by and large, had moved on.

* * *

One of the pleasures of watching *A Woman's Face* several times is to appreciate the command that director George Cukor exerts over so many elements of filmmaking. While often—and rightly—credited for his excellent handling of actors, he is, strangely, often overlooked for his ability as a visual storyteller. This is unfortunate, because he can be quite good, and, in this film, he proves his value in numerous ways.

In the film's very first moments, for example, we see this in how Cukor organizes the blocking of the characters and sets it in relation to the camera. Anna is being escorted by several guards down a succession of halls toward the courtroom. All walk in a very purposeful, subtly synchronized manner. The camera is placed closely behind the group and methodically keeps pace. We don't see the faces of any of these people during these scenes, heightening our curiosity. As viewers, we are effectively joining the group as it approaches and enters the courtroom. Like the others already in the room, we will become observers to the proceedings and, in the process, watch and listen as witnesses tell us the story of Anna Holm. Taking just a few moments of screen time, this is a wonderful way to involve viewers right from the first images they see.

As well as being especially creative in the ways he uses visuals to engage viewers in the story, Cukor, as filmmaker and film writer Karli Lukas notes, "exhibits a great ability to reveal the turning points of character through his use of seemingly understated, but in fact very clever 'mise-en-scene.'"[5] As Lukas continues:

> I love the way that [Cukor] has directed Crawford to dance amongst pools of light and shadow to heighten suspense (and show off her great facial structure). While admittedly borrowing such techniques from the stage, the effect is anything but stagy—instead it lends the film some very noir-esque elements. The scenes where Cukor finally reveals Crawford's scar and her later facial reconstruction are masterful. Equally spectacular is the use of back projection during the cable car and sleigh ride scenes, which once again arguably serve to isolate Crawford's face as she goes through her crises of character.... There are many great scenes in this film....[6]

* * *

Cukor's best-known directorial talent, of course, was his ability to extract exceptional performances from actors. In *A Woman's Face*, much of the discussion over the years has focused on Crawford's portrayal of Anna Holm. This is absolutely appropriate: not only is this performance a major breakthrough for the actress but it also stands as one of the best performances of her career. In addition, Cukor was instrumental in getting fine or at the very least capable performances from virtually everyone else in the cast. Particularly good are Crawford's two male co-stars, Conrad Veidt and Melvin Douglas. Many of the supporting players, notably Albert Bassermann, Reginald Owen, and Marjorie Main, also do fine work.

Coming before Crawford's great performances in such later films as *Mildred Pierce, Humoresque, Possessed,* and *Sudden Fear,* her layered, emotionally spot-on portrayal of Anna must have been startling for her fans to behold. Here, the familiar bright, warm, and spunky Crawford persona, so carefully molded in a succession of romantic dramas during the 1930s, is simply not present. Instead, we see someone quite different: a deeply unhappy, embittered, and hardened—yet also insecure,

Crawford's Anna looks at herself in a series of mirrored reflections that seem to extend into infinity as she prepares to visit Torsten at his apartment in *A Woman's Face.* In noir, as in other kinds of films at the time, mirrors were often used to suggest the duality of human nature, a theme that is central to Anna's personal journey (MGM/Photofest).

vulnerable, and sometimes even pitiful—young woman who undergoes a major personal transformation. It's to Crawford's (and Cukor's) great credit that, whenever we look into the actress's famous eyes as we watch this film, we never see the actress, only the character.

Crawford's portrayal before Anna undergoes the plastic surgery is especially striking. Not only is it extremely disciplined and focused but it manages to reveal important information in very subtle, sophisticated ways. We see some excellent examples of this in the scenes when Anna, the blackmailer, goes to the Segerts' home to sell Vera's adulterous love letters back to her. One is the way Anna chastises Vera for her childish, drivel-filled writing and then contrasts Vera's letters to the "real" love letters of great writers such as George Sand and John Keats. The speech isn't about Vera, of course. It's about Anna's jealousy and anger that Vera can have no idea about what real love is but still have lovers, while she, who truly knows what love is, has long been denied. The tougher Anna sounds, the more pitiable she seems.

Another example is marvelous bit of acting that occurs a few moments later. Gustaf has returned home and has caught Anna trying to escape. He notices the scar, is intrigued by it, and tells her that he is a plastic surgeon who can repair her face. At first, she simply scoffs at the thought that someone can help rid her of the scar, but, as film writer Sheila O'Malley suggests:

> [T]here's something deeper going on in the scene, and you just need to keep your eyes fixed on Crawford's face to discern it. The thought that someday she might NOT have a scar has never occurred to Anna Holm. But now, suddenly ... it does. Instead of leaping for joy, she is almost devastated by it. Because what will it mean? Her whole life is about having that scar. Who will she be without a scar? There's a certain sense of loss there as well. It is as though she feels her whole identity *is* her scar.[7]

Once Anna undergoes the surgery, her life dramatically changes, and Crawford shows Anna's emerging outward confidence and inner softening in numerous ways, most notably through her wonderfully expressive face. She is excellent at little touches, such as when she realizes that she doesn't need to hide the once-scarred part of her face anymore because it repels people. She is also excellent at showing her growing fondness both for Consul Barring and little Lars-Erik. She does it with great subtlety because anything direct or effusive would be inconsistent with Anna's character, at least at this point in her transformation. Finally, she is excellent when, on the tram with Lars-Erik, her face shows the enormous conflict churning within her: Does she kill the boy to fulfill her agreement with Torsten, the man she believes she loves, or does she spare the boy and lose Torsten?

Although Crawford, as she sometimes acknowledged, had a tendency to overact, she absolutely understood the power of suggestion and understatement, and, with Cukor's help in *A Woman's Face*, she more than proves her mastery of film acting. To watch her in this film, Sheila O'Malley adds, "is to see a giant talent at work, an actress who knew what she was good at, knew what she was capable of, and had the ambition and guts to mess with her own persona when called upon to do so."[8]

Often good acting performances are inspired by good interacting with other performers, and this is certainly true in *A Woman's Face*. Of particular note, are the two leading men, Conrad Veidt and Melvyn Douglas.

Veidt (1893–1943), best known today as Major Strausser, the villainous Nazi in Michael Curtiz's classic *Casablanca* (1943) had a storied career in German silent and early sound films before leaving his homeland after Hitler took power in 1933 and settling in the U.K., where he made several films. In 1940, he moved to the U.S., where he made nine films before his death from a heart attack in April 1943. *A Woman's Face* is the second of these, and his work in it could very well be his best performance in a U.S.-made film. What is especially good about his Torsten is how suave, charismatic, and seductive he is while also being so menacing and evil. Two scenes in which he is particularly effective are the two visits Anna makes to his lavish residence, the first before her surgery and the second soon afterwards. In both, he underplays brilliantly, subtly conveying an intense sexual energy that is simultaneously alluring and perverse.

Douglas (1901–1981), one of many actors who came to Hollywood from the stage soon after the film industry's sound revolution in the late 1920s, was a familiar presence in films from 1931 until his death in 1981. Highly respected for his intelligent, no-nonsense acting style, he won two Best Supporting Actor Academy Awards later in his career for his work in *Hud* (1963) starring Paul Newman and *Being There* (1979) starring Peter Sellers. In *A Woman's Face*, he does a superb job of bringing the combination of intelligence, authority, kindness, and shrewdness to Gustaf, a fairly bland character who might have been totally forgettable in a lesser actor's hands. Douglas is particularly effective in Gustaf's scenes with Anna soon after it's clear that her surgery has been successful, wondering if she will see her new face as a chance to start a new life more connected with human society or if she will remain cold and aloof and return to her criminal activities. We know that he is fascinated by her and rooting for her to change, but that he also doesn't quite trust her to do so. Here, Douglas does a fine job of mixing skepticism with hope.

As is usually the case in a Cukor film, the supporting players in

A Woman's Face are also quite effective. Among them, noted German actor Albert Bassermann, British character actor Reginald Owen, and longtime MGM contract player Marjorie Main deserve kudos for delivering very thoughtful, understated performances. Especially notable here are the efforts of Owen and Main, who could both "ham it up" on occasion. Their precise, honest portrayals might indeed be the results of Cukor's strong directorial hand.

Finally, much of the credit for the film's noirish look and dark tone needs to go to cinematographer, Robert Planck (1902–1971), who worked on more than a hundred Hollywood films from the late 1920s to the late 1950s. Better known for his contributions to splashy MGM musicals such as *Royal Wedding* (1951) and *Gigi* (1958) than to melodramas or noirs, he ably underscores the story's dark tone from the initial scenes of Anna entering the courtroom to the pivotal conversation between Anna and Torsten in Barring Hall's forbidding attic.

A Woman's Face does have a few shortcomings that some film writers can't resist pointing out. Among these are the gingerbread-like exteriors of the restaurant where Anna and Torsten first meet (which might better suit a film version of the *Hansel and Gretel* story) and the faux–Swedish costumes and folk dancing routines at Consul Barring's birthday party. All things considered, though, these are very minor hiccups in an otherwise strong and compelling film.

◆ ◆ ◆

A Woman's Face is an enormously significant career milestone for Joan Crawford. As an actress, she had proven that she could ably handle serious, complex roles. As an auteur, she was acquiring a much better sense of the kinds of stories and roles through which she wished to express her art. Finally, as a contributor to noir, she was, for the first time, delving deeply into the complex characterizations and dark themes that would be emblematic of her work for the next decade and a half.

She was also, as she fervently hoped, on her way to more career triumphs.

Reality, however, didn't cooperate, at least at first. The professional accolades and other good roles she had longed for didn't come, and Crawford increasingly found herself on the sidelines as the sought-after female roles in MGM films went to other, up-and-coming actresses.

As was the case when she had been branded as box office poison in 1938, it was clearly time for her to do something different. But, this time, what could that be?

2

"I love you, Mother, really I do. But let's not be sticky about it"

Mildred Pierce (1945)

As many people familiar with Joan Crawford's life know, the lead-up to, and then the enormous success of, her 1945 film *Mildred Pierce* is one of the great career comeback stories in Hollywood history. With the help of a few key figures such as agent Lew Wasserman, studio head Jack Warner, producer Jerry Wald, and director Michael Curtiz—and, as always, propelled by her own indomitable will—the actress rose from her professional death bed. Her career wasn't merely revived, either. It was reignited, and, in the next decade, her continuing efforts would result in a remarkable string of commercial and critical successes, which include much of her best work as an actress.

One great irony in this stirring story is that Crawford was able to revitalize her career almost entirely through stories of defeat and desolation: specifically, a series of dark, despairing noirs and noir-tinged melodramas that focused on obsession, betrayal, jealousy, and exploitation and resulted in murder or suicide. Among the best, and the bleakest, of these are the three films beginning with *Mildred Pierce* (1945) and continuing with *Humoresque* (1946) and *Possessed* (1947).

While *A Woman's Face* has many noir characteristics, its happy ending does detract somewhat from its noir standing because it doesn't deliver on the pre-ordained doom or damnation many believe to be the essence of noir.[1] These three films, however, don't skimp one bit on the doom or damnation part. In many ways, they are as dark and disturbing as the blackest, bleakest noirs out there.

Let's begin with the first and most celebrated of these three,

Mildred Pierce, and let's start off by touching upon the lead-up to what may be the most dramatic of all storied Hollywood comebacks.

◆ ◆ ◆

Professionally, the period between the May 1941 release of *A Woman's Face* and the September 1945 premiere of *Mildred Pierce* might best be described as Joan Crawford's wilderness years.

For the first two of those years, she continued on at MGM, where all the good roles that she had hoped would come her way after her critical success in *A Woman's Face* never materialized. Her next four films— *When Ladies Meet* (1941) *They All Kissed the Bride* (1942, on loan-out to Columbia), *Reunion in France* (1942) and *Above Suspicion* (1943)— while marginally successful at the box office, were far from compelling. "I think Joan was just about at the end of her rope," actress Natalie Schafer, who also appeared in *Reunion in France*, once noted about this period in Crawford's career. "I think she knew her days were numbered at MGM."[2]

Many have pointed to Crawford's age (her mid– to late thirties) as a major factor for her declining status at the studio. This is very likely. Examples of Hollywood's ageist attitudes, especially toward actresses, are amply documented. At this time, too, the studio was intensely focused on "reloading" for a new era. Crawford's studio contemporaries, and for years her main competitors for top roles, Norma Shearer and Greta Garbo, had both followed through with their retirements in 1941, and more of the attention and good roles were now going to younger female stars such as Hedy Lamarr, Ava Gardner, and Lana Turner.

In addition to Crawford's age, other factors may have been in play. One is that many at MGM now saw Crawford as a star more closely identified with past eras, an actress who had made her mark first as a dance-happy flapper in the go-go 1920s and then as the ambitious but principled young woman in 1930s Joan Crawford pictures. Another, and related, factor may have been changing times and tastes. In the early 1940s, as the U.S. shifted from the Depression-era to wartime, female audiences were increasingly drawn to films about noble, self-sacrificing women, films at which another rising MGM star, Greer Garson, excelled. Interestingly, Garson and Crawford were about the same age, but, from the studio's perspective, Garson had two advantages: new to films (her previous work had been almost entirely on the British stage), she was a fresher face to U.S. audiences, and she may have simply been better suited for the moment. Crawford lobbied hard to be cast as the noble female leads in films that eventually became two of the studio's biggest early 1940s hits, *Random Harvest* (1942) and *Madame Curie*

(1943). Neither part, of course, was right for her, and, to no one's surprise, both roles went to Garson, who was quite good in them.

Accounts about particular details vary, but, by the middle of 1943, Crawford and Louis Mayer had reached an agreement in which she could opt out of her MGM contract. On the morning of June 29, the actress drove to her studio dressing room for one last time, packed up her personal items, loaded them in her car, cleaned up after herself, and drove out the studio gates. There was no fanfare or goodbye party. Considering that she had been at MGM for eighteen and a half years, and had, during this time, appeared in about sixty films that had, all totaled, made *many* millions of dollars for the studio, this must have been an enormously sad and lonely day for her. At the time, too, she had no professional prospects and no idea where, if anywhere, her career might be headed. She had, however, just signed with a new agent, the now legendary Lew Wasserman, and was hopeful he could find work for her.

Then, only two days after MGM's door had closed on Crawford, another door officially opened. Wasserman had been hard at work, and, on July 1, 1943, she signed a three-picture, $500,000 deal with MGM's arch-rival, Warner Brothers. In addition, the contract included other terms the actress found quite desirable. While not getting complete artistic control over her films, she would be able to make significant contributions to every aspect of production from script development to art direction, wardrobe, cinematography, and editing.[3] For any major Hollywood studio in 1943, this was an enormous concession, and, for Crawford, who had long wanted a greater say in the artistic direction of her films, this must have seemed like a great victory.

Warner Brothers' interest in Crawford—now seen in some film circles as a "has-been,"[4] as the studio's top director Michael Curtiz famously referred to her in 1944—is quite intriguing, too. According to some accounts, Jack Warner, the studio's politically savvy head of production, was looking for leverage to use against his biggest and most demanding female star, Bette Davis. With Crawford in the fold, Warner is said to have calculated, Davis might have to face some high-powered female competition in a studio acting company dominated by male stars such as Humphrey Bogart, James Cagney, Errol Flynn, and John Garfield. In turn, this competition might make the ever-confident and often difficult Davis feel just a little less indispensable.

Regardless of why both Crawford and Jack Warner agreed to terms, this contract—even when put in the context of the long and eventful film industry careers both had—turned out to be one of the better decisions either of them ever made. For Warner, signing Crawford gave his studio's talent pool added depth and breadth and enabled its creative departments to move into new story territories especially during the time that ultimately became the glory days of the film noir era. For Crawford, a new start at Warner Brothers turned out to be nothing less than career resurrection. First, the studio was a great place for a person in films to be in the mid- and late 1940s—perhaps the most vital period in its long and enormously successful history. In addition to Curtiz, its stable of very able in-house directors at this time included John Huston, Raoul Walsh, Jean Negulesco, Curtis Bernhardt, Vincent Sherman, and others. Bogart, Cagney, Flynn, Garfield, and its other male stars were at their height. The studio's assemblage of superb supporting players ranged from Claude Rains and Sydney Greenstreet to Virginia Mayo, Jack Carson, Alan Hale, Sr., and many others. And its behind-the-scenes staff included scores of the film industry's most accomplished artists and artisans. Second, the studio's punchy, irreverent writing style; mastery of moody black-and-white cinematography; sharp, hard-edge editing; and relentless, driving story pacing all combined to be a superb fit for noir, which, at this time, was busting out all over Hollywood. Finally, as Crawford soon learned, she was a superb fit for the edgy, fast-paced, melodramatic, foreboding noir style that Warner Brothers would soon excel at. This was one of those very infrequent cases when the right person had come to the right place at exactly the right time.

When they signed their contract, however, neither Crawford nor Warner knew the future. The two were gamers willing to take calculated risks, and, for both, this agreement was clearly one of them.

For the next two years, the two didn't know if this gamble would pay off, either. Although Warner Brothers quickly started sending scripts to Crawford to evaluate, she was disappointed with everything she read. She knew that now, more than at any other time during her nearly two decades in Hollywood, if she were to survive professionally, she needed a hit—a big one. So, for roughly the next year and a half, she bided her time, reading—and rejecting—scripts that, for her, didn't measure up.

Then, in late 1944, she found her path out of the wilderness.

◆ ◆ ◆

In February of 1944, Jerry Wald, one of Warner Brothers' up-and-coming in-house producers, had purchased the screen rights to *Mildred Pierce*, a 1941 novel by James M. Cain (1892–1977), a Maryland-based journalist and fiction writer, who, from time to time, also wrote for the movies. The novel, which chronicles the journey of a separated then divorced working-class mother who struggles during the Great Depression to make ends meet for herself and her two daughters, is a fascinating and at times disturbing look at various social inequities, especially for women, and how they clash with the rosy promise of the American Dream. Cain, widely regarded today to be one of the literary godfathers of film noir, wrote two other novels, *The Postman Always Rings Twice* (published in 1934) and *Double Indemnity* (published in 1936) that were also made into classic film noirs in the 1940s. His influence is also unmistakable in numerous other noirs that followed in the late 1940s and 1950s and in many neo-noir films such as *Body Heat* (1981) and *The Last Seduction* (1994).

As soon as he had purchased the rights to *Mildred Pierce*, Wald—who had quickly gained a reputation at Warner Brothers for his ability to mount fine female-centered films starring such actresses as Ann Sheridan, Ida Lupino, and Joan Leslie—was eager to start work on the screenplay. The producer already had some definite ideas about changes to the story both to build up the drama and to accommodate the film industry's strict censorship guidelines at the time. These ranged from softening some of the crudeness and "lower-middle-classness" of the Mildred character and making her nobler and more refined to darkening the characters of Veda, Mildred's older daughter, and Monte Beragon, Mildred's second husband. By far the most radical changes he proposed, though, were to begin the film with the murder of Monte and then to tell the majority of the story using a flashback structure, neither of which is in the novel.

In addition, Wald had an unusual way of working with writers on scripts. Rather than assigning a team of writers to work together on a draft or taking an unsatisfactory script away from a writer in mid-draft, as other producers often did, he assigned drafts to individual writers and let each deliver a completed script. He then took what he considered each writer's good ideas and incorporated them into a kind of master script.

As time went by, quite a number of writers were involved. Cain himself got first crack at a treatment but quickly dropped out of the project. Wald then turned to a series of in-house writers, which included at different times Margaret Gruen, Albert Maltz, Louise Randall Pierson, Margaret Buell Wilder, Thames Williamson, Catherine Turney, Ranald MacDougall, and the celebrated novelist William Faulkner. One of the major contributors was Turney, a playwright as well as a screenwriter. Employed by the studio between 1943 and 1948, she had quickly gained a reputation for developing effective scripts featuring strong, independent female characters who also had a sense of humor. After spending a great deal of time on the effort, she and Wald ultimately disagreed on many of the story elements, and she left the project. Faulkner's script also proved unsatisfactory to Wald. Yet, one significant change he made—the addition of Lottie, Mildred's African American maid—did make it into the finished film. Eventually, MacDougall, a twenty-nine-year-old screenwriter who had recently impressed Wald with his work on *Objective, Burma!* (1945) a war film starring Errol Flynn, was brought in. MacDougall accommodated Wald's requests and made other refinements such as sharpening much of the story's dialogue.

Finally, in September 1944, key elements of the project were beginning to fall into place. After seven months and various writers, Jack Warner gave an enthusiastic thumbs-up to the screenplay, which was now credited solely to MacDougall. By this time, too, Michael Curtiz, fresh from his Oscar win the previous March for directing *Casablanca*, had been assigned to direct.

Wald had both the script and the director he wanted, but there were many pieces to the puzzle that still weren't in place. One of these was the actress who would play Mildred. Bette Davis, Warner Brothers' reigning female star, was the logical first choice. Accounts vary about why she didn't end up with the part. According to one report, she passed on the project because she didn't want to play the mother of a teenage daughter. According to Davis' own account, though, she was never given the script to read. At various times, Warner contract actresses Ida Lupino and Ann Sheridan were also considered. Another serious contender was Barbara Stanwyck, who had recently received rave reviews for her work in Billy Wilder's film version of Cain's *Double Indemnity*, released that July. Curtiz thought she would be an excellent choice, and she was quite interested. "I knew what a role it was, and I knew I could handle every facet of Mildred," she recalled. "I laid my cards on the table with Jerry Wald.... I felt Mildred was me."[5]

Then Wald suggested Crawford, who by this time had been at Warner Brothers regularly turning down scripts for about fifteen months. At first, Curtiz thought this was a terrible idea, making his famous "has-been" remark and adding that he wouldn't work with her "high-hat airs and her goddammed shoulder pads."[6]

But Crawford—who had also read the script, loved it, identified with Mildred, and saw the plum part as *her* ticket back to the top tiers of stardom—was again actively campaigning for the role. To prove to a skeptical Curtiz that she could play Mildred, she even agreed to do what was then unthinkable (and thought by some to be demeaning) for an actress of her stature and years of industry experience: she took a screen test. The strategy worked. Curtiz saw something in her acting that he hadn't appreciated before, and she won the role.

Knowing that screen chemistry between actors was essential to a

On the set of *Mildred Pierce* (1945), Crawford and director Michael Curtiz
(right) discuss aspects of the film that was both a major triumph for him
and nothing less than a career resurrection for her. While both initially
disliked working together, they quickly grew to respect each other's talent
and work ethic (Warner Brothers/Photofest).

film's success, Crawford also agreed to test with several of the actresses
trying out for the critically important role of Mildred's older daughter
Veda. Among them, Ann Blyth, the sixteen-year-old who was eventually
cast in the part, appreciated the older actress's interest and help, saying

years later that Crawford was "the kindest, most helpful human being I've ever worked with."[7]

In addition to Crawford and Blyth, several more actors from Warner Brothers stable of talent were added to the main cast. These included Zachary Scott, Bruce Bennett, Jack Carson, and Eve Arden.

Filming began on December 7, 1944, coincidentally, three years to the day after the attack on Pearl Harbor that had led the U.S. into World War II, and continued through the beginning of 1945. According to Crawford, Wald, and Curtiz, the first weeks of shooting were quite trying, with the director regularly berating his star in front of the whole cast and crew. Reportedly, Crawford wanted Curtiz fired and replaced "with a human being."[8] Wald quickly intervened, however, and soon tensions between Curtiz and Crawford cooled and the two were able to manage a more civil relationship on the set.

◈ ◈ ◈

In addition to being Crawford's first starring vehicle[9] at Warner Brothers, *Mildred Pierce* is also the first film she worked on with several people who would make important contributions to her work in other noir films and, in a couple of cases, films she made after the noir cycle had run its course.

Perhaps the most important of these was Jerry Wald (1911–1962). Along with Crawford, of course, he was one of the first people to envision her in the title role of Mildred. He had seen right away how much the Joan Crawford pictures at MGM had resonated for the actress and resulted in many of her better performances, and he knew how closely aspects of Mildred's story fit into this formula. He had also sensed that Crawford was a good enough actress to do justice to this very complex, nuanced character. Her eventual triumph in the role is in many ways a testament to Wald's faith in her, a fact that she never forgot. After *Mildred Pierce*, Wald and Crawford worked together on her next four Warner Brothers films: *Humoresque, Possessed, Flamingo Road* (1949), and *The Damned Don't Cry* (1950). After they both left Warner Brothers in the 1950s, Crawford and Wald reunited for two more films, *Queen Bee* (1955) and *The Best of Everything* (1959). For *Queen Bee*, the star specifically requested that Wald produce. In addition to his work with Crawford, Wald had many other film successes. He was nominated for Academy Awards (as a producer) four times: for *Mildred Pierce, Johnny Belinda* (1948), *Peyton Place* (1957), and *Sons and Lovers* (1960).

Another key contributor to Crawford's career during the noir cycle was Ranald MacDougall (1915–1973). After his success at bringing in a final script for *Mildred Pierce* that satisfied Jerry Wald, Jack Warner, and Joan Crawford, the actress turned to him several more times in the succeeding years. Along with writer Sylvia Richards, he shares the screenplay credit for *Possessed*. He also directed and wrote the screenplay for *Queen Bee*. In addition to his work with Crawford, he directed several other films and wrote (or contributed to) screenplays for such efforts as *The Unsuspected* (1947) with Claude Rains, *June Bride* with Bette Davis (1948), and *Cleopatra* (1963) with Elizabeth Taylor. Between 1971 and 1973, he also served as the president of the Writers Guild of America West.

Michael Curtiz (1886–1962) worked with Crawford only on *Mildred Pierce* and *Flamingo Road*, but his impact on her career, especially during the late 1940s, was enormous. By doing such an excellent job managing the production phase of *Mildred Pierce*, he played a key role in setting her up for her now-legendary run of fine films that followed. Much like George Cukor had done at MGM, he knew how to direct Crawford to get the best possible results from her. The two never shared a warm friendship like she and Cukor did, but, after their rocky start, they learned how to work together, and, in the process, the quality of her work reached new heights. An émigré from Hungary who came to the U.S. in the 1920s, Curtiz is often, and unjustly, overlooked when film historians rank the outstanding directors of Hollywood's classic era. He was not an auteur with his own personal vision in the way that Chaplin or Hitchcock were. Instead, he was, for more than twenty-five years, an in-house director at Warner Brothers who took his assignments from the boss. That said, he was a skilled and resourceful artist who knew how to leverage the resources of a major Hollywood studio to the fullest to create great films as well as anyone else did during that era. The list of masterpieces he directed ranging from *Casablanca* and *Mildred Pierce* to *The Adventures of Robin Hood* (1938), *Angels with Dirty Faces* (1938), *The Sea Hawk* (1940), *Yankee Doodle Dandy* (1942), and others speaks for itself. After leaving Warner Brothers in the early 1950s, he freelanced for Paramount and other studios and production companies, delivering such successes as the musical *White Christmas*, the highest grossing film of 1954.

A fourth key contributor to Crawford's noir career was the brilliant cinematographer Ernest Haller (1896–1970), who, six years earlier, had won an Academy Award for his work photographing *Gone with the Wind*. Working mostly at Warner Brothers from the 1930s to the 1950s, Haller developed a reputation for his skill at photographing both Bette Davis and Crawford in ways that pleased the actresses while also reinforcing the narratives of the films. After the success of *Mildred Pierce*, Crawford insisted that he work with her on her next project,

Humoresque. When Davis and Crawford united to make *Whatever Happened to Baby Jane?* in 1962, Haller was also the natural choice to be the film's cinematographer, and, for his efforts, he received his sixth (and next to last) Academy Award nomination.

❖ ❖ ❖

In true noir style, the film version of *Mildred Pierce* begins with gunshots in the dark as we look at a plush Malibu beach house from the outside at night. Inside the beach house, the victim, Monte Beragon (Zachary Scott), utters the single word "Mildred," falls to the floor, and dies. Then, we see a woman whose face we can't identify leave the house and drive away.

The scene shifts to a pier overlooking the ocean, Mildred Pierce Beragon (Crawford), clearly distraught, looks down into the water, perhaps contemplating suicide. A cagy policeman senses what's happening, calms her down, and convinces her to leave. Instead, she enters a seedy restaurant on the pier operated by Wally Fay (Jack Carson), a long-time acquaintance who has made it a lifetime practice to make unwanted sexual advances towards her. This time, however, she invites him back to her beach house for a drink and perhaps more. Wally can't resist and drives them there. Once at the beach house, however, she locks him in and departs in his car. As he tries to find a way out, he stumbles on Monte's body and realizes that Mildred is trying to frame him for the murder. Finally, he breaks out and runs along the beach to the road. As he does, two patrolmen in a passing police car, suspecting that he might be a thief, stop him. As one of the patrolmen searches the house, Wally tells the other, "You know, this is a pretty big night for you—lots of excitement. There's a stiff in there."

Meanwhile, Mildred (apparently ditching Wally's car) arrives at her large, well-appointed home in a cab and learns from her daughter Veda (Ann Blyth) that the police want to interview her. Once outside, the police officers tell her that her husband has been murdered.

As Mildred waits to be interviewed at the police station, she runs into her longtime business associate and friend Ida Corwin (Eve Arden), Wally again, and her ex-husband Bert Pierce (Bruce Bennett), all of whom are also there to be questioned. When she enters the office of the police detective handling the investigation, Inspector Peterson (Moroni Olsen), he tells her that they already have the murderer and that it is Bert. Mildred immediately objects to this conclusion, saying that Bert, whom she separated from four years earlier and then divorced, is too "gentle and kind" to do such a thing. Peterson, however, says that he had the motive, jealousy toward Monte, and the means: Bert's gun was the murder weapon. This prompts Mildred to begin to tell Peterson her and her family's story for the past four years.

The film now dissolves to the first of what will be its three flashbacks, with Mildred providing occasional voiceover narration.

It is now four years earlier. She and Bert live in a modest tract house in Glendale with their two daughters, Veda and Kay (Jo Ann Marlowe). Bert and Wally Fay, who have been in the real estate business together, have just dissolved their partnership, and Bert is now out of work. There is obvious tension between Bert and Mildred. He resents her fanatical, almost masochistic subservience to their two daughters, especially Veda, the older one. She resents that he isn't aggressively looking for a new job, and she is suspicious of his relationship with a neighbor named Maggie Biederhof (Lee Patrick), which he insists is purely platonic. One day, they have a major argument, and Bert packs his clothes and leaves. Afterwards, Mildred tells Veda and Kay "We'll have to get along by ourselves now."

Here, we get some insight into both daughters. Kay is caring and kind, sad that her parents have separated. Veda, on the other hand, is snobbish, selfish, scheming, and cruelly inconsiderate, calling Maggie Biederhof "distinctly middle-class" and then mercilessly criticizing a dress Mildred has bought for her.

Later that night when the girls are in bed, Wally unexpectedly calls, hears that Bert has left, and immediately begins to put the moves on Mildred. She resists, eventually gets him to leave, and heads upstairs where she notices Veda still reading in bed. Veda says that she'd overheard her and Wally talking downstairs and suggests that, if she wanted to, she could marry Wally and then they could have more. "It's just that there are so many things that I—that *we*—should have and haven't got," she adds. Mildred promises that she'll find a way to get Veda those things, says goodnight, and tells Veda that she loves her. "I love you, Mother, really I do," Veda says. Then, as Mildred hugs her, she adds, "But let's not be sticky about it." This subtle rejection cuts to Mildred's core.

Mildred realizes now that, with Bert both out of work and gone, she must get a job. After a long day of looking for work, she meets Ida Corwin, the hostess/manager of a busy, understaffed restaurant, and asks her to give her a chance waiting on tables. Ida reluctantly agrees, and Mildred quickly becomes an excellent waitress. Already an accomplished baker, she supplements her waitress's wages by baking pies for the restaurant. Soon, she's bringing in enough money both to support her and her daughters and to put some away in a savings account. She has bigger plans, however, and visits Wally to propose her idea to

Assisted by Butterfly McQueen's Lottie (left), Crawford's Mildred makes pies to help supplement her waitress's salary so she can provide more of the niceties of life to her two daughters, especially the relentlessly demanding Veda in *Mildred Pierce* (Warner Brothers/Photofest).

purchase a property to turn into a restaurant. Admiring her spunk, Wally finds the owner, a land-rich but cash-poor playboy named Monte Beragon; they sell the idea to Monty; the deal is finalized with Wally getting a one-third share of the business; and Mildred begins work on the restaurant. Wally does mention to Mildred, however, that, to protect herself financially, she will also need to divorce Bert. When Bert hears that she wants a divorce, however, he is hesitant.

Soon, two major developments occur. Mildred and Monte begin a relationship, and Mildred and Bert's younger daughter, Kay, suddenly dies of pneumonia. Mildred is crushed by Kay's death, but also reacts by saying, "Oh please, God, don't ever let anything happen to Veda."

Despite her grief, Mildred, with Ida now at her side, forges ahead to open her restaurant, which is a stunning success. On the first night of business, Wally, Veda, and Monte are all there to wish Mildred well. After Wally and Veda have left, Mildred and Monte embrace and Bert comes in. He tells her that he's impressed by what she has accomplished and that she can have the divorce. Monte, however, makes a tasteless remark that spurs the usually placid Bert into a jealous outburst.

We now flash forward to Inspector Peterson's office. Peterson tells Mildred that she still hasn't given him a good reason to believe that Bert didn't kill Monte and that, in fact, she has provided additional evidence that jealousy was indeed Bert's motive. Mildred then claims that it was she, not Bert, who killed Monte. Skeptical, Peterson then asks why, and Mildred continues her story, now hopeful of convincing him of her guilt.

We flash back again to the past. Mildred's one restaurant quickly turns into a very successful restaurant chain. "Everything I touched turned into money," she says in voiceover. "And I needed it. I needed it for Veda. She was becoming a young woman with expensive tastes."

Increasingly, Veda and Monte enjoy the good life together while Mildred works. Also, Monte depends more on Mildred for financial handouts. Mildred doesn't like where this is leading, and severs ties with Monte by paying him off.

With Monte out of her life, Veda, without Mildred's knowledge, marries a young man from a rich family and claims to be pregnant by him. With Wally's help, they negotiate a $10,000 payoff. Later, when they are at home alone, Veda reveals in a smirky manner that the pregnancy isn't real and then tells Mildred that the main reason she wanted the money was to get away "from you and your chickens and your pies and your kitchens and everything that smells of grease." After further arguing, Mildred takes the payoff check from Veda's purse and rips it up. Enraged, Veda slaps Mildred across the face. Mildred, with unusual fury, says, "Get out, Veda. Get your things out of this house right now before I throw them into the street and you with them. Get out before I kill you!"

Distraught, Mildred travels to Mexico but cannot let go of Veda emotionally. Eventually, she returns, telling a skeptical Ida that she'd like her daughter back. Ida responds, saying, "Personally, Veda's convinced me that alligators have the right idea; they eat their young."

Soon, Bert contacts Mildred, asking him to meet her at Wally's seedy pier restaurant. By now, Bert is no longer seeing Maggie Beiderhof and has finally found work, a good job at an aircraft company. At the restaurant, Mildred discovers what Bert had wanted her to—that Veda is now singing there. Shocked, she begs Veda to return home with her, but Veda says she will do it only if Monte is part of the package and the two of them can resume living their extravagant lifestyle. Mildred then proposes a marriage of convenience to Monte, who is now hurting even more financially. He agrees, only if he gets a one-third share of her

Definitely the odd woman out in this scene from *Mildred Pierce*, Crawford's Mildred looks on as Zachary Scott's ne'er do well Monte Beragon (left) and Ann Blyth's Veda (center) reunite after Veda has come back to live with Mildred (Warner Brothers/Photofest).

business. She agrees, and, when he tries to kiss her, she blocks him and coldly says "Sold. One Beragon." Very quickly, they are married.

With Bert's help, Mildred and Veda are also reunited, and, as a result, so are Veda and Monte. Mildred's bills again begin to pile up. Then, unknown to Mildred, Monte decides to sell his one-third of the business. Wally realizes that he needs to do something or risk losing his one-third as well, so he cuts a deal to take over the business. Mildred is out. Furious at both Monte and Wally, but especially Monte, Mildred goes home, takes a gun out of a desk drawer, and drives to the beach house.

Now, we return to the present. In Peterson's office, Mildred says, "I went to the house. Monte was alone. And I killed him."

Peterson immediately rejects this confession, however, and at this point the door to his office opens and Veda walks in accompanied by two police officers. She had been picked up trying to board a plane to Arizona. Peterson then begins to question Veda and tricks her into admitting the murder. Mildred begs her not to say anything, but it is too late.

With difficulty, Mildred continues, saying that, although she'd assumed that Monte was alone at the beach house, Veda was actually with him.

The screen dissolves to the third and final flashback. Mildred, now in the beach house, enters a room to see, in startling black silhouette, Veda and Monte embraced and kissing. Defiantly, almost proudly, Veda admits to having an affair—and a long-term one at that—with Monte and says that Monte is going to divorce Mildred and marry her.

Mildred pulls the gun out of her coat pocket, but Monte stops her, causing the gun to fall to the floor. Horrified by all of this, she runs out of the house and toward her car.

Inside, Monte snaps at Veda, "Just where did you get the idea I would marry you? ... You don't really think I could be in love with a rotten little tramp like you, do you?"

Veda then shoots Monte six times, he mutters the one word "Mildred," and falls to the floor dead. Mildred, trying to start the car, hears the shots, returns to the house, sees what's happened, tells Veda she can't get her out of this jam, and phones the police. She can't, however, report what's happened. "Just give me another chance," Veda pleads. "It's your fault I'm the way I am. Help me."

Again, the scene dissolves back to Peterson's office. Mildred tells Veda she's sorry, that she did the best she could. Veda says, "Don't worry about me, Mother. I'll get by." Then she is led away.

It's dawn now. Peterson stands up and raises the window shade. "We need some fresh air in here," he says. "You know, Mrs. Beragon, there are times when I regret being a police officer."

Mildred walks out of the police offices and sees Bert, who has been waiting for her. Then, the two walk together into the new day.

❖ ❖ ❖

When *Mildred Pierce* was released, it was an enormous hit. Crawford's legion of female fans, who had been waiting for more than two years to see her star in a new film, came to the theaters in droves. In addition, an aggressive studio marketing campaign, featuring such provocative poster headlines describing Mildred as "The kind of woman most men want—but shouldn't have!,"[10] lured in many more viewers. In all, the film made more than $5.6 million, about four times its production costs. Although the critics weren't unanimous, they generally praised both the film as a whole and the performances of Crawford and others in the cast. People throughout the film industry also saw *Mildred Pierce* as a serious Academy Award contender in several categories, much of the buzz centering around Crawford's chances at winning an Oscar for Best Actress. This last detail is a fascinating development because by this time Crawford had been making movies for twenty years and was widely respected by many peers, but she had never even been nominated for an Academy Award in either the Best Actress or Best Supporting Actress category. One key reason for this is probably rooted in the Oscar campaign strategies of Crawford's old studio, MGM. It routinely backed other contract actresses such as Shearer, Garbo, and Garson, who regularly made "prestige pictures," and overlooked Crawford, whose films were often considered lighter and less significant. In contrast, Warner Brothers went all-out for both the film and its star.

When the Academy Award nominations were announced in early 1946, it was clear that her new studio's efforts had paid off. *Mildred Pierce* earned six nominations in all: Best Picture (Wald as producer), Best Actress (Crawford), Best Supporting Actress (both Blyth and Arden), Best Screenplay (MacDougall), and best Cinematography— Black and White (Haller). A few weeks later, Crawford, capping off her amazing comeback, won the Oscar for Best Actress.

While all this Academy Awards notoriety is impressive, three more contributors to *Mildred Pierce* also deserved Academy recognition. One, of course, is Curtiz, whose direction throughout is superb. The second is actor Jack Carson, who shines as the utterly shameless but disarmingly likeable Wally. The third is the film's art director Anton Grot, whose arresting expressionistic designs were highly effective and widely praised.

All totaled, *Mildred Pierce* deserves the vast majority of the attention and acclaim it received when it was first released and has continued to receive in the decades since then.

One of the film's most notable strengths is the final script, which— despite all the writers involved in its development—is an inspired example of film adaptation. Based on a fine novel, which is much closer to mid-twentieth-century feminist social realism than to a noir-melodrama, the script incorporates a number of major changes that help transform it into a darker, more compressed, and ultimately more tragic story, but one that also preserves the essence and most of the strengths of the original.

When discussing these changes—such as the murder of Monte and Veda's subsequent arrest—many film historians have focused on the studio's need to accommodate the film industry's Production Code, which at the time was very strict on matters of morality.[11] Characters who did bad things had to face sobering consequences. This explanation is certainly true, but it is also incomplete. These changes also enriched the quality of the finished film in numerous ways.

First, the addition of a flashback story structure, the darkening of both Veda and Monte's characters, Monte's murder, Mildred's willingness to take the blame for it, Veda's arrest, and other changes greatly heighten the drama. The human stakes are incredibly high, and, as result, the story becomes a much more compact, focused, and suspenseful experience.

Second, although departing from the novel, the screenplay does an excellent job of also retaining many of its key aspects. Among these are Mildred's obsessive, perhaps masochistic, motherlove; the darker elements of the American Dream such as the myth that wealth naturally brings greater happiness; and the special difficulties that women endured in mid-twentieth century U.S. society. The ability to translate so much that is fascinating about the novel into cinematic terms gives the film a psychological dimension, an emotional depth, and even a layer of social criticism that most other noirs don't have.

Third, once the murder becomes an essential part of the story, the screenplay is, in noir terms, uncompromising in taking Mildred, Monte, and Veda to their own tragic ends. In other words, Mildred's obsession for Veda leads not only to her own financial collapse, but also to Monte's death and Veda's arrest and (probably) long imprisonment. There is a slight hint of a possible reconciliation between Mildred and Bert in the film's final scene, but, for all practical purposes, the ending is noir at its bleakest. As opposed to the rags-to-riches story arc of many of Crawford's 1930s MGM films, *Mildred Pierce*—as designed for the screen—extends the trajectory from rags to riches and ultimately to ruin.

Finally, the finished script is quite well crafted. In true Warner Brothers style, the characters are well delineated and the scenes move briskly and naturally from one to the next, often crackling with sharp, edgy dialogue. One excellent "lighter" scene, for example, is when Wally visits Mildred right after Bert has moved out of the family home and lets her know that he would be *very* interested getting to know her better. After she rebuffs several of his advances, they continue to spar:

MILDRED: Wally, why don't you make an effort to grow up?
WALLY: Why don't you make an effort to forget Bert?
MILDRED: Maybe I don't want to.

WALLY: But you'll be lonesome, Mildred. You're not the kind of a woman who can get along by herself.

MILDRED: Well, I can try.

WALLY: Oh, come on, get wise. (He tries to kiss her but she pushes him away.)

MILDRED: Wally! You should be kept on a leash. Now why can't you be friendly?

WALLY: But I am being friendly.

MILDRED: Now I mean it. Friendship is much more lasting than love.

WALLY: Yeah, but it isn't as entertaining.

✤ ✤ ✤

Attending to the film's visual presentation, Curtiz, Haller, Grot, and their teams did a superb job of integrating all the various story-telling components to provide a highly engaging experience. This was the director's first noir, and owing to his European roots and famil-iarity with German expressionism, he quickly integrated his own quasi-expressionistic visual style (for example, he loved to project enlarged black shadows on walls behind characters to convey threat or danger) with many of the familiar expressionistic and other visual ele-ments of noir. During the filming of *Mildred Pierce*, he worked closely with Haller to reinforce meaning with noir touches such as provocative dark lighting and disorienting camera angles. In the scene when Mil-dred discovers Veda and Monte embracing, for example, we see them first in deep black silhouette, a classic noir touch, to emphasize their pure evil. The other key partner in this process was Anton Grot (1884–1974), a fellow European émigré of Curtiz (Grot was Polish), who worked with Curtiz on fifteen films between the 1920s and 1940s and is often credited with greatly influencing the director's own personal style. One of the contributions to the film Grot has often received praise for is his design of the interior of Monte's beach house, especially its spiral stair-case and overall maze-like look—his attempt to build, as he once put it, "menace into the sets."[12] This design is especially effective, for exam-ple, in the scenes when Wally, after finding Monte's body, appears to be trapped in the beach house and frantically tries to get out.

Another interesting element about *Mildred Pierce* is the use of audio in creative expressionistic ways to enrich the narrative. The police station scene early in the film is an excellent example of this. As Mildred waits anxiously for her interview with Inspector Peterson, neither she nor others present are allowed to talk. So, as they sit silently, we become especially aware of the other sounds around the room—the ringing of a telephone, the churning of a pencil sharpener, the rustle of newspa-per pages being turned, the shuffle of footsteps, and so on. In the relative silence, these sounds are emphasized, sometimes even exaggerated, creating an even greater sense of tension for Mildred, who is already experiencing much fear and anxiety, and, by extension, heightened suspense for viewers.[13] It's an excellent touch, reminiscent of some of the creative ways normally innocuous sounds were used to great effect to enhance the narrative in Orson Welles's *Citizen Kane* four years earlier.

One component of *Mildred Pierce* that has also received praise is its musical score, which was written by the legendary film composer Max Steiner (1888–1971). Steiner, who is perhaps best known for his iconic score to *Gone with the Wind*, quickly adapted his work to film noir in the 1940s. Along with his score for Howard Hawks' *The Big Sleep* (1946), his score for *Mildred Pierce* is considered one of his best in the noir style. And, while much of it is quite good in its own right and appropriate to the story, its rousing, romantic main theme—even though it is memorable and quite gripping as a stand-alone piece of music—seems oddly out of place for the dark, bleak storyline. The first time we hear it, for example, is over the film's opening credits—just before the action shifts to gunshots ringing out from Monte's beach house and then to the images of Monte clutching his wounds and falling to the floor dead.

◆ ◆ ◆

The acting in *Mildred Pierce*, especially from several of the principal players, is exceptionally good. For this, Curtiz, as well as the actors, deserves great credit.

Topping the list, of course, is Crawford's definitive portrayal of Mildred. It is outstanding: understated, utterly believable, and often quite moving. Many reviewers have said that the role was a natural for the actress because of the many similarities (struggles to succeed, bad relationships with men, etc.) that she shared with the character in her own life. This may be true, but it's also dismissive considering the high quality of her performance. She creates a character who is quite complex: neurotic in her impossible quest to win the love of the selfish, narcissistic Veda, yet also extremely capable, determined, well-intentioned, and committed to seeing her course of action through—someone we can easily sympathize with. She also plays it without a false note throughout. In scene after scene—as she considers suicide on the pier, fends off Wally's advances, struggles to learn how to be a waitress, tries to get the smallest crumb of affection out of Veda, negotiates her marriage of convenience with Monte, and so on—she is on point and highly effective, often saying a great deal in a single facial expression or body movement. Crawford has been criticized for bringing too much glamour to the part. (Mildred is the person, of course, that Veda at one point calls a "common frump.") At the same time, Mildred is by no means ordinary or mediocre. She is, after all, a person who quickly transforms from a housewife with no formal business experience into a successful entrepreneur. She also needs to be attractive enough to catch the eyes of three different men, including the debonair Monte. As conceived for the screen, Mildred needs to have intelligence, presence, and some amount of glamour—attributes which Crawford ably delivers.

Although many critics praised Crawford's portrayal of Mildred, perhaps the greatest testament to its quality came from the writer who created the original character, James M. Cain. After he had seen the completed film, he sent the actress a signed copy of the novel with the inscription "[T]o Joan Crawford, who brought Mildred to life just as I had always hoped she would be, and who has my lifelong gratitude."[14]

As Veda, young Ann Blyth got to play the role of a lifetime and excelled in it. Her Veda is perfection: the character's distain for her easily manipulated mother is always just below the surface until their famous "Get out before I kill you" blow-up late in the film. In film noir parlance, Veda is the story's femme fatale, the evil woman who leads the hapless hero to ruin and/or death. The twist here, of course, is that the femme fatale is not the male protagonist's romantic interest but the female protagonist's daughter. It's a pity that Blyth (1928–), who was known for her wholesome image and cast against type as Veda, did not have more opportunities to play other noir femmes fatales after *Mildred Pierce*, because she is so good in this role. Her film career also turned out to be fairly brief. In 1953, she married a doctor and retired from films four years later to focus on raising what eventually became their five children. Afterwards, she acted only occasionally on television.

Zachary Scott (1914–1965) does quite well as the ne'er-do-well playboy Monte, who is *Mildred Pierce's* homme fatale. As an actor, Scott certainly looked the part. He was suave and handsome, but he also had dark, beady eyes and a face that could easily suggest duplicity and/or weakness. His performance, especially in his early scenes, is often very charming and relaxed, adding to his character's appeal, especially for Mildred. As the story progresses, we (and of course Mildred) see more of Monte's less attractive sides. It's impressive work in a role that could easily turn out to be thankless, and Scott's portrayal garnered him many positive notices. After *Mildred Pierce* (and perhaps because of it), he was often cast in villainous, or at least mysterious, roles.

One of the highlights of *Mildred Pierce* is Jack Carson's portrayal of the conniving and lecherous but still likeable Wally. A character actor with a long list of comical sidekick parts in films, Carson (1910–1963) could also be quite impressive in more dramatic roles, and, in *Mildred*

Pierce, he makes the most out of an opportunity to seamlessly integrate his comic and dramatic talents. In addition to Wally's humor, perhaps his two most appealing qualities are his self-knowledge and his absolute transparency with Mildred. He knows he's a slimeball, seems to thoroughly enjoy being one, and doesn't care who knows. Other dramatic roles where Carson did impressive work are in George Cukor's *A Star Is Born* (1954) and Richard Brooks' film adaptation of Tennessee Williams' play *Cat on a Hot Tin Roof* (1958).

Rounding out *Mildred Pierce's* main cast are Eve Arden and Bruce Bennett as Ida and Bert. Arden (1908–1990), who made a career out of playing wise-cracking supporting characters in films and then went to television, has only a peripheral role in the film, but, with her distinctive delivery of witty one-liners, she turns Ida into quite a memorable part. For example, her offhand comment referring to Veda, that "alligators have the right idea; they eat their young," is one of the film's most frequently quoted lines. Arden worked regularly up until her late 70s. Bennett (1906–2007) was not a great actor, but, as the dull and colorless Bert, he was well cast and did the job. He is quite good, for example, in the scenes when he tries, unsuccessfully, to get Mildred to see the truth about their two daughters, especially Veda. Bennett worked regularly in films and then television from the early 1930s until the late 1960s.

❖ ❖ ❖

Over the years, some noir purists have resisted calling *Mildred Pierce* a bona fide example of the style. Their arguments, however, are usually rather weak: that the protagonist is not a man; that the story lacks a conventional femme fatale; that the film is more of a woman's picture than a true, full-blooded noir; and so on.

In the important ways, however, *Mildred Pierce* is noir at its purest and darkest. A basically good and very capable person pursues the wrong course of action, and she and others around her reap the grim consequences. In the end, she is left with little more than the stark realization that all her efforts have resulted in death and other tragedy, that her own American Dream has become a nightmare.

By turning the screen version of *Mildred Pierce* into what we now call film noir, Wald, Curtiz, Crawford, and the film's other collaborators also showed—and in quite a stunning way—that, rather than being relatively fixed and rigid, the noir style could accommodate a much wider range of storytelling options. Why can't a woman, for example, be a noir protagonist? Why can't her downfall be as dark and desolate as any man's? Why can't noirs explore troubled mother-daughter relationships? Why can't a femme fatale be the protagonist's daughter instead of a romantic interest? Why can't noirs include elements of female-centered melodramas or even 1930s-style Joan Crawford pictures? Just as noir was beginning to proliferate in U.S. films, *Mildred Pierce* helped to unlock new creative doors for filmmakers, one they could pass through in pursuit of a wide variety of new story ideas and themes.

For Crawford, who understood the fleeting nature of fame as well as anyone, the stunning success of *Mildred Pierce* shifted her career focus from getting back on top to staying there. Now she was determined not to follow an accomplishment as big or as important as this with anything sub-par or even fair-to-middling. As she noted years later, "My gamble on abandoning straight-line glamour girls had paid off, but you don't stop there. A star has to keep in the race every minute."[15] Her next project had to be special: similar to *Mildred Pierce* in some ways but also intriguingly different. She quickly went to work, and even before she received her Academy Award and other accolades for her astonishing comeback of 1945, she was immersed in an effort that would ultimately be her next noir triumph.

3

"You might be sorry
love was ever invented, Paul"

Humoresque (1946)

Knowing that *Mildred Pierce* would be a hard act to follow, Jerry Wald and Crawford were especially careful about choosing both the actress's next starring vehicle and the creative team that would work on it, and, to their great credit, the choices they made were generally excellent. After months of preparation, filming, and post-production, what finally emerged was *Humoresque*, a dark, brooding drama that centers on a doomed love affair between a brilliant, driven violinist and his alluring but neurotic patroness.

Over the years, some critics have dismissed *Humoresque* as overwrought schmaltz, but, by doing so, they've overlooked much of what is distinctive and fascinating about it. More accurately, this film is a skillful and often highly stylized blend of the Wald-Crawford melodrama/noir hybrid with great music from the concert hall and grand opera. Here, the familiar melodramatic and noir elements are very much in evidence: the neurotic heroine, the bad personal choices, the sense of preordained doom, and more—all underscored by a flashback story structure and Ernest Haller's dark, often foreboding noir cinematography. This time, though, a principal aim is not, as was the case with *A Woman's Face* or *Mildred Pierce*, for nuanced realism and restrained, understated performances. Especially as the story of *Humoresque* progresses, the aim is sometimes to be extravagantly, unabashedly operatic. In many ways, this film is Puccini's *Madama Butterfly*, Wagner's *Tristan und Isolde*, Bizet's *Carmen*, or any number of other classic operas that focus on tragic love affairs. Like these works, too, the story is driven mainly by the emotional thrust of the music and, only secondarily, by plot and dialogue. It's no coincidence, for example, that key passages from both *Tristan und Isolde* and *Carmen* figure prominently in the telling of the tale. This time, there's also an unusual twist to the noir fixture of the femme or homme fatale who lures the film's protagonist toward personal doom or damnation. It's not the emotional hold of an evil person such as a Torsten Barring or a Veda Pierce over a more vulnerable Anna or Mildred. Instead, it's the intoxicating power that music, and specifically the violin, has over the heroine's lover. As film historian Rudy Behlmer has said, "Love does not triumph in this case; the violin triumphs."[1]

❖ ❖ ❖

Humoresque is based on a 1919 short story by Fannie Hurst (1889–1968), a writer of socially conscious sentimental novels and stories that were quite popular in the 1920s and 1930s. Hurst's version focuses on a large working-class Jewish family in pre–World War I New York. The mother steadfastly supports one son's aspirations to become a violinist and is thrilled when he exhibits exceptional ability. After several years, the son, now a young man, is making enough money from his playing to help the family out financially. At this time, however, the U.S. has entered the war and he puts his violin aside in order to serve, which leaves his mother heartbroken. The story's title, incidentally, refers to the popular piece of music by Antonin Dvorak, which Hurst, in the story, relates to Jewish life and history and, more specifically, to the very strong bond between the mother and her prodigy son.

A silent film version of the story was released in 1920. Directed by Frank Borzage and adapted by pioneering female screenwriter Frances Marion, it stays fairly close to the original story, although a far-fetched happy ending was added to please audiences.

Wald, who was accustomed to juggling film projects for several different stars at one time, thought that an updated, greatly altered version of the story[2] might make a good starring vehicle for actor John Garfield. To work on an adaptation, he assigned two writers then under contract with the studio, Clifford Odets and Zachary Gold. At the time, Odets (1906–1963) was one of the shining lights of the U.S. stage. His socialist-leaning plays from the 1930s—among them *Awake and Sing!*, *Waiting for Lefty*, and *Paradise Lost*—had achieved great notoriety and would later influence the work of Arthur Miller, Paddy Chayefsky, David Mamet, and other major U.S. playwrights who emerged between the 1940s and the 1970s. In the 1940s, Odets worked mostly in Hollywood, writing adaptations for such films as the drama *None but the Lonely Heart* (1944, which he also directed) and the noir *Deadline at Dawn* (1946) as well as *Humoresque*. He continued writing for both the theater and films until his death. Little information about Gold (1918–1953) is available. In addition to his screenwriting work on *Humoresque*, he is credited for his efforts on the Donald O'Connor musical *Top Man* (1943) and the Joel McCrea western *South of St. Louis* (1949).

In one of her memoirs, Crawford tells how she first heard about the 1946 version of *Humoresque*. During a phone chat with Wald and his wife, Wald mentioned that he was reading a script for a new film that would star John Garfield as a violinist and offered to read a scene between the violinist and a new character—"this nymphomaniac, alcoholic woman," as he put it—that Odets and Gold had added to the story. Crawford, who found their writing "exquisite," immediately asked to play the woman. Wald cautioned her, saying that this part was very small, that this woman appeared in only three scenes. "I don't care," she responded.[3]

Wald had been considering other actresses for this role, among them Barbara Stanwyck and Tallulah Bankhead. But, when Crawford,

As Oscar Levant's Sid Jeffers (second from left) and John Garfield's Paul Boray (right) look on, Crawford's Helen Wright and Ruth Nelson's Esther Boray (second from right), Paul's protective, and very concerned, mother, have one of several uncomfortable face-to-face meetings in Jean Negulesco's *Humoresque* (1946) (Warner Brothers/Photofest).

who was getting lots of attention at the time because of *Mildred Pierce*, expressed her interest, Wald opted for her and directed the writers to greatly expand the character's part.[4]

Crawford was also excited about the prospect of working with Garfield. As film writer Frank Miller notes:

> Like her former husband Franchot Tone, [Garfield] had come to Hollywood after work with the pioneering Group Theatre, whose socially conscious plays and deeply personal acting inspired by the writings of Stanislavsky had always intrigued her. At one point in the '30s, she had even considered leaving Hollywood to work with them. She also was attracted to Garfield's brazen masculinity. On their first meeting, he said, "So you're Joan Crawford, the big movie star! Glad to meet ya," and pinched her breast. At first, she bristled, but then she smiled and said, "I think we're going to get along just fine."[5]

With Crawford on board, Wald increased the film's budget and began to assemble a team that would be acceptable to the star. Among those enlisted were cinematographer Ernest Haller and costume designer Adrian (whose real name was Adrian Adolph Greenberg), a favorite of Crawford's who had worked with her on several of her MGM films.

To direct *Humoresque*, the studio (with Crawford's approval, of course) assigned Jean Negulesco (1900–1993). A Romanian-born artist turned film director, Negulesco had begun his film career at Paramount in 1927, working first as a sketch artist for title designs and montage sequences. Gradually, he took on a variety of other production roles from assistant producer to second-unit director. In 1940, he moved to Warner Brothers, where he soon distinguished himself as a director of short subjects and feature-length noirs that were characterized by intriguing camera angles and the dramatic use of shadows and silhouettes. Among the more memorable noirs he had worked on before *Humoresque* were *The Mask of Dimitrios* (1944) with Sidney Greenstreet and Peter Lorre, *The Conspirators* (1944) with Hedy Lamarr, and *Three Strangers* (1946) again with Greenstreet and Lorre. After *Humoresque*, Negulesco continued to direct films until 1970. In 1949, he received a Best Director Academy Award nomination for his work on the 1948 Warner Brothers drama *Johnny Belinda*. A decade later, he again joined forces with both Wald and Crawford for the Twentieth Century–Fox drama *The Best of Everything*.

At first, Crawford, who preferred to have her directors talk her through her roles in detail, had difficulties working with Negulesco, whose approach was to watch the actors do a scene and then to work with what they gave him. After a few frustrating days of rehearsal, she went to Wald in tears, complaining that the director didn't discuss her scenes with her in advance. When Wald relayed this to Negulesco, the director became anxious about how he could get through to her. Then, according to Negulesco, his wife came up with a solution: paint a sketch portrait that conveyed the essence of the character. He did and gave it to Crawford, explaining, "I'm sorry, but I'm not an eloquent man. This is what I think the character should be."[6] This gesture delighted Crawford, who later claimed that, from that point on, she knew precisely what the director was looking for. (The portrait, incidentally, appears briefly in the completed film.)

As preparations for the film continued, one of the great production challenges loomed large for the filmmakers: the music. With twenty-three different pieces of classical music slated to be played during the story, most with major parts for the violin, the need for a world-class violinist became all the more apparent. The first choice to record the music was the reigning violin master, Jascha Heifetz, but his fee was much higher than the tight-fisted Jack Warner was willing to pay. So, composer and conductor Franz Waxman, who selected, arranged, and conducted the various compositions played in the film, went in search of a younger, less expensive violinist who could also deliver the superb result that would be essential for the story to be credible. In San Francisco, he found that person—the then-twenty-five-year-old Isaac Stern (1920–2001), who would go on to become a towering figure on the global classical music scene for the next half-century.

Another fine addition to the effort was the pianist, composer, author, and film and (later) television personality Oscar Levant (1906–1972), who portrays Garfield's sidekick in the film. His highly unusual assignment was to play the piano beautifully while also sprinkling his character's witty, often self-deprecating one-liners into the otherwise serious story.

Filming took place in early 1946, wrapping up by late April.

◆ ◆ ◆

Humoresque opens outside a New York concert hall. As people mill around its front doors, a man comes out and puts a notice saying "PERFORMANCE CANCELLED" across a poster of the featured player, violinist Paul Boray. Immediately, the picture dissolves to Boray himself (John Garfield), brooding in his well-appointed New York apartment. His manager Frederic Bauer (Richard Gaines) is impatient with him for thinking about giving up his career in music. "Music is an obsession, a compulsion with you," he tells Paul. "You'll blow up into a thousand pieces if you don't play it." Paul's more sympathetic friend, pianist Sid

Jeffers (Oscar Levant), tells Bauer to ease up and the two walk out. Now alone, Paul muses about "being on the outside looking in" and "feeling far away from home" and then mutters "I can't get back to that simple, happy kid I used to be...."

Now, the picture dissolves to Paul as a boy (Robert Blake) in a working-class neighborhood in New York in the early 1920s. He enters the local grocery store his father Rudy (J. Carrol Naish) runs, and his mother Esther (Ruth Nelson) announces that papa will be taking Paul to the neighborhood toy store so Paul can pick out his own birthday present. At the store, Rudy tries to get Paul to select a cheap toy, something that costs about a dollar and fifty cents, but Paul is mesmerized by a violin, which costs eight dollars. Frustrated, Rudy tells him he can't have it, and, unhappily, they return home. Esther, however, is adamant that Paul should have what he wants, even if it costs eight dollars. Rudy relents, Paul gets the violin, and he immediately begins to practice on it with great enthusiasm. The years go by, Paul (now played by Garfield) greatly improves, and along the way has ongoing friendships with two other aspiring musicians, Sid Jeffers and a neighbor named Gina (Joan Chandler), who at one point tells Paul that she loves him. Intensely committed to his playing, Paul, while still retaining some of his boyhood sweetness, has now become more self-absorbed, hard-driving, and brash. With his family coping with the Great Depression, he also feels great pressure to earn money but insists that the only way he can do this is by playing the violin. He goes to Sid, who after years of playing the piano, has himself achieved only modest success, and asks him how it's done. At first, Sid helps Paul get a succession of modest jobs. These frustrate Paul, but he continues to improve.

Knowing that Paul will also need money and connections to achieve the kind of success he is aiming for, Sid eventually invites him to come with him to play at the home of two wealthy patrons of the arts, socialites Helen Wright (Crawford) and her older husband Victor (Paul Cavanagh). At the party (excellently staged as a star's entrance for Crawford), Paul impresses everyone with his superb playing. Helen finds him especially intriguing, and, for a bit, they spar verbally. "Why did Helen ride him like that?" one of the guests asks Victor. "She's merely getting interested, that's all," Victor says, alluding to Helen's practice of initiating affairs with younger men.

The next day Paul receives a gift from Helen, a cigarette case, along with a note asking him to forgive her for her bad manners. They meet for drinks, she asks him personal questions but insists that she's only interested in him as an artist. Later, she arranges for the highly respected Frederic Bauer to manage him and for a concert that music reviewers from various New York newspapers will attend. At the concert, Paul plays beautifully. Afterwards, Esther has planned a small party for the family and Gina, but instead Paul goes to a reception the Wrights are hosting. The next morning, as Rudy reads largely glowing reviews from the critics in the newspapers, Esther, who by now suspects that something might be developing between Paul and Helen, indirectly expresses her disappointment that he stood up the family and Gina.

Helen continues to mentor Paul, introducing him to people who can help his career, even buying expensive clothes for him to wear. The sparring between them continues, however. He resents what he considers her patronizing attitude toward him. She resents his lack of gratitude and feels he sneers at her "general uselessness." Still, they continue to see each other personally. As they ride horses during one visit to her beach house, she falls off her horse. He immediately goes to her full of concern and they kiss. Later, after they've made love for what appears to be the first time, they lay next to each other under the stars and talk openly:

> HELEN: You might be sorry love was ever invented, Paul. I'm not a simple person. I have my faults.... Ever since I can remember ... people were stupid enough to put up with me. You never did.
> PAUL: And you liked that?
> HELEN: No, I hated it. I was afraid of it. I still am.
> PAUL: Why?
> HELEN: Oh, it takes a great deal of courage to look at ourselves as we really are. I never wanted to. So, I drank. That's the truth, pure and simple.
> PAUL: The truth is never simple.
> HELEN: I know that. The truth is I love you. I can't fight you any longer, Paul.

Late at night, Paul returns home. Esther is waiting for him. She reminds him that he had had a date with Gina. He apologizes, saying he forgot. She then asks him about Helen. "What do you think, Mom?" he asks. "She's a married woman. What do you think?" she replies sharply. He denies that he and Helen are involved, but Esther isn't buying it. "Be careful," she warns him. "The stakes are big.... This is for life. Think of this year and the year after. Think of your work."

Now the picture dissolves to a montage of Paul Boray concert dates all around the U.S. It appears as though he has been touring for months. Eventually, he arrives back in New York, sees Gina in Bauer's office, and, on the spur of the moment, asks her to join him and Sid for lunch. As they sit at their restaurant table waiting for Sid, Gina tells Paul that success has changed him, admits to being a bit jealous, and adds "We ought to be able to forget old friends—pack them away in some dim corner like last year's souvenirs. That would be the kindest way." A moment later, Sid enters accompanied by Helen, who immediately becomes jealous when she sees Gina, makes an excuse not to stay, and leaves. Immediately, Paul goes after Helen. Gina then asks Sid about Helen, and Sid, sensitive to her feelings for Paul, tries to make light of things. Gina, however, finds the situation unbearable and leaves as well.

Helen and Paul end up at her favorite bar where she acts jealous and petulant, finally throwing her martini glass against the wall. They leave and go to her place. She's angry because she hasn't heard from him and asks him not to close her out of his life but to let her help "in the small ways that I can." He tells her that she is, after all, married. She says that they are "both old enough to vote," suggesting that they can choose to lead their lives in any way they wish. They both share a knowing, more relaxed smile. A moment later, though, she adds, "We don't laugh enough—that's our trouble."

At a concert soon afterwards, Paul plays a lush, romantic piece of music. His family, Sid, and Gina all sit in the orchestra section as Helen listens from a box seat tenderly holding a rolled-up program (yes, a phallic symbol) in her hands. As she listens to Paul play, she seems entranced, perhaps sexually aroused, by the music. From their seats in the orchestra, both Gina and Esther see this and are greatly disturbed by it, Gina so much so that she leaves the concert hall crying and running out into the rainy night.

Paul moves out of the family home and into a small but very up-scale apartment. One day, when he is still unpacking, Esther and Rudy come to visit. Everywhere Esther looks, she sees evidence of Helen and reaffirms her disapproval of Paul's relationship with her. "There's something wrong with a woman like that," she says. They argue, and unexpectedly she slaps him. Immediately, she regrets this, and both feel sad about the incident.

One night in their home, Victor, in a very kind and chivalrous gesture, tells Helen that, even though he still loves her very much, he won't stand in the way of her divorcing him to marry Paul. Thrilled by this development, Helen goes to a concert hall where Paul is rehearsing and writes a note for a stage hand to give to Paul. "Wonderful, exciting news!" it says. "I <u>must</u> see you immediately." When the stage hand delivers the note to Paul, though, he crumples it up and asks the conductor to continue with the rehearsal. Helen is crushed.

After the rehearsal, Paul tries to track Helen down and finally finds her at her favorite bar in the middle of the night. She is very drunk. "I'm tired of playing second fiddle to the ghost of Beethoven," she tells him.

After Paul and Helen leave, one of her friends, also at the bar, remarks, "A French philosopher once listed 300 ways of committing suicide. But he left one out—falling in love with an artist."

At Paul's apartment, Helen has some coffee and sobers up. She tells him that Victor will give her a divorce without any resistance but that marriage still won't work out for them because his music will always come first. "You don't want me, Paul," she says. "I'm too wearing on the nerves." Paul, however, insists that he still wants to marry her.

Soon afterwards, Helen, hoping to convince Esther that she truly loves Paul and wants only the best for him, visits her at the Boray family home. But Esther, barely containing her anger, won't have any of it. "You talk about love," Esther says, "What love? You only make demands. You only think of yourself. You give nothing in return. Leave him, Mrs. Wright. Leave him alone."

Before his next concert, Paul receives a call from Helen, who is at her beach house. He immediately snaps at her, saying he has enough to worry about without always having to wonder about where she is or what she's doing. "Do you want to ruin my concert?" he says. "Ruin my career? Ruin everything?" Instead of making the long drive back to attend the concert, she says that she will listen to the live broadcast on the radio. It's so quiet and peaceful at beach house, she adds. She wishes him good luck, and he curtly hangs up. Alone and distraught, she starts drinking heavily, seeing herself as a burden to Paul and a drag on his career, perhaps even someone who might inadvertently ruin his career. As she drinks, she listens to Paul playing a piece from Wagner's tragic romantic opera *Tristan und Isolde*. Very drunk, she walks along the beach and, looking at the water, senses that, perhaps, she can find a peace in death that she's never had in life. Then she walks into the ocean and to her death.

Paul and Sid visit the site where Helen entered the water. Then later, at his apartment, Paul tells Sid, "It all seemed so simple once—live your life, do your work. As simple as all that. You find out it's not that easy. Nothing comes free. One way or another, you pay for what you are." He looks at his violins. "Tell Bauer not to worry," he adds. "I'm not running away."

In the film's final shot, we see Paul walking down what seems to be a street in his old neighborhood, very likely the one where the family grocery store and home is.

✦ ✦ ✦

Humoresque opened on Christmas Day 1946 to generally favorable notices and a robust box office. *Variety*, for example, called it a "top-quality motion picture" and praised both Garfield's and Crawford's work, noting that Crawford "makes the most" of the challenging role of Helen.[7] Even *New York Times* reviewer Bosley Crowther, who was often harshly critical of Crawford's work, had to admit that the music was "splendid."[8] The film, which was budgeted at slightly more than $2 million, went on to make nearly $3.4 million—a major success for Warner Brothers and additional proof that Crawford was far from being a "has been."

Today, *Humoresque* is generally considered one of Crawford's best films and her portrayal of Helen Wright one of her best performances. Her Helen is certainly a high point in *Humoresque*, but it is only one of many key contributions to the film's success. Superb work was done in virtually every major element of the production: scriptwriting, direction, cinematography, acting, editing, and—of utmost importance—the selection and performance of the film's twenty-three classical music pieces.

Although the final Odets-Gold script is officially an adaptation, it departs so radically from the original story and earlier film that it is actually much closer to an original screenplay. Perhaps the screenwriters' most interesting contribution is the creation of the Helen Wright character. A fascinating mix of self-loathing; desperate cravings to be loved, happy, and useful to others; and numerous other churning emotions, she literally becomes the story's co-protagonist and most vivid character. In addition, the script provides other characters either adapted or created for this version, such as Victor, Sid, Esther, Rudy, and Gina, all with moments that enable us to glimpse into the core of their humanity. These are small or relatively small roles, but they are all fleshed out and none is one-dimensional or stereotypical. Largely because of the creation of Helen, the story's plot, especially after the film's first thirty minutes, is almost entirely new, and it is to the screenwriters' great credit that, despite the story's complexity, events flow so naturally and logically. While the film does contain a few clunky lines of dialogue, these are little more than momentary hiccups.

Negulesco's direction and Haller's cinematography are both quite good. Among the scenes that especially stand out are those when the film's visuals are used along with sweeping, highly charged pieces of music to create unabashedly larger-than-life—grandly operatic—results. In one scene, for example, Paul plays an intensely romantic piece of music with such feeling that Gina—seeing the intoxicating effect his playing has over Helen (also in the audience)—is so distressed that she must run out of the concert hall. In another, we hear the strains from *Tristan und Isolde* as a drunken and desolate Helen considers, and then follows through with, her suicide. In both instances, close-ups and other visuals combine with the music to convey emotion with operatic intensity. Unlike what would occur in an opera, though, neither Gina nor Helen needs to sing about her heartbreak or despair to adequately convey it. Because the medium is film, both women's feelings are self-evident in what the director, cinematographer, and actresses have (and brilliantly, too) chosen to show us. In a sense, the emotions the actresses' faces reveal to us become their characters' songs of heartbreak and despair.

Still another strength of *Humoresque* is the acting, which is excellent throughout.

As noted earlier, Crawford's portrayal of Helen is widely considered to be one of her best performances, and it's almost impossible to argue this point. From the star's entrance she receives in her very first scene when Helen meets Paul until the end of the film, she plays Helen with

Don McGuire's Eddie (center) and Craig Stevens's Monte (right) look on as Crawford's Helen wallows at her favorite bar in *Humoresque*. The lighting in this scene, especially on Crawford, by cinematographer Ernest Haller is characteristic of his contribution to the film: capturing Crawford in ways that accentuate her physical attributes while also reinforcing the story's narrative (Warner Brothers/Photofest).

absolute conviction and authority. In praising her work, Crawford biographers Lawrence Quirk and William Schoell have mentioned the "extra dimension of romantic lyricism and dramatic sincerity" she brought to her portrayal, adding that she "strode through the role with a grand self-confidence and a sweeping grasp of the part's emotional possibilities."[9] Indeed, she has many wonderful scenes in the film from Helen's initial meeting with Paul to the many times that she and Paul try to hash out why they can't be happy together, to her pivotal confrontation with Esther, to her last moments at the beach house and then on the beach before her suicide. Drawing upon her silent film experience, Crawford is also especially good at using her face and body to communicate Helen's often complex thoughts and feelings. One excellent example is the scene when Helen writes Paul a note during a rehearsal to say that Victor will grant her a divorce and then watches as Paul reads it, crumples it up, and then asks the conductor to continue with the rehearsal. It's fascinating to watch the actress's face as Helen's expression changes from excited anticipation to surprise, to confusion, to deep hurt. Another example is the superb way Crawford conveys Helen's near-sightedness. What she does with her eyes and face seems so real it's easy to forget that this is actually an actress conveying an aspect of her character. Some critics have felt that Crawford overacts in some scenes, but, in this film especially, big emotions are clearly warranted. First, Helen is very much a drama queen, and theatrics, such as throwing her martini glass against the bar room wall, are absolutely appropriate for the character. Second, the big emotions complement the film's big operatic moments much better than a more realistic, underplayed approach would.

Because Crawford's performance in *Humoresque* is so dominant, it's often easy to overlook the fine job John Garfield does at portraying the brilliant, driven, self-centered, and conflicted Paul. An artist completely seduced by his "violon fatale," he is, it seems, constantly at odds with all the important people in his life from Esther to Helen. He wants to be both a successful artist and someone who can lead a somewhat normal, somewhat happy life, and he is deeply frustrated because he also senses that, for him at least, this will probably be impossible. Throughout, Garfield communicates all this with great clarity, honesty, and feeling. Garfield and Crawford seem like an unlikely romantic pairing, but the sexual chemistry is definitely there, and the casting works superbly. Unlike other leading men Crawford worked with at this time in her career, Garfield more than holds his own when he shares scenes with her. It's also possible that his strong presence in the film was an incentive for Crawford to up her game so that he would not dominate the proceedings.

A top Hollywood star during the 1940s, Garfield (1913–1952) distinguished himself in noirs and other films for Warner Brothers and other studios, reaching his peak in the post–World War II years. In addition to *Humoresque*, other significant films he appeared in during this time include: *The Postman Always Rings Twice, Gentleman's Agreement* (1947), *Body and Soul* (1947), *Force of Evil* (1948), *The Breaking Point* (1950), and *He Ran All the Way* (1951). Sadly, he died of a heart attack in May 1952 at age thirty-nine. This was the result of long-term heart problems and, according to many close to him, the stress he endured when, because of his liberal sympathies, he was investigated by the U.S. House of Representatives Un-American Activities Committee in the early 1950s.

In addition to Crawford and Garfield's superb performances in *Humoresque*, several of the supporting players deserve special praise for their fine work. Topping the list is Ruth Nelson (1905–1992) as Paul's mother Esther, who combines a deep, possessive love for Paul and an acute understanding of what he needs with a fierce motherly instinct to protect him from Helen, whom she sees as a serious threat to his well-being. Her performance is marvelous as it moves from an instinctive sense that there may be an attraction between Paul and Helen to outright loathing for Helen and, finally, to a brutally frank showdown with her. Another is the versatile J. Carrol Naish (1896–1973), who skillfully portrays Paul's tight-fisted but basically kind, good-hearted, and loyal father Rudy. Another is actress Joan Chandler (1923–1979), who beautifully underplays her character of Gina as she endures years of unrequited love for Paul only to see Helen win him. Still another is Paul Cavanagh (1888–1964) as Victor Wright, the weak, world-weary husband whose great act of strength and love is to let Helen go so she can follow her heart. Finally, there's the young Robert Blake (1933–2023), who plays Paul as a boy with both great sweetness and a single-minded determination to possess and master the violin. Blake is so winning in his small part that his strong first impression as the young Paul helps to make the older, very self-absorbed Paul (after Garfield takes over the role) easier for viewers to accept and sympathize with.

Although nearly all of the other significant contributors to *Humoresque* did fine work on the effort, two more deserve to be singled out for special recognition: film editor Rudi Fehr and music director Franz Waxman.

Fehr (1911–1999) is often credited with helping to pull off one of the great technical feats in *Humoresque*: making it believable to audiences that Garfield, who could not play a violin to save his life, could handle one like a virtuoso. To create the illusion, especially in closeups, Garfield had to keep his arms behind his back while two professional violinists, one perched on each side of him, did the actual fingering and bowing. So, what we see as we watch the film are Garfield's head and the hands of two different violinists on screen at the same time, and what we hear is the playing of real-life virtuoso Isaac Stern, which was recorded separately. This entire effort had to be directed, filmed, performed, and especially edited with great care and skill. As one of the most respected editors at Warner Brothers during the 1940s, Fehr drew the assignment, and his work on *Humoresque* is regarded as one of the triumphs of his career.

In 1954, Jack Warner appointed Fehr head of the studio's post-production, including the editing department, a position Fehr held until his retirement in 1976. He continued to work afterwards, however, first as the head of post-production for Francis Ford Coppola's production company, American Zoetrope, and then as the co-editor, with his daughter Kaja, of John Huston's hit film *Prizzi's Honor* (1985). For their work on *Prizzi's Honor*, both father and daughter were nominated for a Best Editing Academy Award.

Finally, the contributions to *Humoresque* of composer-conductor Franz Waxman (1906–1967) were both substantial and remarkable. As conductor Richard Kaufman has noted, *Humoresque* "is one of the first films—if not the first film—where the music of the concert hall is so important to the story.... The music was really a character in *Humoresque*."[10] This is absolutely true. Not only is the music central to the lives of the film's characters, but it is critically important to underscoring the interplay between them and ultimately to propelling the drama forward. Waxman, a serious composer and conductor who spent much of his career working in films, was the person responsible for selecting, arranging, and conducting the various compositions played in *Humoresque*, when they would be played in the story, and how they would be arranged and performed. And he did an exceptional job of putting it all together. "Waxman had," as concertmaster Bruce Dukov has observed, "a great feel for the dramatic action of the film."[11]

Much of the critical conversation about Waxman's contribution centers on the brilliant way he selected and arranged passages from two great operas about tragic love, Bizet's *Carmen* and Wagner's *Tristan und Isolde*, to highlight the emotions of Helen and Paul. For example, when discussing the choice of *Tristan und Isolde* to play over Helen's suicide scene, film music historian (and son of Franz) John Waxman has said, "It is very dramatic, it is passionate, it is peaceful, it is reflective, and it resolves the relationship for [the characters played by] John Garfield and Joan Crawford."[12] Reflecting on the same music and scene, Richard Kaufman has also said, "I don't think they could have picked a better piece of music, in all of classical music, to use for that moment in the film."[13]

One of the great film composers and arrangers of Hollywood's classic era, Waxman was active in films from the 1930s until he mid–1960s. Along the way, he picked up twelve Academy Award nominations for his work, one of which was for his contributions to *Humoresque*. Two of these nominations also resulted in back-to-back Oscars: one for *Sunset Boulevard* (1950) and the other for *A Place in the Sun* (1951).

❖ ❖ ❖

Once again, Wald, Crawford, and their filmmaking colleagues took a dark, noirish script and—to appropriate the language of the concert hall—played variations on familiar noirish themes. In *Humoresque*, there is not a single noir protagonist but two, a man who loses the woman he loves and a woman who takes her own life because she, as she has put it, she will always be "second fiddle" to his music and ultimately a drag on his career and him. Here, of course, the femme or homme fatale is the violon fatale. And here, the story is driven and enhanced, not by hard-boiled noir dialogue or a crime-centered plot, but largely by emotionally charged, often operatic music that both reflects and reinforces the intense emotions key characters feel and the operatic situations they find themselves in. At the same time, however, many elements that are distinctively noir—from the story's flashback structure and dark, moody cinematography to its flawed characters and atmosphere of preordained doom—remain. In the end, *Humoresque* is a very successful melding of all of the above, and much more. When it was made, there had never been another film, let alone noir, quite like it, and even today it remains highly distinctive and memorable. Once again, Wald, Crawford, and their colleagues extended the boundaries of noir content and, in the process, enhanced and enriched the noir style.

❖ ❖ ❖

Now, as it does for anyone whose work progresses from project to project, the eternal question again emerged for Wald and Crawford—What do we do next? One part of the answer was easy: stick with the female-centered-melodrama/noir template they had developed with *Mildred Pierce* and refined with *Humoresque*. This was, after all, a formula that was working well and could continue to work for a while longer. But what could they bring to the template this time that was new and different? Their answer was to go deep into a very dark territory, one that noir and other post–World War II Hollywood films were just beginning to explore.

4

"I don't know what's wrong.
I don't know why
I am this way"

Possessed (1947)

For her next project with Warner Brothers and Jerry Wald, Crawford accepted a role that she would often refer to in interviews as the most difficult she ever played. The film was *Possessed*,[1] and the character was Louise Howell, a woman who suffers from schizophrenia and slowly deteriorates, becoming more unstable and delusional as the story progresses.

Much as *Humoresque* had done, *Possessed* fit two key criteria Wald and Crawford sought in a new project: familiarity and novelty. First, the story could easily be shaped to fit what was fast becoming their female-centered melodrama/noir, or *"Mildred Pierce,"* film formula with its dark, foreboding tone; complex, long-suffering female lead; edgy dialogue; flashback story structure; and noir-style lighting and camerawork. Second, this project tackled new subject matter for both the producer and the star: the world of a person with a serious mental illness.

While this subject was new for a Wald/Crawford effort, it was, by the mid–1940s, fast emerging as a popular focus for films, especially noirs and noir-tinged efforts. One key reason was increasing popular interest in such related topics as the work of Austrian psychoanalysis pioneer Sigmund Freud and post-traumatic stress disorder, or PTSD, the psychiatric condition affecting U.S. service personnel during and after World War II. Another was growing popularity of noir-style films with their frequent focus on characters who lose their grip on reality and/or control over their lives, characters whose story arcs overlap closely with the nightmarish realities of mental illness.

In response, Hollywood studios began churning out more

"psychological" noir and noirish films. In addition to *Possessed*, just a few of the dozens of those released between 1945 and 1948 include Alfred Hitchcock's *Spellbound*, Edgar G. Ulmer's *Strange Illusion*, Robert Siodmak's *The Dark Mirror*, Edmond Goulding's *Nightmare Alley*, and Anatole Litvak's *The Snake Pit*.

As we might expect, depictions of persons with psychological afflictions vary widely from film to film. These range from sensationalized "scenery-chewing" performances designed mainly to scare or shock to more thoughtful, well-researched portrayals that aimed to give viewers greater insight into, and empathy for, persons suffering from these illnesses. One excellent example of the latter is Litvak's noirish 1948 drama *The Snake Pit*, which is based on the semi-autobiographical novel written by Mary Jane Ward, a woman who had actually been committed to a mental institution. Both an unusually sensitive and moving portrayal of mental illness and an insightful look at the strengths and shortcomings of the mental health system at the time, it was nominated for seven Academy Awards, including Best Picture, Best Director (Litvak), Best Adapted Screenplay (Frank Partos and Millen Brand), and Best Actress (Olivia de Havilland).

Depictions of psychiatrists and other mental health professionals in these films vary widely as well. Usually, these people are portrayed as committed to the well-being of those being treated. Sometimes, though, these professionals use their expertise and/or power to further their own interests rather than those of the people in their care—a very noir-like behavior. A chilling example of this kind of character is Dr. Lilith Ritter in Goulding's very dark 1947 noir *Nightmare Alley*. Played brilliantly by the under-appreciated Helen Walker, Dr. Ritter is a psychologist who conspires with the story's unscrupulous hero to manipulate her patients for financial gain.

Often, too, the mental health professionals perform an expository function in the narrative, helping to cue audiences in on specific patient conditions by using such jargon as "persecution complex" or "schizoid attachment." One shortcoming of this approach, of course, has been that, as psychiatry and other mental health therapies have evolved since the 1940s, the older thinking and the jargon related to it have increasingly struck modern audiences as dated.

Among these films, *Possessed* is clearly one of the more thoughtful and carefully researched. Crawford and everyone else connected with the project went to great lengths to portray her character's schizophrenia in a realistic, sympathetic manner. Throughout, the mental health professionals are also portrayed as dedicated to helping her and other patients. Since the film is at least partially a melodrama, it does have its overly dramatic elements, but, for the time, an unusual level of commitment was made to telling Louise's story as honestly as possible.

For Crawford, especially, who was as determined as ever to show her critics that she could deliver top-tier performances, the chance to tackle psychological noir, this particular story, and the daunting role of Louise was a challenge she relished. While a difficult assignment for her, this was also one of the few roles she ever played that she didn't express some level of dissatisfaction with afterwards. "*Possessed* contained the best performance I ever gave," she recalled years later. "I put so much of myself into it."[2]

❖ ❖ ❖

Possessed is based on "One Man's Secret," a long short story by Rita Weiman (1885–1954) that first appeared in the March 1943 edition of *Cosmopolitan Magazine*. Weiman, a prolific writer from the 1910s through the 1940s, began as a journalist and then wrote for the stage, screen, and various magazines ranging from *Cosmopolitan* to the

Van Heflin's rakish David Sutton (left) finds the obsessive feelings that Crawford's Louise Howell has for him to be discomforting and if not downright suffocating in Curtis Bernhardt's *Possessed* (1947) (Allstar Picture Library Limited/Alamy Stock Photo).

Saturday Evening Post. She was most active in films during the 1920s, when she developed scripts for, among others, producer Samuel Goldwyn and directors William deMille (Cecil's brother) and Frank Lloyd. By the 1940s, her main focus had turned to fiction writing, which she continued to pursue until her death.

Warner Brothers purchased the rights to *One Man's Secret* and, in April 1944, announced plans to produce a film version starring Ida Lupino, Paul Lukas, and Sydney Greenstreet. Producer Jerry Wald, who was heading the effort, assigned in-house screenwriter Silvia Richards to write an adaptation. But after Richards had completed a first draft, Wald—now basking in the success of 1945's *Mildred Pierce* and intent on repeating a winning formula—coaxed Crawford into starring and recruited Ranald MacDougall to do a complete story makeover, turning it into a full-fledged noir. Ultimately, Richards and MacDougall would share screenwriting credit.

To direct, the studio assigned Curtis Bernhardt, who, in only six years at Warner Brothers, had already acquired a reputation both for creatively employing expressionistic film techniques to enhance noir storylines and for getting excellent performances from strong actresses such as Ida Lupino, Barbara Stanwyck, and Bette Davis. For this project, his talents and experience suited both Wald's and Crawford's interests quite well.

Bernhardt (1899–1981), one of several notable filmmakers to flee Germany after the Nazis came into power in 1933, had an especially interesting personal history. A Jew, he was arrested by the Nazis soon after they came to power, but, in a series of hair-raising episodes, he managed to escape and go to France. For the rest of the decade, he directed films there and in England. With the beginning of World War II in Europe in 1939, he left for the U.S., where, on the strength of one of his French films, the drama *Carrefour* (1938), both MGM and Warner Brothers eagerly sought his services. Although MGM was widely considered the more prestigious studio to work for at the time, he opted for Warner Brothers because he liked its edgier, more hard-boiled style. He stayed there for most of the 1940s and then directed films for MGM, RKO, Columbia, and other studios until his retirement in 1964.

Once again, Franz Waxman was brought in, this time both to write a musical score for the film and to leverage pieces of classical music that could enhance the story's narrative and mirror the feelings of key characters. Much as he had used pieces from Wagner, Bizet, and other composers in *Humoresque*, he made excellent use of an evocative piano piece by nineteenth-century German composer Robert Schumann: Section 12, or the "Chopin" section, of his *Carnaval* Op. 9.

The pre-production, shooting, and post-production phases of *Possessed* occurred mostly in late 1946 and early 1947.

One unusual aspect of this film's production phase is that, at one point, shooting was halted for about six weeks so Crawford and Bernhardt could visit psychiatric wards in the Los Angeles area to observe patients and consult with doctors on aspects of the script in order to ensure authenticity. Curiously, this decision led to additional complications. On one of these visits, the two watched, without the patient's permission, a woman receive electroshock therapy. Claiming that this was an invasion of her privacy, the woman sued Warner Brothers for $200,000. Eventually, though, she settled for far less in damages.

On several occasions, Crawford also exercised the unusual power her contract granted her over creative aspects of the production. In one case, she threatened not to go on with the film unless Warner Brothers' top writing team of Julius and Philip Epstein (who had largely been responsible for the script of *Casablanca*) were brought in to do rewrites on her part. At the time, however, the Epsteins, pranksters who delighted in tormenting production head Jack Warner, had been suspended by the studio. So, to accommodate Crawford, Warner had to temporarily suspend the suspension and give the Epsteins back pay. They did the work and were duly paid, but they did not receive any scriptwriting credit. In another case, the cinematographer was the issue. Bernhardt did not like working with Ernest Haller, who had done such fine work on both *Mildred Pierce* and *Humoresque*, because Haller constantly tinkered with lights between takes, slowing down the shooting process. Crawford agreed to work with someone else but then exercised her right of refusal over every cinematographer the studio suggested. Finally, she agreed to work with Sid Hickok, a respected Hollywood veteran who was especially good at shooting action films. After working on *Possessed* for thirty-eight days, though, Crawford was dissatisfied with his efforts and insisted that he be replaced. Eventually, the studio was able to find a cinematographer who was acceptable to her. He was Joseph Valentine (1900–1949), who had previously had successful collaborations with such directors as Alfred Hitchcock, Sam Wood, and Frank Borzage. Sadly, *Possessed* also turned out to be one of Valentine's last films. In May 1949, he died unexpectedly of a heart attack at age forty-eight. Just two months earlier, he had won his only Oscar for his work on the color epic *Joan of Arc* (1948) starring Ingrid Bergman.

Despite Crawford's dissatisfaction with some aspects of the production, efforts, for the most part, went smoothly. In fact, two of her *Possessed* co-stars, neither of whom had ever worked with her before, found sharing scenes with her quite illuminating. One was Raymond

Massey, a respected stage actor who, by this time, had also forged a very successful career in film, playing roles ranging from the villainous Black Michael in *The Prisoner of Zenda* (1937) to the title character in the film version of Robert Sherwood's Pulitzer Prize winning play *Abe Lincoln in Illinois* (1940).[3] "I never realized until I did [*Possessed*] with Joan what a naturally gifted actress she was," Massey recounted years later. "I had seen and admired a number of her earlier films, but I felt she had developed an expertise in purveying Hollywood artifice, and that her personality, rather than any real talent, carried her. *Possessed* changed my mind."[4] To illustrate, he mentioned a scene in the film in which his character proposes marriage to her character right after she has been rejected by her lover, noting that, as an actor, he found himself "electrified by the white lightning of her ironic laughter"[5] in her response. The other was the highly respected character actor Van Heflin, who was fast on his way to becoming one of the most familiar faces in noir. "Damn, I knew Joan had perfected the art of projecting her personality, but I never took her that seriously as an actress until I found myself up against her in [*Possessed*]," Heflin once observed. "She outplayed me, Raymond, everybody in the cast—and she was up against some experienced competition. Yet she carried the day."[6]

❖ ❖ ❖

Possessed opens ominously, as we hear disturbing, anxiety-filled music and see a woman (Crawford) walking, alone and as if in a trance, through dreary, overcast Los Angeles streets. At a rail-car stop she asks the driver about a man named David, saying she's looking for him. "He ain't here, lady," the driver curtly says before shutting the door in her face. Next, she sees people coming out of a church, asks them about David, and mistakes one man for him. Then, she steps into a diner and has trouble talking and even reaching for a sugar dispenser a man asks for. Others around her wonder if she's sick.

Soon, she is in an ambulance headed for a hospital and then into the hospital's Psychopathic Department. Two tired, overworked psychiatrists come to attend her. The older of the pair, Dr. Willard (Stanley Ridges), complains about how the number of patients they see seems to be going up all the time. "This civilization is a worse disease than heart trouble or tuberculosis, and we can't escape it," he says. The doctors try to learn something, anything, about the woman, but she seems to be unable to tell them. So, they give her a drug (perhaps sodium pentothal) to help her communicate. After the drug is administered, she tells them that her name is Louise Howell and that she has come to Los Angeles from Washington, D.C. "to get away from *them*." She adds, "They must never know." Dr. Willard asks what they must never know, and she refuses to tell him. Trying another tack, he asks who David is. When he says this, we begin to hear a piano piece by Schumann, the "Chopin" section of *Carnaval* Op. 9. It is music Louise has remembered. She tells Dr. Willard about it, and he asks who is playing the piano. She says, "David."

The picture very slowly dissolves into a moment from Louise's past. David (Heflin) is playing the piano in his lake cabin living room as Louise, combing her hair, is preparing to leave after what appears to be a day of swimming and love-making. They chat, pleasantly at first, but Louise soon steers the conversation into uncomfortable territory for David. She loves him and wants to be with him. She adds that, before him, she never felt much either way about other people but that being with him has changed all that. David, however, clearly prefers a more casual, "no-strings" relationship. She eventually says, "Oh, David, I want a monopoly on you." Feeling decidedly more uncomfortable, David tells her that she is too intense. "Everyone wants to be loved," he says, "but no one wants to be smothered." Then he says that it might be better if they didn't see each other, at least for a while. Distraught, she insists that he take her home at once.

They get into his boat and head to a large house on another part of the lake. She gets out, and we find out that she works there as the nurse to Pauline Graham, the sickly, jealous wife of Dean Graham, a wealthy oil man (Massey). Ironically, Pauline despises Louise because she's convinced herself that Louise and Dean are having an affair. After tending to Pauline, Louise suggests to Dean that perhaps it would be best if she left. Dean, however, won't have any of it, saying that he values Louise's work and that Pauline has often, and wrongly, accused Dean of having affairs with former nurses and others.

The next morning, David visits Dean to talk about an opportunity to work for Dean's company on a building project related to its oil activities in Canada. Dean is delighted and agrees to the request. But Louise, who has eavesdropped on the conversation, is not, and, when she and David are alone, she pleads with him to take her along, too. He refuses and then leaves, as she cries uncontrollably at the boat dock.

The scene now dissolves back to the Psychopathic Department at the hospital. Dr. Willard asks Louise about all of this, and she says that David, Dean, and everyone else did this deliberately to hurt her. Conferring with his younger associate, Dr. Clark (Don McGuire), Dr. Willard sees what he calls "the beginnings of the persecution complex." Dr. Clark adds that Louise has also revealed a clear symptom of schizophrenia—the inability to feel either great joy or sadness—before she met

David. They agree that "the seeds" for the mental illness were there and that her obsession for David only made them grow. Then they return to her and ask her to continue her story.

The screen now dissolves to the lakeshore around the Graham house at night. Row boats are in the water and police officers and others, including Louise and Dean, are on shore. Soon, the body of Pauline is retrieved from the water, an apparent suicide.

Because of Pauline's death, Dean has asked their two children, twenty-year-old daughter Carol (Geraldine Brooks) and younger son Wynn (Peter Miles) to come home from her college and his boarding school to be with him. Carol tells Louise she believes she has schemed to replace her mother in her father's affections and that her mother's suicide was a direct result of these schemes. Dean overhears these accusations and is quite upset, telling Carol that it might be better if she returned to her college campus immediately.

Months go by. Dean, young Wynn, and Louise have moved to Washington, D.C., with Louise, at Dean's request, working as Wynn's governess. Louise doesn't feel needed but agrees so that she might, she hopes, have a better chance of seeing David sometime in the future.

She gets her wish when David returns from Canada for a short business visit with Dean. As soon as they are alone, Louise approaches David. "Go ahead and kiss me," she says. "You don't have to mean it." He obliges but with no emotion. "I didn't expect you to mean it that little," she says. As they continue to talk, he repeatedly makes it clear that they are finished, but she can't accept this. Finally, he leaves.

Later, Louise and Dean talk. "You've become very necessary here," he tells her. "You're a part of my home and very much a part of my life." He asks her to marry him, she says she doesn't love him, he says he will do everything he can to make her happy, and she agrees.

Louise visits Carol at her college to tell her that she and Dean plan to be married. Carol, while admitting that she had wrongly believed the worst about Dean and Louise, still doesn't warm to the idea. Louise then plays to Carol's feelings of guilt over hurting her father, and Carol relents, agreeing to accept Louise.

At Dean and Louise's wedding reception, an uninvited guest turns up—David. He flirts with Carol, and she is charmed. Louise, however, tells him to leave and to stay away from her new stepdaughter.

Soon afterwards, Louise and Carol run into David by chance at a piano concert. Carol invites David to sit with them. But, when the pianist plays the same Schumann piece that David played for Louise at his lake cabin long ago, Louise becomes very distressed, pretends to have a headache, and leaves.

At home, Louise continues to hear this piece of music in her head. Then the sounds of a ticking clock and her own heartbeat seem exaggerated. She hears a car pulling up. It is David dropping Carol off from the concert. They kiss and laugh at the doorway, and she calls him "darling." After David leaves and Carol walks up the stairs to her bedroom, Louise grabs her. They argue about David and about Pauline's death. Carol walks away, but Louise pursues her to the top of the stairs and hits her. The force of Louise's blow knocks Carol down the entire flight of stairs, and she lies still at the bottom, appearing to be dead.

Then, the front door opens. Carol enters and offers a friendly, non-romantic goodbye to a person we assume to be David. The body at the bottom of the stairs disappears, and Louise realizes that the argument with Carol and Carol's fall down the stairs have been hallucinations.

Quite distraught, Louise goes to see a local doctor, who confirms what she had suspected: that she suffers from schizophrenia. He offers to recommend a psychiatrist for her, but she simply walks out the door in despair.

Louise then tells Dean that she wants a divorce, saying she feels uncomfortable replacing Pauline. Dean refuses to accept this and insists that they go to the lake house together. "There's only one way to solve a problem," he says, "and that's to face it."

At the lake house, though, Louise again has hallucinations, believing that Pauline is talking to her and wants her to kill herself, to drown just like Pauline did. After Dean calms her, she says that she was responsible for Pauline's death, that she helped her kill herself. He convinces her that that was impossible, that she was elsewhere, in town to be specific, when Pauline died. As Louise absorbs this, she feels relieved and at last, happy.

She and Dean return to Washington, D.C., exhilarated and decide to go to a nightclub. There, however, they meet David and Carol, who are on a date. Later, Louise learns that David and Carol have become very close and tells Carol that she dislikes David intensely. She adds that David is not in love with Carol but with her. Carol finds this ridiculous. She and David talk to Dean, who again becomes quite concerned about Louise. He tells her he's arranged for her to see a psychiatrist. At first, she resists, but then she admits, "If only you could [help me]. I don't know what's wrong. I don't know why I am this way."

As soon as Dean leaves, however, Louise goes to where David is staying. They argue, she tells him not to marry Carol, and then she pulls out a gun to emphasize how serious she is about this matter. Although the gun makes him feel a bit uncomfortable, David tries to make light of the situation. "It's silly of you to kill me, Louise," he says. "There's still a lot of pain and unhappiness in store for me. Now, you wouldn't want me to miss all that, would you?" He then makes light of her ability to shoot him and tries to grab the gun. She shoots him once. Shocked, he falls to the floor. Pointing her gun down toward him, she fires four more bullets.

Now, the screen dissolves back to the Los Angeles hospital. "I killed him!" Louise screams. After she is subdued, Dr. Willard goes to his office and speaks to Dean (who has come from Washington, D.C.), telling him that, while the process will be long and arduous, he believes that Louise's mental health can be restored. Dean brings up David's murder and need for a trial. Dr. Willard says that, while he can't predict the outcome, he believes that "Louise is neither mentally or morally responsible for any of her actions."

Dean asks to see Louise. They go to her bed where she is now sleeping. Dean looks down at her and asks what the recovery process will be like.

"It's pain that made her his way," Dr. Willard says, "and it's only through greater pain and suffering beyond belief that she'll get well again."

"I'll be there no matter what happens, no matter how much she suffers," Dean says.

"I was rather hoping you would say that," Dr. Willard responds.

Dean asks to stay with Louise for a while. Dr. Willard gently says "Why yes, of course" and then leaves.

◆ ◆ ◆

Possessed opened in late July 1947 to a fairly robust box office and mostly positive reviews. The film, which was budgeted at slightly more than $2.5 million, earned more than $3 million worldwide. It was a hit, but not one on the scale of *Mildred Pierce* or *Humoresque*. The critics were also quite complimentary, especially toward the film's star. "Most of [*Possessed*] is filmed with unusual imaginativeness and force," wrote James Agee in *Time Magazine*. "The film is uncommonly well-acted. Miss Crawford is generally excellent, performing with the passion and intelligence of an actress who is not content with just one Oscar."[7] Herman Schoenfeld of *Variety* was of a similar opinion, noting that "[Crawford] cops all thesping honors in this production with a virtuoso performance as a frustrated woman ridden into madness by a guilt-obsessed mind. [The] actress has a self-assurance that permits her to completely dominate the screen even vis-a-vis such accomplished players as Van Heflin and Raymond Massey."[8]

As with *Mildred Pierce* and *Humoresque*, the work of many talented people contributed to the success of *Possessed*.

Once again, the film's final shooting script, while an adaptation, is vastly changed from the original story in order to accommodate the style and goals of the Wald-Crawford noir-melodrama. Since one of Wald's aims here was to re-capture much of the magic and box-office success of *Mildred Pierce*, the decision to have MacDougall write the final version of the script is obvious. Throughout, we can see the distinctive and often quite stylish and effective MacDougall touches. Instead of being told in one extended flashback, for example, the story is told, much like *Mildred Pierce*, in three distinct flashbacks, each functioning much like an act in a play or chapter in a novel. This technique also helps to ground viewers, periodically bringing them back to the real-time problem that began the film. In addition, the story is again told by the troubled heroine, and the final, shocking revelation is withheld until the very end. Finally, *Possessed* includes a good share of the sharp, insightful MacDougall dialogue that greatly enhanced *Mildred Pierce*. Among many memorable lines in *Possessed*, for example, is Louise's overture to David upon his return from Canada, "Go ahead and kiss me. You don't have to mean it." As well as being strange and jarring, this line superbly captures her increasingly needy, desperate state of mind and plummeting self-esteem.

Bernhardt's direction and Valentine's cinematography both deserve high praise, too. One great strength of *Possessed* that sets it above most films of the time that focused on mental illness is its ability to convey the disorienting, dreamlike tone often found in noir. Bernhardt and Valentine do this in several ways. One is by shooting Louise's hallucinatory scenes in a very straightforward manner, thus blurring the distinction between reality and her delusions. This is done superbly, for example, in the sequence when Louise imagines arguing with Carol and then pushing her down the flight of stairs, perhaps even killing her, and then watching as Carol actually arrives home from a concert a moment later. The effect is to put us, the viewers, inside Louise's head to experience first-hand the same disorientation and terror that she feels. Another is by jarring the viewer through the use of disturbing point-of-view shots. One fine example of this is when we see Louise wheeled into the hospital on a gurney near the beginning of the film. First, we are watching her much as a bystander would. Then, we suddenly see everything— the hospital's entrance, its hallways, passing personnel, ceiling lights— from Louise's vulnerable perspective as the gurney takes her to an examination room. The effect, of course, is to give us as viewers a much more visceral sense of the fear and uncertainly that Louise obviously feels during those moments. In addition to these expressionistic visual touches, Bernhardt cleverly employs exaggerated sounds of voices and commonplace noises to give us a more immediate sense of what Louise is hearing in her mind at certain times. Two examples are the harsh, grating sounds of Pauline Graham's voice and her bedroom buzzer to reinforce both how unpleasant it has been for Louise to care for her and, later, the trauma Louise feels over not being able to stop her from committing suicide.

Still another great strength of *Possessed* is the acting, especially among the principal players.

Knowing that Louise would be a particularly difficult role, Crawford, in addition to visiting mental health facilities to observe patients and consult with doctors, spent countless hours working on the part in order to get Louise's descent into full-blown schizophrenia just right. As a result, each step in the character's downward arc is meticulously crafted. Barely detectable at first, we see Louise's gradual but unstoppable unraveling: her paranoia, fixations, and hallucinations. Crawford captures all of this with great aplomb while also portraying Louise in a sympathetic light, as a person acutely aware that something is very wrong but unable to do anything about it and, quite understandably, terrified. As film writer Gwen Ihnat has observed, "It's the subtlety of her performance that's chilling: off-kilter glances and a scene where Louise's bright chatter gradually slips into mania are as unnerving as any expression of the outlandish behaviors associated with mental illness in the mid-century."[9] Film writer David Krauss has also noted the "heartbreaking vulnerability that's so raw it's difficult to watch" which the actress brings to the performance.[10] He adds, "Rarely, if ever, does Crawford beg for affection in her films, so her impassioned pleas for David's love seem doubly pathetic. When she madly shrieks, 'David, listen to me! You mustn't treat me this way! Don't leave me! Take me with you, David! David!!!,' the brazen emotion sends a chill down our collective spines."[11]

While there is much to praise about Crawford's performance in *Possessed*, it isn't always pitch-perfect to the degree her performances were, say, in *Mildred Pierce* and *Humoresque* are. Several critics have felt that the actress occasionally resorts to histrionics to get certain points across, and their comments are well taken. On balance, however, Crawford's portrayal of Louise is quite intelligent, sensitive, and well-orchestrated—an enormous achievement at a time when Hollywood films were just beginning to take on the extremely complex and still relatively little-known subject of mental illness.

Although Crawford was riding high on the strength of *Mildred*

Pierce and *Humoresque* when she made *Possessed*, she did not succumb to the temptation to play it safe, and she deserves additional credit for taking this major career risk. Still widely considered to be a "glamour queen" rather than a serious actress, she not only committed to playing the very troubled Louise Howell but she also went all out to portray her as realistically as possible. A startling example of the degree of this commitment is the film's very first sequence, as we see her, drably dressed and completely without make-up, wandering like a lost child through the streets of Los Angeles. The contrast between this entrance and, say, her Tallulah Bankhead–like movie star entrance in *Humoresque* is both stunning and startling.

In early 1948, Crawford received another Best Actress Academy Award nomination for her work in *Possessed* and, in some quarters, was considered a front-runner for that year's Oscar. Ultimately, she lost to Loretta Young for her performance in the comedy *The Farmer's Daughter*. Years later, however, Crawford did receive some recompense when Robert Osborne of the Turner Classic Movies channel declared her performance in *Possessed* one of his "should have won an Oscar" picks.[12]

Among the other principal players, two also deserve special kudos.

One is Van Heflin (1908–1971), who is excellent as the charming, cultivated, notoriously uncaring, and disarmingly self-aware David Sutton. For David, Louise is merely a fling, one of many in a lifetime devoutly committed to non-commitment. The more obsessed she becomes with him, the more repulsed he is by her neediness. As is his nature, he moves on to the next woman, who this time happens to be the young, pretty, and rich Carol. By this time, he sees Louise as little more than a pathetic joke, that is, until she—to his great surprise—shoots him. This is an unusual role for Heflin, but he inhabits it with ease and plays it with great verve.

Already the recipient of a Best Supporting Actor Oscar for his work in the noir *Johnny Eager* (1941), Heflin continued to perform in films and then for television until his untimely death from a heart attack at age 62. Among his best-known roles are the drab but steadfast ranchers in two classic westerns, *Shane* (1953) and *3:10 to Yuma* (1957).

The other is Raymond Massey (1896–1983), whose Dean Graham is a fascinating counterpoint to both Louise and David. At first, we see Dean as stern and remote, but, after his wife dies and his feelings for Louise grow, we see him blossom as a very decent, kind, and caring person. Unlike Louise, who is falling apart, Dean seems to grow stronger. And, unlike David, who wants nothing to do with Louise, Dean rallies to her side, helping her with great patience and love. Dean is not nearly as colorful a role as David is, but Massey manages to make the character quite engaging, appealing, and thoroughly credible.

After *Possessed*, Massey continued to work in films and on television for another twenty-six years before retiring from acting in 1973. Perhaps the best-known role of his later career is Dr. Leonard Gillespie, which he played from 1961 to 1966 on the television series *Dr. Kildare*.

Much as he did in *Humoresque*, Franz Waxman brilliantly mixed pieces of classical music with his own film score to reinforce the narrative in numerous ways. One wonderful contribution, of course, is the repeated use of the "Chopin" section from Schumann's *Carnaval* to suggest, what for Louise is, both the agony and the ecstasy she feels over her relationship with David. This piece is a superb choice, and it is used just often enough and in just the right places to have a very powerful impact.

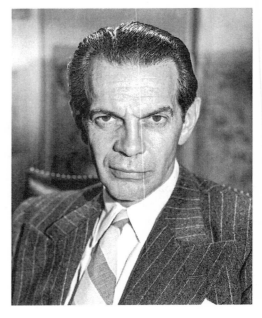

Raymond Massey, who played the role of Dean Graham in *Possessed*, was a highly respected theater, film, and later television actor whose career spanned from the 1910s to the 1970s (Allstar Picture Library Limited/Alamy Stock Photo).

❖ ❖ ❖

While not a first as a female-centered noir, a noir-melodrama hybrid, or a film depiction of a mental illness, *Possessed* does represent real progress in the ways noir was presented and perceived in the mid–1940s. The efforts of Wald, Crawford, Bernhardt, Richards, MacDougall, Valentine, and others to approach the story's disturbing subject matter as honestly and sympathetically as possible are worthy of high praise. *Possessed* could have been a simple, suspenseful noir with a scenery-chewing-crazy-lady thrill angle, but it aspires to be and do much more. Specifically, it explores the causes and effects of a serious mental illness, and it takes the afflicted character through her downward arc in great detail and with great care. Generally, it succeeds, and because it does, it is both a very satisfying film in its own right and one that clearly helped pave the way for the more serious explorations of mental illness in many noir and noir-tinged films that followed over the next decade. With *Possessed*, Gwen Ihnat wrote, "Joan Crawford elevated noir."[13] This is a strong claim to make, but it's one that is almost impossible to dispute.

◈ ◈ ◈

Soon after completing *Possessed*, Crawford played a pivotal role in working out an arrangement in which Warner Brothers would "lend" her to rival Twentieth Century–Fox for a one-picture deal. She would star in a film based on a novel that had intrigued her since it had first been published in early 1945. She would also work with a brilliant, demanding, and sometimes imperious producer-director, who—since his first major critical and commercial hit, a groundbreaking 1944 noir—had intrigued her even more.

5

"I love you, too, I guess"
Daisy Kenyon (1947)

Looking back, it's fascinating that none of the principals involved with Crawford's next project, an adaptation of the best-selling 1945 novel *Daisy Kenyon*, seems to have been very excited about it. "*Daisy Kenyon* wasn't a great movie, but I think it was a good one," Crawford once noted.[1] Her co-star Henry Fonda acknowledged that the story simply wasn't "his cup of tea."[2] The film's producer-director Otto Preminger added that "we couldn't make a masterpiece out of what we had."[3]

Audiences and critics at the time of *Daisy Kenyon's* initial release seemed to share these lukewarm feelings. The film made a modest profit, and newspaper reviews were often carefully balanced. The *New York Times*, for example, praised the film for being "somewhat more mature and compelling" than other romantic dramas while also criticizing the screenplay's inability to solve a central plot problem, "at least, not with any noticeable ingenuity."[4]

Over the years, however, *Daisy Kenyon* has gained steadily growing respect from classic film aficionados and scholars alike for its many fine qualities. Crawford biographers Lawrence J. Quirk and William Schoell have called it one of the actress's "most interesting pictures."[5] Film critic Molly Haskell has described it as a "Preminger gem."[6] Crawford biographer, Donald Spoto, has said that the film "not only offers one of Joan's most forthright and moving performances, but also showcases her in a story of striking complexity and maturity...."[7] Film writer Dan Callahan has added, "*Daisy Kenyon*, which was generally dismissed as a slick triangle melodrama, has emerged as one of the most adult of all post-war noirs...."[8]

It's also fascinating to try to come to grips both with why so many people, including the film's director and star, were dismissive of *Daisy*

Kenyon when it was first released and with why respect for it has grown so much in the decades since then.

The film certainly has its shortcomings, especially in some writing and plotting that occurs near the end of the story, and these could at least partially explain why Crawford, Preminger, and others had some reservations about the effort overall. Today, however, proponents of the film generally acknowledge these shortcomings while also saying that they are relatively minor detractors when balanced against the film's many strengths.

Another possibility might be that, as a mainstream Hollywood film, *Daisy Kenyon* was, in some respects, well ahead of its time. Although several of the story's key characters behave in morally questionable ways, the film never judges them—making it clear-cut who is good and who is bad—as was the case with most other films of the time. Instead, it adopts an unusually detached, non-judgmental point of view. Many people in late–1940s U.S. audiences, long accustomed to Hollywood films making moral judgments for them, may have found this approach unsettling, if not downright disturbing.

Still another possibility might be the film's richness and nuance both in terms of the story and the visual presentation. As is true with many of Preminger's, and Crawford's, best films, repeated viewings reveal more and more of what's actually there to take in and think about. To Preminger and his team's credit, the film is beautifully crafted with a script that brims with intelligence and sensitivity, gorgeous and suggestive noir cinematography, thoughtfully adorned settings that also tell us much about the characters who inhabit them, and strong, disarmingly honest performances by Crawford and the other actors.

Daisy Kenyon is not Crawford's best film, but it is one of her most thought-provoking and under-appreciated efforts, a fine blend of provocative issues, vivid characters, and numerous noir shadings that together make for a better, more challenging film than either she or Preminger may have recognized at the time.

✦ ✦ ✦

The story of the film version of *Daisy Kenyon* begins with the 1945 publication of the novel on which it is based. The book, which became an immediate best seller, was written by a second-time novelist named Elizabeth Janeway (1913–2005). The wife of noted economist Elliot Janeway, she was a prolific writer whose output eventually included five additional novels, several non-fiction books on feminism, numerous book reviews for the *New York Times*, and many other published works.

The novel *Daisy Kenyon* follows a love triangle involving the title character, a successful magazine illustrator who is unmarried, and two men, Dan O'Mara, an unhappily married Manhattan corporate lawyer, and Peter Lapham, a widower who works as a magazine art editor. At first glance, this storyline might sound like just another formulaic piece of romance fiction, but there is much more going on here. One element that especially struck readers was the complexity of the story's three main characters: the depth of their thinking, the intriguing ways in which they interacted, and the curious paths they all took to work through their issues. Unlike the stock characters in most romance novels, these were smart, interesting people who were conflicted, ambivalent, flawed, often unpredictable, and thoroughly credible. As book reviewer Octavia Randolph once noted, "The interior world of Daisy, Dan, and ... Peter is so richly drawn that we feel ourselves changing along with them—coming to the same conclusions, making the same discoveries about [ourselves] and others."[9]

Among those greatly impressed with *Daisy Kenyon* was Crawford, who was, of course, always on the prowl for good stories with strong female characters she might play in film adaptations. She quickly made plans to buy the novel's screen rights. Unfortunately for her, though, Twentieth Century–Fox beat her to the deal, paying $100,000 for the rights in early 1945.

Another person who found the novel quite enticing was Otto Preminger (1905–1986), then a contract producer/director at Twentieth Century–Fox. Fresh off the enormous popular and critical success of his film noir *Laura* the year before, he was quickly establishing himself as one of Hollywood's top directors and would remain a major film industry force into the 1970s.

It's not difficult to understand Preminger's attraction to the novel, either. A lawyer by training with a high regard for the U.S. trial-by-jury system,[10] he disliked films that did the thinking for the viewers and greatly preferred ones that effectively turned viewers into jurors, people whose job it was to weigh the evidence that's presented and judge for themselves. He also had a rebellious streak. He detested the U.S. film industry's restrictive Production Code,[11] and *Daisy Kenyon's* ambiguous morality would likely present him with a golden opportunity to do battle with the industry's censors.

Initially, actresses Gene Tierney (who was under contract with Twentieth Century–Fox at the time) and Jennifer Jones were the front-runners to play Daisy. Ultimately, however, both actresses were involved with other projects when Preminger was finally available to begin work on the film adaptation in 1947.

True to character, Crawford saw her opening and aggressively

pursued the part. One version of the story is that she saw Twentieth Century–Fox's studio head Darryl F. Zanuck at a party one night, brought
the subject up, and emphasized how much she would like to play the
role. Another version is that she personally pleaded with Preminger for
the part. In any case, an arrangement was made for Warner Brothers to
"loan" her to Twentieth Century–Fox for the one film.

A major concern Twentieth Century–Fox had in casting Crawford was her age. In the novel, Daisy is thirty-two, and Crawford was
then about decade older than that. Apparently, though, she convinced
the appropriate decision makers that, between her acting and the right
make-up, wardrobe, lighting, and camera angles, she could credibly play
the younger woman.

As her leading men, Crawford, who insisted on having her say

Crawford's Daisy must choose between long-time lover, Dana Andrews's
Dan (left), and new husband, Henry Fonda's Peter (right), in Otto
Preminger's *Daisy Kenyon* (1947), a film that writer Dan Callahan
has called "one of the most adult of all post-war noirs" (Twentieth
Century–Fox/Photofest).

about acting choices at Twentieth Century–Fox as well as Warner Brothers, was adamant about casting two of Fox's biggest male stars at the time, Dana Andrews to play Dan and Henry Fonda to play Peter. Neither actor, however, was thrilled either with his assigned role or with the prospect of working with Crawford, who, with rare exceptions at this time, dominated her films and worked with second-tier leading men who usually played subordinate roles. Since the two actors were under contract with Twentieth Century–Fox and eager to fulfill their obligations to the studio and move on, however, both realized that resistance was counterproductive and agreed to play the roles.

At this point, the script adaptation had gone through several revisions. Instead of setting the story at the beginning of World War II, for example, the story was updated to post-war 1947. As well as being a widower, Peter Lapham is also a returning war veteran who, in addition to grieving over his wife's death, suffers from PTSD. To open up the story more, some scenes were set in Massachusetts' Cape Cod (although the film was shot entirely at Fox's studio) and Peter's occupation was changed from magazine editor to boat designer. Another fascinating addition to the story is a subplot in which Dan takes the case of a decorated Japanese-American war veteran whose farm was taken away from him when he was fighting for the U.S. in Europe and who is now suing to get it back. At the time, this was a controversial subject for many Americans, who still felt great hostility toward the Japanese, even those who were loyal U.S. citizens.

❖ ❖ ❖

The film opens as Dan comes to visit Daisy at the Manhattan apartment that doubles as her home and work office. We quickly learn that he and Daisy are in a long-term extra-marital relationship (he's married, she's not) and that she is tired of constantly seeing each other on the sly. She talks about breaking their relationship off but in a very ambivalent manner. Charming but also quite arrogant and entitled, Dan dismisses the thought, saying that he doesn't want to have that conversation again just then. Daisy also announces that she has a date that night with another man. As Dan leaves, he and Daisy's date, Peter Lapham, meet and Dan immediately lets Peter know that he has just come from Daisy's apartment, rattling Peter a bit. Before they head out for their date, Daisy learns that Peter, who is currently in the army but will be discharged soon, was a boat designer before the war and that his wife had been killed in an automobile accident five years earlier.

At Dan's home, we are introduced to his wife Lucille (Ruth Warrick) and their two daughters Rosamund and Marie (Peggy Ann Garner and Connie Marshall). Lucille constantly fidgets and appears disturbingly insecure, both as a wife and as a mother. She clearly knows about Dan's relationship with Daisy, and, at one point, she slaps Marie for being disrespectful towards her. Dan seems constantly to be playing the role of peacemaker between his daughters, whom he loves and feels the need to protect, and Lucille, whom he barely tolerates.

Later that night, Peter walks Daisy home from their date, unexpectedly tells her that he loves her, and then quickly leaves. They plan another date, but, when the time comes, Peter stands her up. Later, he comes to Daisy's apartment and, in a very touching speech, proposes marriage. Needless to say, Daisy has misgivings: he's too impetuousness, he's unreliable, and he may still be in love with his late wife. Despite these misgivings, however, she wants to keep seeing him.

Meanwhile, Dan does something that seems quite out of character: he agrees to represent a Japanese-American whose farm was taken away from him when he was serving in the U.S. Army during World War II. There is no money in it for Dan, and he understands that, considering the intense prejudice toward the Japanese (even loyal U.S. citizens of Japanese descent), there is every chance that he will lose the case.

After a whirlwind courtship, Daisy marries Peter, although she feels that she still might love Dan. She also supports Peter's plans to leave the service and resume his career as a boat designer, and the two agree to move to Cape Cod, where Peter had once lived with his wife. As she gets to know him better, however, Daisy is increasingly concerned that Peter, after having experienced both the loss of his wife and traumatic experiences during the war, might be using her to prop himself up emotionally.

Dan loses in his effort to help the Japanese-American and turns to Daisy to talk about it. Hearing him on the phone, Lucille eavesdrops on another phone and breaks into the conversation. When Dan hears her, he comes to her, takes the phone away, and says, "For a long time I didn't think you were worth killing, but you are."

This brings all of Dan and Lucille's bottled-up rage towards each other to a breaking point. Lucille files for divorce and demands full custody of their two daughters as a way to punish Dan. If Dan doesn't agree, Lucille will make the divorce as ugly as possible, making Dan's relationship with Daisy a central issue in what promises to be a highly publicized court battle.

In a curious move, Dan meets with both Daisy and Peter to ask if Daisy would be willing to have her name dragged through the proverbial mud. She quickly agrees to help. During the conversation, however, Peter offers a surprising perspective, saying that he no longer needs

Daisy to support him emotionally and will not stand in her way if she loves Dan and wishes to be with him instead. He then leaves and indicates that he will simply wait for her answer.

Dan and Lucille's divorce trial begins, but, after some courtroom nastiness, Dan cannot stand how the experience is hurting Daisy, stops the proceedings, and agrees to Lucille's terms. Lucille has hopes for a reconciliation, but Dan sees this as impossible.

Soon, Daisy returns to Cape Cod alone to try to think through which suitor she wants: Dan, Peter, or neither. She's only there a brief time, however, when Dan and Peter arrive together, Dan, especially, intent on pressing her for an answer. At first, Daisy tells them that she doesn't want either of them. Peter says that he is willing to divorce her if she asks him for one directly. She pauses for a second, perhaps reflecting. Peter leaves to let Dan say what he needs to say. Again, Dan talks about reuniting, perhaps going away to the Bahamas together to rekindle their love. Then Daisy says, "I stopped being in love with you a long time ago, Dan, but memory lingered on and kept me mixed up." She is also concerned that he seems to be abandoning his daughters just to be with her and says that he shouldn't do this, that it's simply "running away from responsibility." With great finality, she says goodbye to him. Sadly, he accepts her decision and leaves.

Unexpectedly, Peter returns, and Daisy realizes that he loves her and has understood all along that the only way to win her love has been not to press aggressively as Dan has done but instead to let her sort through her feelings by herself. "When it comes to modern combat tactics," Peter tells Daisy, she and Dan are "both babies compared to me." The two embrace and kiss.

◈ ◈ ◈

For many viewers, *Daisy Kenyon* is difficult to categorize, and often discussions center around just what kind of a film it is—a female-centered melodrama, a film noir, or a hybrid of both.

Is *Daisy Kenyon* a female-centered melodrama? Well, yes and no. Its story, which focuses on a love triangle and the emotional pangs the three main characters go through, clearly resembles the popular kind of female-centered melodrama in which the heroine must choose between two or more suitors. At the same time, however, the film rarely seems typical of melodrama. The distinctive, well-drawn characters here, even in several of the key supporting roles, bear little resemblance to the stock characters that often appear in these kinds of stories. Throughout the film, too, these characters are treated in Preminger's very detached, non-judgmental way that rarely tries to manipulate viewer attitudes.

Again, this is atypical of the genre. If this is a melodrama, the material, for the most part, is presented very un-melodramatically.

Daisy Kenyon is also infused with ample noir content. It is largely shot in the dark, moody noir visual style. And it covers uncomfortable subjects often treated in noir such as adultery, racism, and the plight of traumatized servicemen returning from World War II. At the same time, though, the plot doesn't follow the classic downward noir trajectory; no typical noir crime such as murder is committed (though, considering the increasingly hostile relationship between Dan and Lucille, we sometimes think that one easily could be); and the characters, because they are so distinctively drawn, don't fit the conventional noir mold.

Considering all of this, it might be more helpful to view *Daisy Kenyon* in somewhat different terms, mainly as a serious character-driven relationship drama that is peppered with melodramatic and noirish elements. This is a film that's much closer in spirit and tone to an articulate, straightforward character-centered drama such as William Wyler's 1936 *Dodsworth* than to a manipulative melodrama or a textbook noir. *Daisy Kenyon's* characters, as conceived and written—as well as the exquisite craftmanship that Preminger, the actors, and others bring to support the way these characters' stories are conveyed—are what give the film its most important distinguishing qualities and are ultimately its main drawing card.

Film writer Zach Campbell has called the three lead characters in *Daisy Kenyon* "the key to unlocking [the film],"[12] and it's difficult to disagree. All three appear to be fully formed while also shrouded in ambiguity and mystery. We want to know more about them, and repeated viewings only leave us with additional questions to ask. At the same time, they, not intricate plotting or some other storytelling element, are what we are naturally drawn to; they *are* the essence of the film.

Daisy, for example, is a serious professional woman who is tired of being the other woman in an extramarital relationship and unsure about what her next steps should be. "I can't wander all my life," she says in frustration after Peter stands her up for their second date and she asks her friend Mary Angeles (Martha Stewart) to take in a film with her. "I have to be going somewhere," she adds, "even if it's just to the movies." She is also ambivalent about her feelings for Dan, responding to his declaration of love during a phone call by saying, "I love you, too, I guess." Throughout the story, too, her feelings for Peter seem just as ambivalent.

As we watch the film, the questions about Daisy keep piling up. Why has this smart, independently minded, self-supporting woman stuck with Dan for so long? What are her feelings for either suitor, or does she even know herself? Her feelings (or at least our perception of them) always seem to be in flux. Also, what kind of a relationship will she have with Peter after the action of the film ends? There is much to wonder about here.

Dan can be arrogant, patronizing, entitled, and controlling. One interesting behavior is that every time he enters Daisy's apartment and music is playing, he immediately turns it off. It's as if he is demanding Daisy's full attention and will not tolerate any distractions, even innocuous background music. On the other hand, Dan can also be very charming, he shows an idealistic streak by agreeing to defend the Japanese-American, and he loves his two daughters deeply. In one scene we even see him shed a tear when he realizes that Lucille has hit their daughter again. Dan's big challenge, as Daisy emphasizes at the end of the film, is to learn how to be a more responsible adult, a challenge he has long avoided facing.

During the action of the film, Dan makes many changes, and we wonder what kind of a person he will be as he moves forward in his life. A more attentive father? A lawyer who takes more pro bono cases to help right injustices? A less selfish, more caring person in general? None of these? It's difficult to tell.

Peter is haunted by past traumas and not above using Daisy as his lifeline, but he is also kind, insightful, understanding, patient, at times witty, and at other times a bit of a poet. We see his insight early on when Daisy wonders if he wants to be with her mainly because he needs her as an emotional crutch.

"You're using me, sort of," she says in her characteristically ambivalent fashion.

"Do you love him?" he asks about Dan.

"Yes, I do love him."

"But it isn't enough or I wouldn't be here, would I?"

Here, Peter not only questions Daisy's feelings for Dan, but he also suggests that Daisy, for her own reasons, may be using him, too. He is a very shrewd student of behavior.

Peter's feelings for Daisy and his own emotional state are interesting subjects for speculation as well. We know that, initially, he needs Daisy, but, by the end of the story, has he—as he tells Daisy and Dan—really moved beyond that? Also, has he sufficiently conquered his personal demons and is now able to lead a happy life with Daisy?

Daisy Kenyon is also enhanced by the presence of several unusually interesting supporting characters.

One is Dan's wife, Lucille. She vents her rage at Dan by slapping their daughter, which is clearly child abuse. Yet, we also sympathize with the depth of hurt she feels because of Dan's adultery, her nervousness (which sometimes seems to be verging on hysteria), her complete lack of self-esteem, the pitiful position she now holds in their family, and her equally pitiful hopes for a reconciliation with Dan after he stops the divorce proceedings. Will the break-up of her marriage help her to change for the better or not?

Another is Daisy's co-worker, friend, and, at one point, roommate, Mary Angeles. She is an interesting mix of understated caring for Daisy, understated dislike for Dan, and sassy wit. "You cook like you paint, honey," she tells Daisy as they share a meal together, "fast, colorful, and glib." She seems to be the one that Daisy relies on in a pinch more than either of her male suitors, and it would be fascinating to know more both about her and her relationship with Daisy.

Still another is a character few people ever mention in discussions of the film. This is Will Thompson (Griff Barnett), an aging civil rights attorney who asks Dan to defend the Japanese-American robbed of his farm. Appearing in only one scene and for less than two minutes of screen time, Thompson is more interesting and more fully formed than the vast majority of characters in the vast majority of films. When Dan dismissively tries to brush him off, saying, "That's not my kind of case," Thompson, barely containing his indignation, tells him, "It isn't anybody's kind of case. It is an unpleasant, thoroughly thankless kind of case, O'Mara, but it's representative of almost every [Japanese-American] who fought in Europe. I used to feel a sort of pleasant dignity knowing that I could always be called upon to protect a democratic idea. I'm a tired and angry man now, Mr. O'Mara, but you are an unspent and very wealthy man. Maybe you could use some of that sort of pleasure." This short speech alone suggests so much about this man. Again, it would be fascinating to learn more about him.

Adding to the richness of the film's characters, of course, are all the efforts that were put into making them and their stories appear even more real and relatable. For this, Preminger and the film's many other contributors deserve much credit.

Taking their cue from Preminger, the three lead actors deliver strong, thoughtful, understated performances.

Crawford, in a very honest, precise, and focused effort, does an excellent job of conveying Daisy's intelligence, pride in being a self-sufficient woman, dissatisfaction with her personal life, uncertainty about where her life is headed, and ambivalence about her feelings for her two suitors. One scene in which Crawford excels early in the film when Daisy lays out to Dan her misgivings about their relationship. In what is essentially an exposition scene, she does a fine job of conveying both her deep feelings for Dan along with her equally deep frustration with him and their current arrangement. Another is when Daisy finally rejects Dan at the end of the film, credibly conveying her growing confidence and clarity in her dealings with her two suitors.

Henry Fonda (1905–1982), one of the great actors of the classic Hollywood era, is marvelous at conveying the emotionally haunted, eccentric, caring, and whimsical sides of the intriguing and unpredictable Peter. He is exceptional, for example, at conveying a range of emotions from great tenderness in the scene when Peter proposes marriage to Daisy to the trauma of PTSD in the scene when he wakes from a war-inspired nightmare. Already respected for his superb performances in films such as *Young Mr. Lincoln* (1939), *The Grapes of Wrath* (1940), and *The Ox-Bow Incident* (1943) when he made *Daisy Kenyon*, Fonda worked in films until the early 1980s, ending his career on a high note with a Best Actor Oscar for his work in *On Golden Pond* (1981).

Dana Andrews (1909–1992), too, is especially effective, in his case at conveying both Dan's selfish, manipulative, and at times even cruel sides as well as his brilliant, charming, caring, idealistic, and even vulnerable sides. In the final scenes of the film, for example, Andrews is so good at communicating with his eyes and body language the profound sense of loss Dan feels when Daisy says goodbye for good that— even if we don't like Dan as a person—it's almost impossible not to feel great sadness for him. Andrews was always an under-appreciated actor. This is a shame, too, because at times such as this he is superb. His Dan in *Daisy Kenyon* is not one of his best-known performances, certainly not as well-known as his roles in *Laura* or William Wyler's masterpiece *The Best Years of Our Lives* (1946), but it is one of his best. A major star throughout the 1940s, Andrews continued to work until his retirement in 1985. After the early 1950s, however, most of his roles were in less distinguished films and on television shows.

The portrayal of the pitiful but always potentially destructive Lucille by Ruth Warrick (1916–2005) is worth noting as well. Another actress could have easily overplayed this small but critical role, but Warrick's ability to convey the various sides of this basically unlikable character in such an emotionally true and affecting manner is to her great credit. One of Orson Welles's Mercury Players, Warrick, who played Kane's first wife in Welles's *Citizen Kane*, eventually moved from film to television roles where she is best known for her thirty-five-year run (from 1970 to 2005) on the daytime soap opera *All My Children*.

Because *Daisy Kenyon* so heavily emphasizes characters and their relationships, Preminger also took great pains to give the characters

With the successful noirs *Laura* (1944) and *Fallen Angel* (1945) on his resume, producer-director Otto Preminger, was just coming into his own when he made *Daisy Kenyon*. Never one to shy away from taboo subjects from adultery to drug abuse, to rape, to homosexuality, Preminger would remain a major creative figure in Hollywood until the late 1970s (Photofest).

added texture in as many ways as possible.

One was to photograph scenes in ways that give more emphasis to the conversations and interactions between the characters and less on manipulative, melodramatic effects. This, he believed, better enabled audiences to view the film in the more detached, dispassionate manner he preferred they do and then draw their own conclusions about the characters and their actions. More so than many directors, for example, he preferred extended medium and long shots that would, say, include both parties in a two-person conversation. He considered this far superior to the norm at the time, which was to put more emphasis on closeups and cutting between characters. He felt that this more popular approach was both disruptive to the flow of conversation and an easy way, if a director were so inclined, to manipulate the emotions of viewers.

Another way was the use of noir-style lighting and photography, especially when the action is in and around Daisy's apartment. Many film writers have noted that this was probably done to help make Crawford look younger so she could be more believable in the role. This may be true, but the darkly lit scenes also serve a more artful purpose: they visually reinforce key aspects of major characters, especially Daisy and Peter. Daisy, of course, is living a life in the shadows. Although she is not a kept woman, she is effectively a rich married man's mistress. Both she and Dan must always be discreet. They only socialize with two other friends, the couple who had introduced them and who know about and accept the relationship. This can make for a lonely existence for Daisy, one that the film punctuates in a brief, beautifully photographed scene that shows her sitting in her dark apartment as rain pours down outside and with only her dog as company. Peter lives in a different kind of darkness. Still recovering from the double trauma of his wife's death and the horror he saw in the war, he has dark, depressed moods. It's interesting, too, that certain scenes set in Cape Cod, including one in which Peter experiences a bad nightmare and its aftermath, are shot in very noirish fashion, perhaps suggesting that, at least at this point the story, the darkness still follows Peter wherever he goes.

Much of the credit for both the effectiveness and the beauty of many of the noir-tinged scenes goes to cinematographer Leon Shamroy (1901–1974). A master at both black-and-white and color filming, Shamroy, whose Hollywood career extended from the mid–1920s to the late 1960s, shares the records for both the most Academy Award nominations (eighteen) and Oscar wins (four) for cinematography. A magnificent example of his skill photographing in color is his work on the Gene Tierney film *Leave Her to Heaven* (1945), for which he won one of those four Oscars.

Still another way Preminger gives additional texture to the characters is in how he uses sets and furnishings that suggest things about the characters who inhabit those settings. His films put much more thought into this aspect of production than most films of the era, and, in *Daisy Kenyon*, many set elements from furniture to art pieces tell us a great deal. One example is the new suite of offices Dan moves into after he leaves his father-in-law's law firm. As opposed to the very dark, formal, old-fashion offices he has just left, these are bright, more relaxed looking, and contemporary—exactly where Dan wants to be as he plans a new start for himself. Also, an especially interesting decorative item we see later in the film is a justice scale in Daisy and Peter's Cape Cod home. Knowing about Preminger's lifelong interest in justice and the law, and seeing this scale emphasized visually more than once, we know it is there for a reason. Perhaps it suggests a commitment by Daisy and Peter to find a fair and equitable solution to their respective personal quandaries. Perhaps it suggests something entirely different. At the very least, it's something to consider, and Preminger, as we know, was constantly looking for ways to get viewers to think about, and grapple with, what they are seeing and listening to.

❖ ❖ ❖

Overall, *Daisy Kenyon* is a largely successful character-driven drama with significant noir shadings that underscore the narrative in highly effective ways. The key to appreciating the film on its own terms, of course, is to focus on its characters: carefully drawn, distinctive, intelligent, flawed, utterly relatable and, at the same time, ambiguous and elusive. They captivate us during the film, stay with us afterwards, and then call us back for repeated viewings.

Although *Daisy Kenyon* was not a hugely influential film when it was released, its adult nature, well-drawn characters, non-judgmental approach to morality, and emphasis on a variety of women's perspectives and issues all represent forward progress in noir's continuing expansion into new storytelling territory. Crawford, as a key contributor to the effort, was again testing the limits of female-centered noir and noir-infused films and, in the process, expanding the possibilities for noir content.

6

"You just wouldn't believe how much trouble it is to dispose of a dead elephant"

Flamingo Road (1949)

In 1947, the same year that Crawford worked on *Daisy Kenyon*, she adopted two more children, baby girls she named Cindy and Cathy, and, when the film wrapped, she took more than a year off to focus on what was now her growing family. When she wasn't working, however, she wasn't making money, and, as a single parent, she was also the family's sole breadwinner. So, in the fall of 1948, she returned to Warner Brothers and prepared to star in a new project, a film based on the novel and play *Flamingo Road*, a sensationalized story of political corruption, sex, and various other matters in a fictional Florida town.

Although the film that emerged from this effort is often regarded as one of the Crawford–Warner Brothers noirs of the mid- and late 1940s, it is more a mix of noir and melodrama with the emphasis on the melodrama. It certainly has a good share of noirish elements—from its dark, shadowy cinematography and claustrophobic-looking scenes to its themes of political corruption and doomed love—to qualify as a legitimate example of the style. At the same time, though, it doesn't contain many of the classic noir elements we see in Crawford's three previous Warner Brothers films such as a femme or homme fatale figure, the seemingly doomed or damned female protagonist, or the imaginative use of flashbacks to reinforce an air of inevitable doom or damnation. In addition, its protagonist, Lane Bellamy, is a strong, grounded, and largely self-assured person who in the end gets the man she loves and happiness—all quite different from the more noirish personalities and story arcs of the neurotic Mildred Pierce and Helen Wright and the deeply disturbed Louise Howell.

Whether we see it as noir or simply noir-tinged, however, *Flamingo Road* remains quite interesting to this day for its curious mix of strengths and shortcomings as well as for the wide diversity of responses it has elicited since its release. These responses have ranged, for instance, from the ecstatic praise of the celebrated German filmmaker Rainer Werner Fassbinder to the harsh criticism of Crawford, who once admitted that, by stepping into the project, she'd "screwed up completely."[1] At the very least, *Flamingo Road* deserves a close look, both for its commendable elements and for thoughts about why, after more than seventy years, people remain so deeply divided over it.

◆ ◆ ◆

The novel of *Flamingo Road* was first published in 1942 and immediately became a bestseller. Its author was Robert Wilder (1901–1974), who, before turning to writing, had worked in such jobs as a soda jerk, ship fitter, theater usher, shipping clerk, radio executive, and publicity agent for actress Claudette Colbert. In addition to his novels, among which *Flamingo Road* is the best known today, Wilder wrote articles for the *New York Post*, stories for *The New Yorker* and other magazines, Broadway plays, and a few Hollywood screenplays. After the success of the novel of *Flamingo Road*, he and his wife Sally adapted the story for the stage, and, in 1946, this version opened on Broadway. It wasn't nearly as successful as the book, however, and closed after only a few performances.

Despite the failure of the theatrical version, Warner Brothers, seeing the story as a promising vehicle for actress Ann Sheridan, bought the rights. Wilder was hired to work on the screenplay and was assisted by talented in-house screenwriter Edmund H. North (1911–1990), who would later work on scripts for such classic films as *In a Lonely Place* (1950), *The Day the Earth Stood Still* (1951), and *Patton* (1970).

While the screenplay of *Flamingo Road* doesn't change the basic nature of the original story as much as, say, the screenplays for *Mildred Pierce* or *Humoresque* do, numerous changes were made. Perhaps the most significant were those that softened the book's more scandalous elements in order to pass muster with the film industry's censors. In the book, for example, the heroine, Lane, works as a prostitute for a time and the character of Lute Mae runs the local bordello. In the film, Lane works as a waitress and Lute Mae's establishment is simply referred to as a "roadhouse."

When Sheridan read the script, however, she was not impressed and shortly afterwards passed on the project.

As nimble as ever, Jack Warner quickly pivoted and decided to take another shot at trying to re-create the success of *Mildred Pierce*. To assist in the effort, he enlisted five key contributors to the studio's 1945 hit: Wald, Crawford, actor Zachary Scott, composer Max Steiner, and director Michael Curtiz. By this time, Warner had given Curtiz his own in-house production unit, and the director was looking for an appropriate project. For him, the timing couldn't have been better. In addition, he seemed to relish the challenge of returning to the kind of female-centered melodrama/noir he had helped to create and to prove, yet again, that Crawford was still a major star.

A very significant addition to the production team was veteran cinematographer Ted McCord (1900–1976). McCord, a personal favorite of Curtiz, would eventually work with the director on nine films. *Flamingo Road* was also the first of what would eventually be four collaborations at Warner Brothers between him and the very demanding Crawford. His camerawork, very much in the studio's captivating visual style of the period, is exceptionally effective in its use of lighting (especially in his use of deep shadows) and camera placement and movement to reinforce the narrative. He seemed to be the ideal choice for a project in which Curtiz wanted to enhance the noirish and other visual qualities of the story and Crawford wanted to be as credible as possible playing a character who is much younger than she was at the time.

While not as well-known today as Gregg Toland, James Wong Howe, Jon Alton, or other cinematography stars of the period, McCord was responsible for the exceptional look of dozens of fine films (in both black and white and color) between the 1920s and 1960s. In addition to *Flamingo Road*, just a few examples include John Huston's 1948 *The Treasure of Sierra Madre*, Elia Kazan's 1956 *East of Eden*, and Robert Wise's 1965 *The Sound of Music*. "A dedicated artist," one online film reviewer once wrote about McCord, "[he] could make a meatball look like filet mignon."[2]

✦ ✦ ✦

"There's a Flamingo Road in every town," the opening narration for the film (delivered by Crawford) begins. "It is the street of social success, the avenue of achievement, the golden goal for all who struggle and aspire to reach the top and sometimes find that, from the top, there's no other place to go...."

The words then introduce us to the small town of Boldon in an unnamed state in the American South.[3] In a montage we see a few of the places that will figure in the story from the front porch of the Palmer House Hotel to the bar and dancefloor at Lute Mae's roadhouse, to a traveling carnival that comes through town once a year.

It is at the carnival that the narration ends and we hear real-time voices and other sounds. We see three "exotic" dancers, one of whom is Crawford, and we soon learn, when she does, that the carnival is immediately pulling up stakes because it can't pay its bills and, and, if the whole operation doesn't quickly get over the state line, the local sheriff will confiscate all its assets. "Get yourselves together, girls," the carnival owner tells them. "The sheriff's breathing down our necks."

The picture cuts to a sheriff's patrol car pulling up to the Palmer House and an old, fat, and vaguely scary man getting out. He is Sheriff Titus Semple (Sydney Greenstreet). Soon his young deputy, Fielding "Field" Carlisle (Zachary Scott), joins him, and Semple tells him to serve legal papers on the carnival. In addition, the sheriff notes that, down the road, he also has great plans for the younger man. As the conversation ends, we meet Field's long-time girlfriend Annabelle Weldon (Virginia Huston), a very sheltered young woman who seems to be much more interested in Field than he is in her.

Field goes to deliver the papers to the carnival owner only to find

out that the carnival has left town, all of it, that is, except one of its employees, the dancer played by Crawford. He finds her alone in a tent singing along with music on the radio. She tells him that her name is Lane Bellamy, that she has left the carnival because she is "sick of moldy tents and one-night stands and greasy food—sick of having people look at me and think I was cheap."

Lane says that she will leave in the morning if Field will let her stay in her tent for the night. Instead, he offers to take her to dinner at Boldon's Eagle Café. During dinner, he helps to get her a job as a waitress there and introduces her to another waitress who just happens to need a

After leaving her job with a traveling carnival, Crawford's Lane Bellamy decides to settle in the town of Boldon and finds work as a waitress at the town's Eagle Café in Michael Curtiz's *Flamingo Road* (1949) (Warner Brothers/Photofest).

roommate. Immediately, Lane is set up in the new town. "For the first time in my life I feel that I belong someplace and that someplace belongs to me," she tells Field later that evening.

One person who doesn't like any of this, however, is Titus, who also meets Lane that evening and treats her coldly.

Lane is put off by Titus as well, telling Field that he gives her "the creeps" and adding "We had better-looking people than that in our sideshows."

Soon, Lane and Field are seeing each other romantically, and one day Titus tells Field that he wants him to meet the state's political boss, Dan Reynolds (David Brian), at the roadhouse run by Lute Mae (Gladys George). He mentions that his plans are to help Field get elected to public office, beginning with state senator, and he stresses that the plans include Field's marrying Annabelle, because a politician needs a "respectable wife," and that they definitely don't include Field "getting mixed up with that stray cat from a carnival."

At Lute Mae's, Titus gets Reynolds's approval to fill the local vacancy in the state senate with Field, and Field is stunned by the ease with which this development has occurred. Soon, Titus also puts added pressure on Field to move on from Lane and propose to Annabelle. Field visits Annabelle and delivers the less-than-impassioned marriage proposal, "They tell me that any young man going into politics is supposed to get married." Thrilled that she will soon be "Mrs. Senator Fielding Carlisle," Annabelle receives the news with much more enthusiasm.

A dejected Field shares this news with Lane, who is sad but understands the situation. Moments later, Lane learns that she is being let go from her waitressing job, a move orchestrated by Titus, and that she likely won't be able to find another job in Boldon. Infuriated, she goes to the Palmer House to speak to Titus:

> LANE: Did you have me fired from the Eagle Café? Did you have it fixed so I couldn't get another job in this town?
> TITUS: It wasn't really anything personal.
> LANE: It's personal to me if I don't have a place to eat or sleep.
> TITUS: I reckon it would be. I'm a quiet man, Miss Bellamy. When I see trouble coming, I try to duck it. Now, with you and Field Carlisle, I can't see nothing but trouble.
> LANE: I don't mean anything to Field Carlisle. If I did, he wouldn't be getting married, would he?
> TITUS: I just don't want to take any chances, Miss Bellamy. Field's going to the state senate, and one of these days, he's going to be governor. A man like that has got to get married ... stay married ... happily married.
> LANE: That's fine, but I've got a right to live, too.

TITUS: You know, when I was a young fellow, I once had a job at a ware-
house. There were rats there. I didn't pay no attention to them. Then one
night there I went to sleep, and a rat half-chewed my big toe off before I
knew what was happening. After that, I went around and plugged up all
the holes. As long as I kept the holes plugged, I didn't have nothing to
worry about. That's how I've kept my toes all these years.

LANE: I won't be run out of town this way. I'm going to stay here and get
another job, any kind of a job. I want to stay here if it kills me.

TITUS: (Leans forward and looks directly into her eyes) It might do just
that, Miss Bellamy. One more move shouldn't be so hard to take, you
being a carnival girl.

LANE: I'm not a carnival girl anymore!

TITUS: You've sure been acting like it with young Carlisle.

LANE: (Slaps him hard across the face) I'm not running. Do you understand that?

TITUS: I sure am sorry you did that, Miss Bellamy.

Soon afterwards, Titus frames and arrests Lane for prostitution,
and she is sent to the local woman's prison farm for thirty days. At the
farm, another woman serving time suggests that, when Lane gets out,
she might try going to work for Lute Mae, whom, she says, nobody—not
even Titus—interferes with. Lane likes the idea. After Lane is released,
Lute Mae hires her, and she meets local political boss Dan Reynolds at
one of his poker get-togethers at the roadhouse. The two are immediately attracted to each other, and Dan takes her with him on an extended
business trip to New York that includes seeing to politics as well as the
running of Dan's construction company.

Several months later, much has changed. Field, is now a state senator, unhappily married to Annabelle, and turning more to alcohol. Lane
and Dan have also married, even though Dan knows that Lane might
still harbor feelings for Field. The couple return to the state's capital,
Olympic City, from New York; Titus runs into them at a nearby restaurant; and he and Lane again spar verbally:

TITUS: (to Lane) I didn't know that you were interested in politics.

LANE: I wasn't until politics became interested in me.

TITUS: The legislature's real interesting to watch. Of course, we officers of
the law ain't as forgetful of our promises as the fellows who make the
laws. Now me, I don't ever forget anything.

LANE: You know, Sheriff, we had an elephant in our carnival with a memory like that. He went after a keeper that he'd held a grudge against
for almost fifteen years. Had to be shot. You just wouldn't believe how
much trouble it is to dispose of a dead elephant.

Soon, Lane and Dan have moved into their new home in Boldon, a
very large and impressive house located, of course, on Flamingo Road.

Titus pays them a visit, telling Dan he wants to run Field for governor in the next election. Dan says that the state machine has promised the job to someone else and that Field can become governor later. Titus, however, doesn't want to wait. Dan doesn't back down, and both know that they are headed for a reckoning.

This reckoning comes soon enough when Titus frames and arrests the son of one of the top managers at Dan's construction company, saying he'll drop the charges if the company uses free convict labor on its projects and gives Titus a big kickback, an illegal practice. This is also what Titus would need, he calculates, to send Dan to jail and wrestle control of the state's political machine away from him.

In the meantime, Titus realizes that Field, who now drinks constantly, is too "soft" and "weak" to be his puppet-governor and decides that he should be the machine's candidate instead. When the other party bosses hear this, they are strongly opposed, but Titus shows them that he has kept records revealing many of their corrupt activities. Dan insists on fighting Titus, but the other bosses believe that Titus is holding all the cards.

Hearing all of this, Lane confides to Dan that Titus was determined to drive her from town because she had once been close to Field. When she tells him this, Dan feels that she has played him for a chump, marrying him for protection against Titus so she might eventually get back together with Field. Lane denies this, but he doesn't believe her and leaves without her for Olympic City.

That night, Field—very depressed, guilt-ridden, and drunk—visits Lane and tells her that Titus has everyone, even Dan, licked. He begs her for a drink, and she agrees, if he will tell her what incriminating information Titus has over Dan. "You're really in love with Dan," he says. Then, as she fixes his drink, he goes into another room and shoots himself.

Learning about Field's suicide, Titus immediately spreads vicious gossip suggesting an extra-marital affair between Lane and Field. A mob is formed to run Lane out of town, and soon a rock goes through the front window of Lane and Dan's house. A furious Lane tracks Titus down at Lute Mae's, tells him to admit publicly that Dan is innocent, pulls a gun on him, and tells him that, if he doesn't comply, she will kill him. Ever the wily one, Titus starts to phone the state's attorney general and then throws the telephone at Lane. She drops the gun, and he picks it up and points it at her. They struggle and, as they both try to take control of the gun, it goes off and Titus falls to the floor dead.

Initially, Lane is jailed. After investigating, though, the local district attorney is convinced that the gun was in Titus's hand and that Lane did not murder him but was instead defending herself in the struggle. Dan comes to her jail cell, she tells him that she now realizes how much he means to her, and he says that, after she's officially cleared, they will begin again—together.

◆ ◆ ◆

When *Flamingo Road* was released in May 1949, audiences were enthusiastic and reviews generally mixed. At the box office, the film brought in nearly $3 million worldwide, roughly double its production costs, which clearly qualified it as a hit. Many of the critics were quite impressed with both the film and its star's performance. *Variety*, for example, called the film "a class vehicle," adding that it "is hooped together by a smart, well-meshed screenplay and reenforced by a strong cast and sound direction."[4] Singling out its stars, the review also noted, "Miss Crawford's portrayal of a demanding, many-sided part is handled with her usual resourceful technique. She imparts convincing personality shadings ranging from strength to tenderness with a continuous and convincing style."[5] Other critics, though, were not nearly as complimentary. Writing in *The New York Times*, Bosley Crowther pulled no punches, calling the film both "a murky thing" and a "jumbled melodrama" and dismissing Crawford's performance "a mechanized demonstration."[6]

As the decades have passed, this significant critical divide has largely remained. While many film aficionados, including some of Crawford's biographers, have quickly dismissed the film, many others have appreciated it, often in very different ways.

Among *Flamingo Road's* most ardent advocates, for example, was the highly respected German film director Rainer Werner Fassbinder, a great fan of Hollywood noirs and melodramas. Fassbinder often praised Curtiz for his artistry, once complaining in an essay that his fellow director had been "cruelly overlooked" by film critics and historians.[7] Although he greatly admired such Curtiz classics as *Casablanca* and *Mildred Pierce*, he saved his highest praise for *Flamingo Road*, which he ranked as one of the top four films of all time. In addition, *Flamingo Road* was quite influential in Fassbinder's work. The opening scene of his 1975 drama *Fox and His Friends*, for example, pays homage to the earlier film's opening scene, in which the seedy carnival shuts down. Echoes of the small-town corruption in *Flamingo Road* are also present in Fassbinder's 1981 drama *Lola*.[8]

Another admirer, film writer Dave Kehr, has also likened *Flamingo Road* to an edgy "Southern gothic." "The film is sweaty, delirious, and purposefully perverse," he notes. "A strange, strange movie, it casts its own type of spell."[9]

Still another interesting take comes from film writer Alan Bacchus. Calling *Flamingo Road* a "terrific Hollywood melodrama" and an example of "the studio system at its best," he is also impressed by what he sees as the progressive thematic elements in the story. "The film is about female empowerment in a sexist age of specifically-defined domestic and gender roles," he writes. "It's an engrossing story of a girl from the wrong side of the tracks who fights prejudice and sexism as she moves up into high society and the corrupt world of American state politics."[10]

Taking into consideration these and other viewpoints espoused over the years, *Flamingo Road* is a fascinating film to try to come to grips with.

On one hand, it has many of the elements of a typical melodramatic soap opera. The plot is overly complicated and often contrived. For the most part, too, the characters lack the distinctiveness and depth of those in, say, *Mildred Pierce, Humoresque,* or *Daisy Kenyon.* Neither Lane's stubbornness at staying in Boldon (even at great risk to herself) nor Field's suicide, for example, seems adequately motivated. In fact, the suicide—one of the film's more sensational twists—comes across as quite forced.

On the other hand, this often-contrived story is presented with generally excellent production values. Credit for this, of course, must go to the talented team that Warner Brothers assembled for the project.

One great enhancement to the story is the additional rewriting that Crawford, exercising the powers granted in her contract, demanded as a requirement for her joining the project. The final version of the script is filled with the cutting, sassy, very noir-style one-liners that often serve to sharpen the distinctions and heighten the conflicts between characters. One of the better and more noirish lines, for example, is when Titus sizes up Field to his face, saying, "Soft and weak—you're just the kind of man I like." Another is when fellow female inmate at the woman's prison farm tells Lane that she's there because "My boyfriend cut himself on a knife I was holding." These kinds of lines also help tremendously in making the verbal sparring scenes between Lane and Titus highlights of the film.

Another major strength of the production is the superb direction and cinematography by Curtiz and McCord, respectively. In their choices of lighting set-ups, camera placement, camera movement, blocking, and other visual elements, they do a great deal both to build atmosphere and to reinforce meaning. As this nicely written entry in the *Pale Writer* web blog notes: "When watching *Flamingo Road,* you can feel the oppressive environment of Boldon, of the heat in the Southern United States and the festering corruption of those in power.

Curtiz's direction is brilliant, as he bathes everything in almost impenetrable shadows that cement the ... noir elements of the film and further the claustrophobic reality that Lane keeps trying to escape from. It seems that the more she tries to fight against Titus, the tighter his grip becomes on her world."[11]

Yet another strength of the film is the consistently good acting both by the leads and by a couple of the supporting players.

Although Crawford's work in *Flamingo Road* has never received the attention or praise that her efforts in, say, *Mildred Pierce* and *Possessed* have, she plays Lane in a very natural and convincing way. She seems quite comfortable inside this character, which is eminently understandable after having played far more troubled individuals in her three previous Warner Brothers outings. Lane is also familiar territory for the actress, harkening back both to her own early life and to many of the poor-but-spunky roles she had played in MGM's formula Joan Crawford pictures a decade or more before. Perhaps her greatest challenge in the role is credibly conveying Lane's strength, fearlessness, and just plain stubbornness to hold her own in her confrontations with the formidable Titus, and she does this admirably. Her line about the difficulty of disposing of a dead elephant, for example, is superb payback for Titus' earlier lines about what he did to keep rats from eating his toes off, and she delivers it in a wonderfully droll way.

Film writer Donna Marie Nowak has observed, "Crawford is the intriguing combination of contrasts that make her so fascinating and powerful a star: elegant but earthy, seductive but girlish, assertive but demure, vulnerable but no one's fool."[12] In *Flamingo Road*, her performance as Lane captures all of these conflicting characteristics in a very easy, natural way. Lane is the underdog we can't help but root for; a grounded, self-assured, and caring person surrounded by compromised people in a town rotten with corruption; a bright light in an otherwise dark, bleak noir world. No matter how formidable her challenges are, we want her—somehow—to surmount them. Among others, incidentally, her performance greatly impressed her highly respected co-star Sydney Greenstreet, who later remarked that she was "a better actress than a lot of people realize."[13]

One distraction in Crawford portraying Lane, however, is the actress's age. She was in her forties at the time, and Lane is clearly someone in her early to mid-twenties. Especially at this point in her career, Crawford was often older than her leading men, and in films such as *Humoresque, Sudden Fear,* and *Autumn Leaves,* her age is not an issue because the stories are about older-woman/younger-man relationships. Here, though, her age does get in the way. The early scene when she is dancing at the carnival with two women both about twenty years her junior, for example, is a challenge to accept. For those who have seen George Cukor's MGM production of *Romeo and Juliet* (1936) seeing Crawford dancing in this scene might even remind them of that film's casting in which the star-crossed teenage title characters were played by Norma Shearer (who was thirty-three at the time) and Leslie Howard (who was forty-two). Once we can get past our self-consciousness about Crawford's age and closely watch how she is tackling her character, however, we can see in the ways she moves, gestures, and talks that, although she is in her forties, she is doing an excellent job of channeling a significantly younger woman.

In addition to Crawford, several of the supporting players turn in fine performances.

One of the more fascinating aspects of *Flamingo Road* is the casting of the rotund, British born, Shakespearian-trained stage actor Sydney Greenstreet as Titus Semple, a crude, wily, and thoroughly despicable Southern sheriff and Lane's main antagonist. Greenstreet (1879–1954)

Three male characters who figure prominently in *Flamingo Road* are Sydney Greenstreet's Sheriff Titus Semple (left), Zachary Scott's Fielding Carlisle (center), and David Brian's Dan Reynolds (right). Greenstreet's vivid performance as Boldon's corrupt and thoroughly detestable chief law enforcement officer is one of the film's highlights (Warner Brothers/Photofest).

had enjoyed a forty-year stage career in both the U.K. and the U.S. before signing with Warner Brothers and shifting to films in 1941. His first film role, the villainous Kasper Gutman in John Huston's classic *The Maltese Falcon*, made a huge impression on audiences and led to a Best Supporting Actor Academy Award nomination for his work. During the 1940s, Greenstreet appeared in twenty-four films in all, mostly in supporting roles. In addition to *Flamingo Road* and *The Maltese Falcon*, some of his better-known portrayals are in *Casablanca*, *The Mask of Dimitrios* (1944), and *Christmas in Connecticut* (1945). Sadly, *Flamingo Road* was one of his last films. In 1949, failing health forced him to shift from films to acting for the radio, and he died four years later.

Greenstreet's Titus Semple isn't as well known as his Kasper Gutman but it is every bit as good. Buffoonish, terrifying, and, as film writer James Quandt has observed, "deliciously malignant."[14] Titus lives for power and revels in his talent for intimidating others so that he can preserve and even enhance his power. We see this in obvious ways such as his determination to run Lane out of Boldon because she may interfere with his plans for Field. We also see this in a number of much subtler ways. In one particularly creepy bit of business, Titus, after agreeing to help Annabelle with a problem, caresses her chin with more than a hint of perverse sexual interest. Annabelle is clearly surprised and repelled by his action, but she is also frightened—which is exactly how Titus wants it.

As written, the character of Titus has been given many idiosyncratic quirks, such as his penchant for drinking large quantities of milk and his delight in hearing the "squeal" of a sheriff's car siren. What's remarkable about Greenstreet's performance is how he manages to integrate all of these quirks and other elements of Titus's personality together in a way that produced a cohesive, credible, and very formidable character. This portrayal was certainly deserving of another Best Supporting Actor Academy Award nomination for Greenstreet. He was passed over, of course, but it would have been nice if he could have closed out his brief but very memorable film career with this extra bit of recognition.

In addition to Greenstreet, Zachary Scott and two actors playing minor parts, Gladys George and Fred Clark, have excellent moments. Scott, who was quite good as the debonair ne'er-do-well Monte Berragon in *Mildred Pierce*, ably portrays the weak and compliant Field Carlisle. While not a stand-out performance, Field is a very difficult role to pull off credibly while also eliciting some viewer sympathy, and Scott manages to do both. Gladys George (1904–1954), a veteran character actress Crawford insisted on to play the small but key role of Lute Mae also does fine work, bringing both authority and humanity to her underwritten character. Finally, Fred Clark (1914–1968), at the beginning of a career as a fine character actor in both films and television, brings a sense of strong, no-nonsense integrity to the small role of Doc Waterson, the crusading editor of Boldon's newspaper.

To complement the narrative, Max Steiner composed a score with a main theme that, while catchy, seems too jaunty and casual in tone to fit well with the story's melodramatic nature and its emphasis on corruption and rot. With a fairly contrived storyline to work with, however, he may have simply decided to fulfill this assignment by writing a serviceable score and then to move on to his next project.

◆ ◆ ◆

In many respects, the film version of *Flamingo Road* is a classic case of the futility of trying to "dress up" so-so material. Unlike *Mildred Pierce*, the compelling story just wasn't there, and unlike *Humoresque*, the original story wasn't totally reconceptualized and rewritten. With this built-in limitation, it appears that those involved with the production then gamely went about trying to make the best film they could with the material they had to work with. Crawford demanded that the script be spruced up, and some sharper, snappier dialogue was added. Curtiz and McCord did a great deal to reinforce the narrative visually, often giving specific scenes a highly effective noirish look and feel. With Crawford and Greenstreet leading the way, several of the actors also gave excellent performances. Yet, while all these efforts resulted in the many notable elements within the film, they didn't result in a particularly enthralling film. We often hear about the whole being greater than the sum of its parts. *Flamingo Road* may very well be a case in which the sum of its parts is greater than the whole.

This viewpoint might also help explain why people such as Fassbinder have held *Flamingo Road* in such high regard. He and others may have been so impressed by the extremely well-executed elements of the film such as Curtiz and McCord's visual rendering of a corrupt, oppressive environment and Greenstreet's riveting portrayal of Titus, that it was easy to overlook the contrived storyline, some thinly drawn characters, and other shortcomings.

◆ ◆ ◆

After finishing *Flamingo Road*, Crawford then plunged into a project that would result in perhaps the purest of all the noirs she ever made. Dark and unsparing, this film was based, not on fiction, but on the real-life story a woman who, in the 1930s and 1940s, was the mistress of several major gangland figures.

7

"You gotta kick and punch and belt your way up, 'cause nobody's gonna give you a lift"

The Damned Don't Cry (1950)

It has been approximately three-quarters of a century since Crawford's next film, *The Damned Don't Cry*, premiered, and, much like *Flamingo Road*, the critical jury is still pretty much divided on it.

The film has had, and continues to have, more than its share of detractors. When it first came out, many critics skewered it for its superficiality, lack of plausibility, and tawdriness. The *New York Herald Tribune's* Howard Barnes, in particular, was put off by the story's "shabby" theme.[1] The passage of time hasn't led to a generally kinder, gentler critical reassessment in other circles, either. Well into the twenty-first century, Frank Miller, writing for the Turner Classic Movies website, called it "a strange, artificial film"[2] and *Slant Magazine's* Jeremiah Kipp declared that it is "hardly memorable and at times putrefying in its reliance on hokum, cliché, and ... sentimentality."[3]

Yet, there's another side to the story, a side that, in some respects, also tracks with *Flamingo Road*. When *The Damned Don't Cry* was released, audiences loved it. The film became a major popular hit for Warner Brothers, making nearly twice its initial investment back at the box office. Today, it continues to remain a favorite among both Crawford and noir fans. One of these is noir historian Eddie Muller, who, while conceding that it might not be Crawford's best noir, has called it his "favorite by far" of all of her noirs.[4] Crawford biographer Donald Spoto has also been quite complimentary, calling the film "first-rate"[5] as well as "provocative and uncompromising."[6]

117

So, why is there such a wide divergence of opinion about this film? How can one perfectly respectable source denounce it as "putrefying" while another calls it his "favorite by far" among Crawford's noirs?

One explanation might simply be viewer preference.

The Damned Don't Cry is very different from *Mildred Pierce* and the other prestige noir melodramas that drew Crawford fans to movie theaters in droves in the mid- and late 1940s. Those films were filled with complex characters, rich storylines, and meaty themes, the stuff we normally associate with art, or at least efforts that aspire to be art.

In stark contrast, *The Damned Don't Cry* doesn't even attempt to aspire to such lofty aims, and, if we apply the same standards to it that we might apply to, say, *Mildred Pierce* or *Humoresque*, it won't come close to measuring up. Instead, this film is much closer to noir at its purest and pulpiest, a tribute to the dark film's trashy crime fiction roots. Little about this story is complex or, unless you are a gangster or a gangster's moll, relatable. Its characters are one-dimensional, its morality obvious and heavy-handed, and its plotting contrived.

But if we accept *The Damned Don't Cry* as high-caliber trash—pulp par excellence, if you will—it succeeds admirably. There is no mystery why lots of people, especially noir and/or Crawford fans, adore it. It gallops from scene to scene, bristles with energy, showcases its charismatic star, and captivates throughout. It might not be high art, but, as a dark, lurid, utterly shameless pulp entertainment, it can be quite satisfying and, especially for those who love to wallow in the whole sordid, doom-obsessed noir experience, lots of fun.

◆ ◆ ◆

The Damned Don't Cry is very loosely based on the scandalous real-life story of Virginia Hill (1916–1966), a poor girl from the American South who became a notorious mob moll in the 1930s and 1940s. As a teen, she left Marietta, Georgia, for Chicago in hopes of entering the pornography business. Instead, she became a waitress at a mob-run restaurant and made extra money moonlighting as a prostitute. This led to a series of relationships with various mob figures both in Chicago and in New York, where she was mistress to Luciano family capo Joe Adonis. During this time, she frequently posed as a Southern society belle who had gone through four rich husbands, leaving each marriage with more money. She also met and soon began a long affair with mobster Benjamin "Bugsy" Siegel, who was instrumental in developing the Las Vegas Strip into a major gambling center. After Siegel was killed in a mob hit in 1947, she radically changed course, marrying a professional Austrian skier, having a son with him, and eventually moving to Europe to avoid being prosecuted in the U.S. for tax evasion. (Another somewhat less fictionalized bio-pic of Hill and Siegel, *Bugsy*, starring Warren Beatty and Annette Bening, was released in 1991.)

Crawford, who had read quite a bit about Hill and Siegel, was fascinated with Hill's story and went to producer Jerry Wald with the idea.[7] Wald, who immediately saw the similarities with Crawford's own personal story, quickly agreed to the project. Then Crawford, as was her practice at this point in her career, became deeply involved in much of the film's pre-production phase. To direct, she recommended veteran studio hand Vincent Sherman, and, to play her four leading men, she recommended actors Richard Egan, Kent Smith, David Brian, and Steve Cochran. All five were quickly recruited for the effort. In addition, she was actively involved in discussions about subjects from her wardrobe to script development, regularly participating in the daily script conferences. Sherman, who had never worked with her before, was quite impressed. "I found her excellent to work with—intelligent, perceptive, and she presented her thoughts in a way that was never high-handed," he recalled.[8] She was also quite impressed with him, and about the time they started the project they also embarked on what became an extended affair.

Of all the people Crawford suggested for the film, perhaps the most interesting choice was Sherman (1906–2006). Today, he is not nearly as well known as other Warner Brothers' contract directors of the era such as Michael Curtiz, John Huston, and Raoul Walsh. He did, however, work steadily at the studio during the 1940s and early 1950s on both budget and more prestigious "A-list" films, quickly earning a reputation as a solid craftsman skilled at reworking flawed scripts and at getting excellent performances from his lead actresses. In the mid–1940s, for example, he directed both Ida Lupino and Bette Davis to Academy Award-nominated performances for their work in, respectively, *The Hard Way* and *Mr. Skeffington*. Both these skills—especially the latter— greatly appealed to Crawford.

For *The Damned Don't Cry*, Sherman's abilities as a script doctor turned out to be especially helpful. Based on "Case History" by Gertrude Walker, a fictionalized short story itself loosely based on Hill's life, the film adaptation needed numerous changes. Some were made to accommodate Crawford's age, which at this time was well into her forties. When the original story begins, for example, the Hill character is a discontented teenager. In the film, the character is a mother and discontented housewife, possibly in her early thirties. Another challenge was to come up with a more manageable script. Writer Jerome Weidman, a novelist working on his first-ever screenplay, had delivered a 300-page first draft, which, if filmed in its entirety, would result in a five-hour movie, about three times the length of a typical feature-length presentation. This left Sherman and the film's other credited writer, Harold Medford, with a major editing task. The film's working title had also been the lackluster *The Victim*. Eventually, Sherman changed it to the more noirish and intriguing *The Damned Don't Cry*, which he also felt, according to writer Frank Miller, "was more descriptive of Crawford's tough title character."[9]

Pre-production and shooting took place in the final months of 1949 both at the Warner Brothers' backlot and at various desert locales.

In this wonderfully realized scene in Vincent Sherman's *The Damned Don't Cry* (1950), Crawford's scheming Ethel Whitehead convinces to Kent Smith's meek accountant Marty Blackford (right) to take a lucrative job with the mob. In addition to Crawford and Smith's fine acting here is Ted McCord's striking noir lighting, which makes the faces of these two characters seem like they are sinking into a sea of black (Warner Brothers/ Photofest).

The Damned Don't Cry opens in classic noir fashion. In the middle of the night, a man's body is dumped unceremoniously out in the Nevada desert. Soon afterwards, perhaps the next day, a surveyor finds him and calls in the law. A local sheriff and his deputy check out the body, an underworld figure they're well aware of.

"Well, he finally got it," the sheriff says.

"Yep, it had to happen sooner or later," the deputy observes.

"He just got it sooner," the sheriff replies.

Soon, the sheriff and others learn that this figure has been associating with a wealthy socialite known as Lorna Hansen Forbes (Crawford). They want to contact her, but can't. In addition, no one—the sheriff, other government agencies, or the press—can dig up any kind of a past on this woman prior to the last two years.

The film then cuts to a car driving up to a sad, dingy house next to a field filled with tall, ugly oil rigs. The woman we've seen in home movies and photos as the glamorous Lorna, parks it, gets out, and enters the house, reuniting with her elderly parents who call her Ethel. Later that night, Ethel sees a photograph—a family portrait of her, a man, and a boy about six years old. As she looks at it, she, and we, flash back several years.

Now, Ethel is in a store with her son (the boy in the photo). He's fallen in love with a bicycle and begs her to buy it for him. After resisting at first because of the cost, she agrees. When her husband Roy (Richard Egan), an oil field worker, learns about this, he is furious and demands that the bike go back. They call to their son to return home. As he is riding back, however, he cuts across the road in front of an oncoming truck he hasn't noticed and is killed. After his funeral, Ethel, declaring that the boy was the only reason she had put up with this hard, dismal life, announces that she is leaving. Roy tries to defend himself, saying that he's done the best he could. "Well, it ain't good enough," Ethel barks back.

After struggling to find work, Ethel lands a job at a dress manufacturer modeling outfits for salesmen. She also meets Martin "Marty" Blackford (Kent Smith), a meek accountant who keeps the company's books, and soon convinces him to moonlight to help straighten out the books for a restaurant owner she knows. His new client is impressed with Marty's accounting talents and soon asks him to attend a meeting, which, Marty is told, could result in enormous new opportunities for him. Marty and Ethel go to the stately home of George Castleman (David Brian) who is hosting the meeting. While Ethel waits in another room, Marty sees first-hand that this is a gathering of major organized crime figures and that Castleman, who has heard of his excellent work, wants him to manage the accounting for a major national organization involved in all kinds of criminal activities from drug trafficking to prostitution. As they drive back after the meeting, Marty, in horror, tells Ethel about this. Far from being horrified, however, she is thrilled, seeing this as a big opportunity for Marty and her. Marty is shocked by her response:

MARTY: You want me to be like them—a criminal?

ETHEL: You bet I want you to be like them—smart. Nothing's going to happen to you. Castleman won't let it.... You're going to be an accountant just like you've always been.

MARTY: There's such a thing as self-respect.

ETHEL: Don't talk to me about self-respect. That's something you tell yourself you've got when you've got nothing else.... Look, Marty, the only thing that counts is that stuff you take to the bank, that filthy buck that everybody sneers at but slugs to get. (Marty looks sickened.) Oh, I know how you feel. You're a nice guy, but the world isn't for nice guys. You gotta kick and punch and belt your way up, 'cause nobody's gonna give you a lift. And you gotta do it yourself, because nobody cares about us except ourselves.

MARTY: It can't be right. It can't ever be right.

ETHEL: I'm not saying it is, but ... there's no other way—not for us.

MARTY: If I could be sure it was for *us*.

ETHEL: Marty, *everything* I've ever done was for us. (They kiss.)

The next day, however, Ethel visits Castleman, using her sex appeal and hoping to position herself with the organization's top figure. He sees great potential in her and oversees an entire personal and social makeover for her, rechristening her as Mrs. Lorna Hansen Forbes, a wealthy and well-bred socialite. Meanwhile, Marty is left with a lucrative but disreputable new position he never wanted and the knowledge that Ethel has merely used him and moved on.

After several months, Castleman, concerned about the loyalty of Nick Prenta (Steve Cochran), the cocky young lieutenant who runs his West Coast operation, sends Ethel out on a special assignment: ingratiate herself with Prenta and relay useful information back to Castleman. She agrees but, in the process, becomes fond of Prenta. Soon, the tension between Castleman and Prenta builds to a reckoning. Marty travels to the desert to tell Ethel that Castleman doesn't think she's telling him all she knows and to convince her that it's in her interest to level with the boss, but she hesitates. Along with Marty, Castleman unexpectedly appears at Prenta's desert home. As Marty watches helplessly, Castleman fiercely beats Ethel up and then shoots and kills Prenta. In the confusion immediately afterwards, Ethel escapes.

Now, the story flashes forward to the present. In her parents' home,

Ethel's mother wakes her up, telling her a man has come to see her. It's Marty, saying that Castleman will soon be coming and that she should leave as quickly as possible. Castleman then arrives and, in a struggle, shoots Ethel. Marty then shoots and kills Castleman, sees that Ethel is still alive, picks her up, carries her into the house, and then apparently flees.

The police and press soon descend upon the house, learn next to nothing from Ethel's parents, and see that Ethel isn't in any condition to talk. Knowing that they are at a dead end, at least for the moment, a reporter and a photographer both leave, talking as they walk out the front door.

"Well, it must be pretty tough living in a place like this," the reporter says.

"Tougher to get out," the photographer says. "Do you think she'll try again?"

"Wouldn't you?" the reporter responds.

◆ ◆ ◆

It might be easy to dismiss *The Damned Don't Cry* as nothing more than a studio-manufactured pot-boiler, but it would also be unfair to Wald, Sherman, Crawford, and others who contributed their talents to it. It's not *Mildred Pierce*, of course, but then it's not trying to be. It's a fast-paced, energetic, well-crafted pulp crime noir/star showcase that both noir and Crawford fans have, for more than seven decades, found engrossing and entertaining. For this to happen, a good deal of artistry and craft had to go into its making.

One person who certainly deserves much of the credit for the film's success is Sherman, who contributed on several fronts. One of these, of course, was his work, with writers Jerome Weidman and Harold Medford, on the script. Compared to the vast majority of crime noirs, the story of *The Damned Don't Cry* is quite well conceived and presented. Action follows action at a breakneck pace, giving every moment a special urgency. Snappy, hard-boiled dialogue is plentiful and fun to listen to. Tension is always present. On another front, Sherman was very talented at staging some of the film's key scenes. An excellent example is when Castleman beats Ethel up late in the film. It is Ethel's comeuppance (or at least the first part of it) for her actions. Sherman wanted to emphasize that she would not be getting off lightly, and he succeeded. Still disturbing to watch today, the scene is brutal, extremely realistic, and quite effective. In 1950, it must have startled and shocked many viewers. On still another front, the film has a clarity and cohesion to it that attests to Sherman's ability to run a focused, well-disciplined operation. He might not have had the visual flair of a Curtiz or a Raoul Walsh, but the finished film is proof that he was in full command of the conception, design, and shooting of every scene in it.

Among the actors, most of the attention usually goes (as it should) to Crawford. From start to finish, this film is her star vehicle, her showcase, and there are several aspects to what she does and how she does it that are worth noting.

One of these is the great amount of overlap between Ethel's journey and Crawford's own life story. In script sessions, Crawford also lobbied hard for changes that would make Ethel harder and more aggressive, someone who, like the actress, truly believed, "You gotta kick and punch and belt your way up...." The film industry that Crawford entered isn't the mob, of course, but the two worlds share similarities (such as the promises of glamour and riches and the realities of exploitation and possible ruin) that certainly weren't lost on her, Wald, or Sherman.

Another aspect worth noting is seeing the Ethel character in a noir context. More than any other noir or noir-tinged film Crawford ever did, *The Damned Don't Cry* probably comes closest to the pure hard-boiled crime noir template. In many of her other noirish efforts, she plays a heroine who contends with a seductive, potentially dangerous man, or homme fatale, such as the characters played by Conrad Veidt in *A Woman's Face* or Van Heflin in *Possessed*. Here, she plays the stock noir femme fatale, but, since this is also a Crawford film, there has to be a twist. In this story, the femme fatale is also the naïve, ill-fated noir protagonist (a character that is almost always a male) who realizes too late that she is in over her head and then pays dearly for her past criminal associations and activities. Setting Ethel up in this way gives her story a fascinating and highly distinctive arc that mixes the journeys and fates of these noir archetypes with those of her 1930s Joan Crawford picture characters. Like her typical 1930s Cinderella heroines, she uses her grit and spunk to rise in the world. Unlike those heroines, however, Ethel throws any kind of decency she might have once had out the window, does shady things, and ends up, as the film's title tells us, "damned." While she manages to avoid a violent death (the fate of many noir protagonists and femmes fatales), she is, with the possibility of prison ahead of her, much worse off than she was at the beginning of her story. In effect, Ethel's journey is, much like Mildred Pierce's: a noirish perversion of the journey taken by Crawford's 1930s heroines.

Still another aspect worth noting is Crawford's portrayal of Ethel. For the most part, film critics have not had kind words to say about her acting in the film, and many of their points are well taken. Most of the time, she is playing a twisted, noirish version of her spunky 1930s character and offering little more. In Crawford's defense, however, Ethel Whitehead is not the kind of thoughtfully developed, well-rounded individual that Anna Holm, Mildred Pierce, Helen Wright, Louise Howell, or Daisy Kenyon is. She is a pulp creation, nothing more, and, rather than attempting a serious acting portrayal, Crawford and Sherman opted for the star to simply pull out the stops—to turn on her charisma and rely mainly on that to get through the proceedings. This was not necessarily a bad choice, either. By relying mainly on charisma, Crawford has some excellent moments. One, for example, is the scene in which Ethel convinces Marty that he should go to work for the mob. Here, Crawford speaks with great conviction, urgency, and forcefulness. It's impossible for us to take our eyes off her, and, even though Marty finds the whole idea repugnant, we also know that it will be impossible for him to refuse her.

It's also worth noting that *The Damned Don't Cry* marks the beginning of a trend that will continue throughout most of the 1950s in Crawford noirs and other films in which she plays harder, less sympathetic characters. In this film, Ethel's hardness is tempered somewhat by our knowledge of her harsh and painful earlier experiences. These help us understand why she acts in certain ways and, as a result, helps us sympathize with her at least to the point in the story when she dumps Marty for Castleman. In some future films, most notably 1955's *Queen Bee*, there is next to nothing to offset the strongly negative aspects of the characters she plays. The result, at least partially due to these portrayals, is the birth of the "mean girl Joan" stereotype and her rise as a "camp" figure, a phenomenon we'll come back to later in this book.

Crawford, of course, is not the only actor with a significant role in *The Damned Don't Cry*. In fact, one intriguing element of the film is that it includes roles for no fewer than four male romantic leads for her to play opposite: Richard Egan, Kent Smith, David Brian, and Steve Cochran. Usually, her films include just two: the man she separates from and the man she eventually ends up with. In *A Woman's Face*, for example, these are the characters played, respectively, by Conrad Veidt and Melvin Douglas. In *Possessed*, these are those played, respectively, by Van Heflin and Raymond Massey. Rather than being a strength in *The Damned Don't Cry*, however, the presence of four lovers actually detracts from the story because these roles are, for the most part, insufficiently developed. Egan's Roy is on screen too briefly to leave any meaningful impression. Brian's Castleman is simply evil and charmless. Cochran's Nick Prenta isn't sufficiently fleshed out. It's interesting, too, that Cochran, who specialized in sexy bad-boy roles at this time in his

Two of the main mobsters in Ethel's life in *The Damned Don't Cry* are Steve Cochran's suave Nick Prenta (lower left) and David Brian's cold and ruthless George Castleman (upper right) (Warner Brothers/Photofest).

career, lacks the screen chemistry with Crawford that she and Sherman were probably hoping for when they cast him.

Of the four supporting male performances, the most intriguing by far is Kent Smith's portrayal of Marty, the accountant. Smith (1907–1985), who had a busy Hollywood career that extended from the 1930s to the 1970s, played a variety of character roles ranging from stern authority figures to cautious, milquetoast types like Marty. While not a household name to movie fans, he was widely respected within the film industry for his ability to infuse humanity into sketchily written supporting roles, giving them greater depth and distinctiveness. In the role of Marty, he does this to great effect. Of all the key characters in the story, Marty, the accountant who manages the money, is the only one who isn't ruled by it—the only one with any real decency or integrity. He is also no match for the relentlessly ambitious Ethel and sacrifices his much-valued "self-respect" just to remain with her. As written, the role, while clearly drawn, is little more than a stereotype. Smith, however, gives Marty a mix of gentleness, quiet dignity, emotional vulnerability, and naivete that make the character quite human and compelling. Although Ethel is usually considered the story's tragic figure, it is much easier in the end to feel the same amount of, if not more, pathos for Marty, and Smith's ability to bring so much to this part is the main reason for this.

In addition to Sherman, Crawford, and the other actors in *The Damned Don't Cry*, numerous Warner Brothers behind-the-scenes personnel made major contributions to the effort.

One was Ted McCord, the Warner staff cinematographer who had recently worked with Crawford on *Flamingo Road*. Here, as in *Flamingo Road*, McCord does an excellent job of underscoring both the themes and the mood of the story through striking visuals. The dark scenes in and around the dingy house next to the oil fields, for example, are especially memorable for how they present the depressed, broken environment Ethel desperately wants to escape from. In addition, they serve as a stark contrast to the elegance and glamor of later moments such as when Ethel and Castleman enjoy an elegant dinner on his balcony and the scenes depicting the high life in the desert. Ominous noir darkness, however, is always either present or looming. In the scene when Ethel convinces Marty to go to work for the mob, for example, the lighting is stunning. It's set at night in the backseat of Castleman's limo, and most of what we see throughout are Ethel and Marty's faces both lit dimly in a sea of black—more than a suggestion that the two are surrounded by, and helpless to withstand, the forces of darkness.

Another key contributor was Rudi Fehr, the excellent film editor who, four years earlier, had accomplished the very difficult task of making John Garfield look like a world-class violinist in *Humoresque*. Although his work on *The Damned Don't Cry* isn't nearly as well-known as his work in *Humoresque* and other films, it is quite good. His editing is always tight and exacting, keeping the film moving at an almost manic pace and reinforcing Ethel's deeply held conviction that she doesn't "have any time to waste" in her quest for wealth and position. Working with Warner Brothers technicians, Fehr also helps to create very compelling montages during the film. For example, the montage in which both the authorities and the press are trying to learn what's really behind the story of Lorna Hansen Forbes is exquisitely put together and absolutely riveting to watch.

Still another important contributor was Daniele Amfitheatrof (1901–1983), a Russian-born composer and conductor, who, after years of preparing to be a serious musician, relocated in Hollywood shortly before World War II. For the next twenty-six years, he composed scores (some credited and some uncredited) for more than fifty films. Twice nominated for Academy Awards for his work, he later regretted his association with Hollywood, believing that it ultimately tarnished his reputation as a serious composer. Among his better-known film scores are those for *Lassie Come Home* (1943), *Song of the South* (1946), *Letter from an Unknown Woman* (1948) and *Human Desire* (1954). For *The Damned Don't Cry*, Amfitheatrof's score does an admirable job of complementing the story's lurid and ominous but still glamorous focus as well as enhancing the sense of anxiety and urgency we feel throughout. From beginning to end, it is quite effective.

◆ ◆ ◆

"The thrill of noir is the rush of moral forfeit and the abandonment to titillation," crime fiction writer and editor James Ellroy once observed. "The overarching joy and lasting appeal of noir is that it makes doom fun."[10]

Of all Crawford's noir and noirish films, *The Damned Don't Cry* probably comes closer than any other to delivering on these essential truths. At its pulpy core, noir is escapism, pure and simple. As viewers, we live vicariously through the tainted characters we see on the screen. Then, when it's time for them to face their dark destinies, we breathe an enormous sigh of relief that we will not have to experience what's in store for them. *The Damned Don't Cry* may lack many of the qualities of Crawford's earlier noir melodramas, but, as pure noir, it more than satisfies by giving viewers the thrill and the joy of watching others as they travel down the dark road to rot and ruin. Yes, if you are in the appropriate frame of mind, doom can be a lot of fun.

◆ ◆ ◆

After *The Damned Don't Cry* was completed, Sherman and Crawford, still in the throes of their affair, made two more films together, both film versions of successful stage plays. The first, *Harriet Craig*, is a drama based on the 1925 play *Craig's Wife* by George Kelly, which had already been filmed twice (in 1928 with Irene Rich and again in 1936 with Rosalind Russell). The story focuses on its title character, a manipulative, controlling perfectionist who winds up alienating her husband and others around her. The second, *Goodbye, My Fancy*, is a romantic comedy based on a 1948 play of the same name by Fay Kanin. In this story, Crawford plays a liberal congresswoman who visits her former college and reunites with two former flames. Both films received tepid reviews and proved disappointing at the box office, *Goodbye, My Fancy* barely making back its production costs.

Soon after *Goodbye, My Fancy* wrapped, Sherman and Crawford also said goodbye to each other, ending both their personal and professional relationships.

Sherman went to MGM to direct *Lone Star* (1952), a western starring Clark Gable and Ava Gardner, and then to Columbia to direct *Affair in Trinidad* (1952), a noir starring Rita Hayworth and Glenn Ford. After these films, and with the Hollywood blacklist at its height, he had trouble finding work for several years because of his left-wing political sympathies. Beginning in the late 1950s, however, he did make a few more notable films. Among them is *The Young Philadelphians* (1959), a well-received legal drama starring Paul Newman and Barbara Rush. In the 1960s, he shifted to television and worked on both made-for-TV movies and episodes of several TV series, ranging from the wholesome family drama *The Waltons* to the gritty crime show *Baretta*. His last directing credits are two episodes of the medical series *Trapper John M.D.*, which he worked on in 1983 when he was seventy-seven years old. In his last years, he was often interviewed for documentaries and DVD special features and was quite candid about both his professional and personal relationships with Crawford as well as other actresses such as Hayworth and Bette Davis. He died in 2006, less than a month shy of what would have been his one-hundredth birthday.

With one more film commitment remaining on her Warner Brothers contract after *Goodbye, My Fancy*, Crawford weighed her future prospects at what, for the past eight years, had been her home studio. Now sensing that the luster was wearing off her brand with the studio's powers that be, she was beginning, once again, to think in terms of new professional possibilities.

First, though, she had to do that one last film at Warner Brothers, an experience she would quickly come to dread.

8

"I'm sure your life is going to be much brighter from now on"

This Woman Is Dangerous (1952)

When brilliant eye surgeon Dr. Ben Halleck (Dennis Morgan) removes the bandages from the eyes of patient Beth Austin (Joan Crawford) after a high-risk operation in Felix Feist's 1952 crime noir-melodrama hybrid, *This Woman Is Dangerous*, the two learn, and then absorb, the result. Against all odds, Beth's eyesight, once nearly lost, has been fully restored. With gentle assurance, Halleck then tells her, "I'm sure your life is going to be much brighter from now on."

Certainly, for many people who've watched this film, this line has triggered laughter of the you've-got-to-be-kidding kind. "Yes, doctor," an incredulous viewer might imagine responding, "pretty much anything is brighter than blindness."

Unfortunately for Crawford, Morgan, and most of the other people working on *This Woman Is Dangerous*, the film was one of those studio assignments they dreaded but had to complete anyway. The main problem with the effort was a script that could have benefited greatly from a couple of serious rewrites. As it stands, the story's plot is formulaic, the characters underdeveloped, and the dialogue, as exemplified above, riddled with cliches. Instead of the skillful and highly effective blending of noir and melodramatic elements that are at the heart of Crawford's best Warner Brothers films, this is a clumsy grafting.

Curiously, when we learn a bit about Crawford's professional circumstances at the time, Dr. Halleck's prediction of a brighter life ahead also, and somewhat ironically, mirrors reality. By 1951, she felt that her tenure at Warner Brothers was coming to an end in much the same way her long run at MGM had done nearly a decade before. Again, the warning signs were there: she was no longer getting plum roles, the studio was focusing more on promoting its younger actresses, and the behind-the-back whispers about her advancing age and declining box-office clout seemed to be everywhere.

Especially sensitive to what she interpreted as disrespect, Crawford must have been deeply hurt and angered by the whole business. In just six years, she had made a succession of critically acclaimed and enormously popular films for the studio and, in the process, picked up a pair of Best Actress Academy Award nominations and an Oscar for *Mildred Pierce*. Her only real box-office dud had been her most recent effort, the poorly received romance, *Goodbye, My Fancy*.

Tensions apparently came to a head when production head Jack Warner offered her *This Woman Is Dangerous*, a clearly inferior project, in hopes that she would reject the role. This would enable him to suspend her and stop paying her high salary. To Warner's surprise, however, Crawford accepted the assignment. At the same time, she instructed her agents to negotiate a way out of her Warner Brothers contract. She would leave on her terms, not Jack Warner's.

Ever the planner, she was already looking to the future. Instead of signing with another studio as she had done after leaving MGM, her strategy this time was to work on an independent project she was quite excited about, an adaptation of the 1948 suspense novel, *Sudden Fear*. The hope, of course, was that, just as her professional life had brightened considerably after MGM, it would brighten again post–Warner Brothers.

First, though, Crawford would have to slog through the dark time of making *This Woman Is Dangerous*, the film, which, in an often-cited tidbit of trivia, she called the worst movie she'd ever made. Considering that this comment came late in her life, after she'd made such indisputably terrible films as *I Saw What You Did* (1965), *Berzerk!* (1967), and *Trog* (1970), that's quite a statement. She must have really hated it.

Yet, Crawford's negative feelings toward the studio's treatment of her at the time may have colored her perspective on the whole experience. *This Woman Is Dangerous* is clearly not one of her stellar Warner Brothers efforts, but it is, on the critical spectrum, nowhere near *Trog* territory, either. More accurately perhaps, it is an example of sub-par work from a major studio in its heyday. The project needed more pre-production development, especially with the script, just to make it into a solid, but routine, noir thriller. At the same time, though, the film includes contributions from several top talents in Warner Brothers' impressive stable of artists and artisans, people who approached the dubious material with their usual high level of professionalism and made positive contributions to the production. It's not deathless art, but it's also not as bad as Crawford made it out to be.

❖ ❖ ❖

The story of *This Woman Is Dangerous* opens as Beth Austin—by all appearances, a cultured woman of means—learns that she is rapidly going blind and that perhaps the only doctor who can save her is eye surgeon Dr. Ben Halleck at the Halleck Clinic in Indiana. She then meets up with Matt Jackson (David Brian), a rough, hot-tempered thug, and we learn that Beth is both Matt's girlfriend and the brains behind a gang of robbers that also includes Matt and his younger brother Will (Philip Carey). She tells Matt that she's moving up plans to rob an illegal gambling casino at midnight that night. When the time comes, they pull the robbery off quite neatly. It's a clever operation. Beth, dressed like a socialite, gets the proprietor to open his safe to get more money for her just before the gang members, dressed as police officers and carrying

Dennis Morgan's renowned eye surgeon Dr. Ben Halleck (right) checks the declining vision of Crawford's Beth Austin before agreeing to operate on her in Felix Feist's *This Woman Is Dangerous* (1952) (Warner Brothers/ Photofest).

guns, enter, close down the casino, and take all the money from the safe. The next day, Beth meets with Matt to discuss the gang's next steps and to tell him that she needs to go to Indiana to get the eye operation. Matt immediately becomes jealous, assuming that there is another man

Unknown to Dr. Halleck, however, the elegant Beth is also the brains behind a gang of notorious robbers that includes David Brian's psychopathic Matt Jackson (left) (Warner Brothers/Photofest).

involved. She assures him that there isn't and pleads with him to lie low until she returns. He promises to do so.

At the Halleck Clinic, Beth meets Dr. Halleck, who warns her that this surgery will involve both great risk and a long recovery period and require tremendous patience, discipline, and courage. She soberly takes in this information and insists that they move forward. Halleck, impressed with her courage, agrees to proceed, and the operation takes place. As Beth recovers, she and Halleck begin to fall in love. Both are also thrilled when it's clear that the operation has been a success. A little later, Halleck even takes Beth home to meet his young daughter, Susan, explaining that his wife had walked out on the two of them years earlier and that he has been a single dad ever since. Soon, however, Beth, fearing both that she will be bad for Halleck and that, unless she goes back to Matt, he will come after Halleck, breaks it off with the doctor.

Meanwhile, Matt kills a police officer and he and Will become the targets of a major FBI manhunt. This, however, doesn't concern Matt as much as the thought that Beth might be with another man, so he goes to Indiana to see for himself what's going on. Also, the FBI has connected Beth with Matt and Will but not with the murder, has tracked her down, and is keeping tabs on her during her recovery in hopes that she will eventually lead them to the desperado brothers.

Eventually, the action leads everyone to a hospital where Halleck, assisted by four other doctors, is operating on another patient. Convinced that the doctor has lured Beth away from him, Matt waits in the observation gallery above the operating room, planning to kill Halleck as soon as the operation is over. Beth, Will, and Will's wife all arrive at the hospital to pick up Matt. Beth goes to find Matt, leaving Will and his wife behind. The FBI agents show up. Will instinctively pulls out his gun and is killed in a shootout. By now, Beth has found Matt in the observation gallery. She has come to plead with him, telling him that she has rejected Halleck to be with him. But he's not buying it. When the operation concludes, Matt looks at the five doctors (all of them wearing surgical masks) standing around the operating table and demands to know which one is Halleck. Bravely, Halleck takes off his mask, but, before Matt can shoot him, Beth goes for his gun and Matt shoots her instead, wounding her. At this point the FBI agents come in and shoot it out with Matt. He dies, falling, in very dramatic fashion, through the observation gallery's glass windows and onto the operating room floor. Halleck tells the lead FBI agent of Beth's courageous effort to save him, and the agent suggests that she will likely get a lenient sentence. Soon, it seems, Beth will be free to start a new life with Halleck.

❖ ❖ ❖

As this plot synopsis suggests, *This Woman Is Dangerous*, like most other Crawford films of the late 1940s and early 1950s, is a hybrid of elements from both the crime noir and female-centered melodrama worlds. The part of the story that involves Beth and the Jackson brothers is pure pulp noir. Along with other typical noir elements, it features a robbery, two murders, an FBI-led manhunt, a certifiable psychopath, a climatic shootout, and some attempts at hardboiled dialogue such as Will Jackson's very odd line, "We're so hot from the cops, we're smokin'." The other main story thread is an intriguing mix of two kinds of storylines common in female-centered melodramas, one in which the heroine has a serious health affliction and the other in which she must make a major sacrifice. Beth, a woman with a serious health affliction, is cured by Dr. Halleck and falls in love with him. Soon though, she fears for his safety because her other boyfriend is a hyper-jealous psychopathic killer. She then concludes that she must sacrifice her happiness by leaving Halleck so that boyfriend number one (who by now is also public enemy number one) doesn't rub the good doctor out.

Unlike *Mildred Pierce* and other Crawford films that deftly knit their noirish and melodramatic elements together to produce a single, unified storyline, *This Woman Is Dangerous* often comes across more as two entirely different stories that have been clumsily spliced together. Watching it can sometimes be jarring, an experience akin to switching constantly between two television programs as they air simultaneously on different channels. Curiously, though, this spliced quality also offers a fascinating perspective on what it must be like to be Beth as the story unfolds. One minute she worries about going to jail. The next minute (literally), she is in Halleck's beautiful suburban home helping his sweet, charming daughter prepare dinner. While this can be disconcerting for the viewer, it also underscores Beth's highly fragmented, almost surreal existence as she tries to navigate between the two very different worlds and, in the process, actually furthers the story's interests.

❖ ❖ ❖

Despite the unkind words Crawford and others have heaped on *This Woman Is Dangerous*, the film overall is surprisingly watchable and engaging. The acting, cinematography, pacing, music, and other contributing elements all help to mask or at least to soften many of the story's shortcomings. Again, the operative word here might be the "professionalism" that was typical of production staff members during the studio era. Even if they had little confidence in the project as a whole, they usually wanted to make sure that their contributions looked good, or at least not embarrassingly bad.

Taking into account the film's underwritten characters and often clunky dialogue, the actors, for the most part, do the best they can with the material they are given. Crawford and Morgan have fairly good screen chemistry and effectively underplay scenes that could easily have gone awry with too much hand-wringing and emoting. It's amazing, for example, how Crawford can deliver a line such as, "Don't you see that you're tormenting both of us?" and somehow pull it off. Morgan is so understated that film writer Glenn Erickson once called his performance as "bland as skim milk."[1] It's true that Dr. Halleck might not be wildly exciting, but he is thoughtful, kind, stable, and exactly what the story needs—a clear counterpoint to raging psychopath Matt Jackson—and Morgan ably conveys all these qualities. In the supporting roles, most of the actors perform well or at least competently. Philip Carey's Will (the supposedly more sensible Jackson brother) has a few fine moments when we see that he can be scary-crazy, too. A major shortcoming, however, is David Brian's Matt. Although he, like the other actors, is saddled with a sketchily drawn character, Brian plays Matt in such an over-the-top, ham-fisted manner that he quickly becomes tedious and annoying.

Perhaps the greatest strength of *This Woman Is Dangerous* is the cinematography of Ted McCord. His camerawork—as in both *Flamingo Road* and *The Damned Don't Cry*—is exceptionally effective in its use of lighting and in camera placement and movement to underscore the narrative. In the scene when Beth learns that her surgery has been a success, for example, the visuals beautifully reflect her sense of uncertainty and then the joy she feels when she understands what this means for her. In another fine scene, as Halleck operates on a child in an impoverished family's home, there is a dark, dramatic quality in the visuals that greatly heightens the intensity of the moment and reinforces the operation's enormous importance for the family.

Two of Warner Brothers' other great strengths during the late 1940s and early 1950s were the fast-paced editing and musical scoring of many of its films, especially action pieces, to provide constant forward movement and often amp up the tension. Sometimes, if the story is found wanting in certain respects, the contributions of the film editor and the composer could go a long way in improving the viewing and listening experience. This is definitely true with *This Woman Is Dangerous*. It was edited in the crisp, fast-paced Warner studio style by James C. Moore, who would soon go on to work on Nicholas Ray's 1955 classic, *Rebel without a Cause*, and then as the supervising editor on hundreds of episodes of such hit Warner television shows as *Maverick* and *77 Sunset Strip*. The film's music, intended both to complement the action and to build suspense whenever appropriate, was composed by David Buttolph, a veteran who had done film scores for such directors as Andre DeToth, Raoul Walsh, John Ford, and Jean Renoir.

Altogether, the work of these contributors—as well as the contributions of director Felix Feist, art director Leo Kuter, and others—combine to give *This Woman Is Dangerous* a handful of first-rate scenes that really do click.

One of these is when Halleck is summoned to a woman's prison to see a patient and leaves Beth in his car to wait for him. As she sits, elegantly dressed and leisurely smoking a cigarette, a prison van enters the yard and parks. She watches a group of tough-looking woman depart from the back of the van and an even tougher looking female matron realize that one of the prisoners has been smoking, which is against the rules for prisoners at these times. The matron then lines all the woman up, demands that the guilty woman come forward and, when no one does, inspects the hands of all the prisoners. When she finds no evidence, she takes the smoking privileges away from all the women. What the matron hasn't seen but what Beth notices is that the prisoner who had been smoking has put her cigarette out with her bare fingers, burning them, and then hid the cigarette in her belt. The camera cuts back to Beth, appearing quite agitated, and we see that, although she is wearing gloves, she has also snuffed her cigarette out with her fingers. It's a startling moment. Is Beth reliving a similar experience she had when she'd served prison time before joining up with the Jacksons? Is she thinking that, very soon, she could again be in prison and treated just like these women are being treated? Are both thoughts running through her mind? The entire scene, which is slightly less than two minutes, is wonderfully realized—the visual storytelling, shot selection, camera placement, and music all perfect for the moment. It's interesting, too, that the scene does nothing to advance the plot and could easily have been edited out of the film. It was kept in, of course, for what it tells us about Beth's past and current state of mind and because it is simply a great couple of cinematic minutes.

Another excellent scene is the climactic shootout in the observation gallery at the end of the film. Established earlier in the story, the gallery set is narrow and tall and even has a ladder and portal leading to the roof, giving viewers a kind of skyscraper-like effect. It's especially eerie how Matt, like a bird of prey, patiently watches the surgery from his high perch above a massive wall of glass, waiting for the operation to end so he can find out which of the masked doctors is Halleck and then kill him. The narrowness of the gallery also gives the scene a claustro-phobic quality, especially after Beth and then the FBI agents enter, giving Matt the look of a caged animal who will instinctively feel trapped and strike back. Finally, there's the climactic moment when Matt is shot, falls through the wall of glass, and lands dead on the operating room floor with pieces of broken glass scattered all around him. We might be expecting that something like this will happen; still, when we actually see it, it is quite shocking.

✦ ✦ ✦

Although *This Woman Is Dangerous* could have been better, it could, without its talented contributors, have also been much worse. Unfortunately, its reputation suffers today both from Crawford's low assessment of it and from comparison with the succession of excellent films she had done at Warner Brothers just a few years earlier. It wasn't up to those standards, and, ever the perfectionist, she wasn't happy about that one bit. Still, the film does have some fine moments, and it does give Crawford and others in the production the chance to explore once again yet another variation of the crime noir/female-centered melodrama hybrid.

In the end, of course, Crawford got her wish: the release from her Warner Brothers contract on terms that were acceptable for her as well as the chance to assert more control over her film projects and ultimately her professional destiny. The plans for her first independent feature film, an adaptation of the novel *Sudden Fear*, had already been percolating in her head for months. Now, the dream could become a reality, and perhaps her professional life was, in Dr. Halleck's words, "going to be much brighter from now on."

9

"Lester, I have a gun"

Sudden Fear (1952)

As we watch the opening credits of Crawford's next film, the independently made thriller *Sudden Fear*, one very interesting slide pops up. It is titled, "Miss Crawford's Wardrobe." Underneath is a list:

- Gowns designed by.... Sheila O'Brien
- Furs designed by.... Al Teitelbaum
- Lingerie and Hostess Gowns by.... Tula
- Hats by.... Rex, Inc.
- Jewels by.... Ruser

As we peruse these credits, it immediately becomes clear just who was running this show, which is, perhaps, exactly how its star, prime mover, and de facto producer wanted to be perceived.

Although it is not as well known or as widely discussed as *Mildred Pierce* or other mid– to late–1940s Crawford triumphs, 1952's *Sudden Fear* is, from several perspectives, one of the most significant achievements of her career. First, it was the commercial and critical hit she needed (once again) to put her back on top in Hollywood and help assure a steady stream of film offers for the next few years. Second, it was a venture for her into a different kind of noir, the woman-in-distress thriller, a noir category that includes such fine films as *Gaslight* (1944) with Ingrid Bergman, *Sorry, Wrong Number* (1947) with Barbara Stanwyck, and *Whirlpool* (1959) with Gene Tierney. Again, she was extending the reach of cinema's dark art by taking many elements of the Crawford noir-melodrama into new storytelling territory. Finally, and perhaps most important for her, it represented an enormous step forward in her longtime quest to have greater control over *all* facets of a film's artistic development. At long last, she was truly the auteur, the person with both the vision for a major film project and virtually all the power and resources needed to turn that vision into a compelling celluloid reality.

◆ ◆ ◆

According to Crawford, her relationship with *Sudden Fear* began with a "Eureka!" experience she had late in the summer of 1951. With the lackluster *Goodbye, My Fancy* still fresh in her mind, and the prospect of doing the deeply flawed *This Woman Is Dangerous* just ahead, she desperately needed a hit. At this point, Warner Brothers, seeing her as past her prime as a box-office draw, was of little help. So, she realized that, once again, it would be up to her to find the right story and do everything she could to turn it into an excellent film.

That summer, she took her children, along with a wide assortment of scripts and books, with her to the ocean-side town of Carmel, in Central California. During the days, they swam and played together on the beach. At night, as the children slept, she reviewed the various story properties. For weeks, nothing really clicked for her. Eventually, she brought the children back to Los Angeles for school and then headed back to Carmel with another load of books. None of these impressed her, either. Then at midnight one night she picked up one novel, a recently published romantic thriller by Edna Sherry with many unexpected twists. "[I] couldn't put it down until I read the last page at 4:00 a.m.," she recalled. "Sleep was out of the question. I arose and walked along the sea. By daybreak I had *Sudden Fear* shot and ready for release."[1]

Turning all the thoughts then swirling around in Crawford's head into a successful film, however, would not be nearly so easy. She soon learned that Joseph Kaufman, an independent film producer with nine, mostly undistinguished, films to his credit, had already secured the film rights to the book. She contacted him and began discussions about a film version of the story they could collaborate on. Eventually, they arrived at an arrangement which, while involving financial risks for her, gave her the kind of filmmaking power she had longed for during much of her career. In effect, they agreed to co-produce. He would raise the money needed for the production. She would help keep the budget to a reasonable sum by waiving her customary salary and instead taking forty percent of the film's profits (that is, if the film made money). He would focus on marketing and promotional efforts. As well as starring in the film, she would supervise virtually all facets of production, assuming a degree of control that far exceeded any she had ever had. In addition, she formally severed her ties with Warner Brothers.

Again, Crawford was without a studio. This time, however, she was perhaps better prepared and positioned than at any time in her career to be the master of her destiny. In nearly every meaningful production respect, *Sudden Fear* would be her movie. Its success or failure (as well as her financial well-being) would depend on the people she chose to work with her and her abilities to communicate her vision for the adaptation, to convince everyone involved of the soundness of her thinking, and then to get the results she wanted. After more than a quarter-century in the film business, the actress—now bound to *Sudden Fear* as closely as such legendary auteur-producers as David O. Selznick and Val Lewton were committed to their projects—had effectively joined their ranks.

From that night in late-summer 1951, Crawford saw the adaptation in a certain way. She believed that some key parts of the story could play well with little or no dialogue and a strong emphasis on visual communication, much in the way silent films had done. She also liked the ideas of complementing the story with an energetic, contemporary-sounding musical score and placing the story in picturesque San Francisco, which at the time was fast becoming a popular setting for location shooting.

To direct, she hired David Miller (1909–1992), an under-appreciated journeyman filmmaker she had known since he had been a film editor at MGM in the 1930s. She trusted his judgment, valued his thinking, and felt that they could work well together. Along with his creative talents and level-headed personal style, she was impressed with his ability to cut as he shot, leveraging his experience as an editor to minimize the number of camera set-ups and amount of film needed to get a shot right. This would save both time and money, a big plus in a limited-budget independent production. In turn, Miller quickly grew to appreciate how well Crawford understood not only acting but other aspects of filmmaking as well, once noting, "She knew more about lighting and camera angles than anybody I ever met."[2] A director of more than twenty feature films from the 1940s to the 1970s, Miller would work again with Crawford in the drama *The Story of Esther Costello* (1957). In addition to his collaborations with her, he is perhaps best known today for his superb modern-day western *Lonely Are the Brave* (1962) with Kirk Douglas and Gena Rowlands and the noir-tinged thriller *Midnight Lace* (1960) with Doris Day and Rex Harrison.

The first step in translating *Sudden Fear* from the page to the screen, of course, was to adapt the novel into a camera-ready script. Two writers eventually received script credit, Lenore Coffee and Robert Smith. Of these two, the one who likely exerted the greater influence over script development was Coffee (1896–1984), who had worked in Hollywood since 1919, writing or co-writing nearly eighty scripts for MGM, Warner Brothers, and other studios. Crawford had collaborated with her at MGM on the 1931 film *Possessed* and had great confidence in her abilities both as a visual storyteller (she had ample experience in silent films) and as someone who could effectively develop strong, sympathetic women's characters. In addition to Coffee and Smith, both Crawford and Miller were actively involved in the script development process, attending meetings, reviewing script changes, and offering suggestions and other ideas of their own. Several accounts credit both with making significant contributions to the finished script.

The changes the writing team made to the original plotline by Edna Sherry (1885–1967), an English professor who had turned to writing novels later in her life, were fairly modest, certainly compared with the changes that were made to the original versions of *Mildred Pierce* and *Humoresque*. One was to make the story's main character, Myra Hudson, less intimidating and more likeable. Another was to make several changes to the storyline involving the novel's second most important female character, the scheming Irma Neves, giving her more of a personal history with the story's main male character, Myra's duplicitous husband Lester Blaine, and a different first name, Irene. Perhaps the greatest scriptwriting challenges, however, were to make the novel considerably more cinematic in order to fit Crawford's vision of the film, developing major sections that communicated almost exclusively in visual terms, much like silent movies had done.

To handle the cinematography, Crawford enlisted another industry veteran, Charles Lang (1902–1998), who had been working in Hollywood since the 1920s and, at this point, had received seven Academy Award nominations for cinematography to his credit. (He would eventually receive eighteen nominations in that category, tying for the record with Twentieth Century–Fox's Leon Shamroy.) A master at black-and-white camera work, Lang was known for a range of talents from a knack for making a film's female stars look their best to an ability to integrate a film's visuals seamlessly with other story elements in order to serve the interests of the entire story, not just the cinematographer's art.[3] At the time, he was receiving high praise for his efforts in other noir films such as Billy Wilder's *Ace in the Hole* (1951). Greatly impressed with his talents, Crawford would later recruit him for three more noir-tinged films, *Female on the Beach* (1955), *Queen Bee* (1955), and *Autumn Leaves* (1956) as well as several 1950s and 1960s television appearances.

In contrast to her choices of seasoned film industry veterans Miller, Coffee, and Lang, Crawford chose the young composer Elmer Bernstein (1922–2004) to develop the contemporary, jazz-infused score she envisioned to complement the story. *Sudden Fear* was only Bernstein's third film in a fifty-year career that would include more than 150 other (and often quite memorable) big-screen credits—such as *The Man with the Golden Arm* (1955), *The Magnificent Seven* (1959), and *To Kill a Mockingbird* (1962). Along the way, he picked up fourteen Academy Award

Gloria Grahame's Irene Neves (left, front) and Jack Palance's Lester Blaine (right, rear) play the two main antagonists to Crawford's Myra Hudson in David Miller's brilliant woman-in-distress noir thriller *Sudden Fear* (1952). Palance's performance in this film led to a Best Supporting Actor Academy Award nomination and was instrumental in launching a highly productive film career that would continue until 2004 (RKO Radio Pictures/Photofest).

nominations and one win (1967's *Thoroughly Modern Millie*) for his compositions.

Other critical choices for Crawford included the various cast members, especially the roles of the two villains in the story, Lester and Irene. The wonderful Gloria Grahame (1923–1981), who was at the height of her career and in great demand to play noir bad girls, was a natural to play Irene, and Crawford quickly arranged for her to join the cast. Selecting an actor to play Lester, however, was far more difficult. According to several accounts, both Clark Gable and Marlon Brando were approached and turned the role down. Gable, a long-time friend and on-again, off-again lover of Crawford's, may have been a sentimental choice, but he was both too old and not at all a good fit for the character. A 1952 version of Brando, though, might have been quite interesting in the role. It's intriguing to imagine how he would have interpreted the character and played various scenes.

Discussing the selection one night at Crawford's house, Miller suggested Jack Palance (1919–2006), who had recently turned in a widely praised performance in Elia Kazan's noir *Panic in the Streets* (1950). At this, Crawford became indignant. She was used to acting opposite handsome leading men and considered Palance anything but. Miller persisted, however, stressing the actor's raw masculinity, dangerous look, and captivating tone of voice, all qualities that made him right for the part. Eventually, Crawford agreed, and Palance was brought on board.[4]

In January 1952, Crawford and company began location shooting in San Francisco. She was, according to Miller, "a bit tense at first,"[5] a state of mind he attributed to her leaving Warner Brothers for a risky venture in which, for her especially, much was at stake. Overall, the cast and crew were quite professional during filming. Crawford, as Miller observed, "demanded total perfection from everyone."[6] There was, however, considerable animosity between the star and her two main co-stars. Apparently, Crawford, who, after casting Palance, had grown to appreciate his raw masculinity more fully, wanted to have a fling with him during the shoot. Instead, he rejected her and took up with Grahame, a move that, as one might expect, led to much on-set tension—and a definite case of life imitating art. Shrewdly, Miller took advantage of the real-life hostility between Crawford and Palance to heighten the growing on-screen tension between Myra and Lester, especially during the second half of the story.[7]

◈ ◈ ◈

The film version of *Sudden Fear* opens inside a Broadway theater in New York City. Myra Hudson, a playwright with a long list of hits to her credit (who also happens to be a wealthy heiress), is watching a rehearsal for her new play, *Halfway to Heaven*. On stage, the play's male lead, actor Lester Blaine is delivering a key speech from the play to his character's love interest. Although both the play's producer and director are quite excited about Lester's performance, Myra strongly believes that he just doesn't have the romantic appeal the part requires and insists that he be replaced. After the director fires Lester, the actor angrily confronts Myra and then stomps out of the theater.

Soon, *Halfway to Heaven* premieres with another actor in the lead role and is, as one newspaper reports, a "smash hit." Myra, who is eager to return to her home in San Francisco, boards a train for the transcontinental trip. Soon, she notices, of all people, Lester, who is also riding on the train. When she sees him a second time, she asks to talk to him. He is cool and clearly still bitter about his firing. Attempting to make amends, she invites him into her room for a drink. Soon, they become fast friends, playing poker, discussing their lives, quizzing each other with quotes from Shakespeare, and more.

They arrive in San Francisco, and, far from being tired because of the travel, Myra is jubilant and suggests dinner and dancing at the swank Fairmont Hotel. She and Lester literally dance the night away, arriving at Myra's home at 5:00 the next morning. She shows him her home office, the room where she writes her plays, and takes a special pleasure in showing him her "dictating machine," an early recording device. The machine is connected to several strategically placed microphones that, when switched on, can record her effectively even as she walks about the room. She then asks him to speak into the device. He responds by delivering the same speech he had delivered when rehearsing Myra's play. This time, she is deeply moved by his rendering. She plays the speech back on her machine as they look directly, and longingly, at each other. At the end of the speech, they kiss passionately.

Soon, Myra and Lester are married, and, at a reception Myra gives at her (and now Lester's) home, a new person arrives on the scene. She is Irene Neves, the date of Junior Kearney (Mike Connors, billed here as Touch Conners), one of Myra's attorneys. She and Lester clearly know each other but both pretend that they are meeting for the first time. Irene says that she has come to settle in San Francisco and coyly mentions the apartment building where she is staying.

Later that evening, Irene returns to her apartment and encounters Lester, who seems furious that she is in town. We quickly learn that they are former lovers who have a long history of conning others for money and that, far from being the sweet, doting man Myra thinks she has married, Lester is a vile, scheming brute. After tossing Irene around a bit, Lester prepares to leave. Irene, however, lures him back, and they have sex.

Soon, Lester and Irene agree to work together to get as much money as they can from Myra. Lester will focus on getting information from Myra. Irene will work on Myra's lawyer, Junior Kearney.

Irene is the first to follow up, telling Lester she has learned that Myra will be giving away a major part of her fortune to a foundation very soon. The two understand that, if they want to get as much as they can from Myra, they must act quickly.

In her home office, Myra meets to go over both the transfer of money to the foundation and her new will with Junior's older brother and law partner Steve Kearney (Bruce Bennett). Steve has proposed terms in her will that she is unhappy with, and she wants to make some changes. He is agreeable but needs her rewritten version right away. Immediately, she begins to dictate the terms she would prefer on her dictation machine. In the meantime, guests have begun to arrive, and Myra asks Steve to look after them while she continues to work on the rewrite.

One of those guests is Irene, who whispers to Lester that they need to talk privately. Lester suggests Myra's office later in the evening. As Myra and her other guests play bridge, both slip into the office.

The next morning, Myra enters her office. Her personal assistant mentions that the dictating machine had been left on the night before and that she had switched it off. Myra is certain that she had done so herself but then considers that maybe she had forgotten to.

Now alone, Myra turns the machine back on to review what she had dictated the evening before. As she listens, she hears a sudden jarring sound on the machine. Then the recording continues, this time with Lester and Irene's voices on it. As she listens, she realizes for the first time that Lester cares nothing for her and that he and Irene are lovers plotting to get her money. They talk about Myra's new will and that it will be signed the following Monday, in three days. They also see the copy of Steve Kearney's draft on Myra's desk. Lester is furious that he is being given so little, but Irene has an idea:

> IRENE: Suppose she isn't able to sign it on Monday. Suppose something happened to her between now and Monday. Who'd get her money?
> LESTER: Her husband, Lester Blaine. I'd get it all. Why not?
> IRENE: Sure. Why not?
> LESTER: Rich. You and me rich!
> IRENE: Lester, I have a gun.
> LESTER: That's no good. It'll have to look like an accident.... We've got three days. I've got to be smart. As her husband, I'd be suspected before she was cold.

IRENE: Three days. We'll work it out. Kiss me. Kiss me. Hard.
LESTER: I'm crazy about you. I could break your bones.

Horrified by what she has heard, Myra retreats to the adjoining bathroom where she vomits. She realizes that she will need the disc with the recording of Lester and Irene's conversation on it to use as proof of their plot. Her hands shaking from fear, she takes the disc from the recording machine. Frantically, she looks about the room for a suitable place to hide it. She decides to put it among some books but drops it instead. It shatters into pieces. Staring at it in fear and despair, she knows that she now has no proof to provide the police of the threat to her life.

Hours later, after absorbing this horrendous shock, Myra, in her disciplined playwright's way, begins to formulate an intricate plan to kill Lester and frame Irene for the deed. The first step is to make a duplicate of Lester's key to Irene's apartment and get Irene's gun, which will be the murder weapon. Myra then forges notes between Lester and Irene telling Lester to come to her apartment at midnight and Irene to be at Lester's garage nearby at that time. In her head, Myra imagines the deadly sequence:

- Lester comes to the apartment at midnight.
- Irene won't be there, but she will.
- She will shoot him with Irene's gun, hide the gun where she'd found it in the apartment, and leave.
- Assuming that Lester has stood her up at the garage, Irene will come back to the apartment.
- Irene, the body, and her gun will all be discovered.
- Ultimately, Irene will be found guilty and given the death sentence for Lester's murder.

In her mind, Crawford's Myra imagines murdering Lester as part of a plan that will also frame Irene for the crime and get them both out of her life for good in *Sudden Fear* (RKO Radio Pictures/Photofest).

At the appointed time, Myra begins to put the plan in motion. Just before midnight, she enters Irene's apartment and hides in the closet. Then, she has a startling revelation. Leaving the closet for a moment, she catches sight of herself holding the gun in a mirror. She is utterly appalled by what she sees. No matter how much she hates Lester and Irene, she cannot bring herself to commit murder. "No, no," she mutters, and she throws the gun down and begins to run out of the apartment. At that moment, however, she sees that Lester is about to enter. Quickly, she returns to the closet and immediately realizes that the gun is still on the floor, in plain sight. If he sees it, he, not her, will be the one with access to the deadly weapon. As Lester waits for Irene, Myra, dabbing the sweat from her brow with a handkerchief, waits for a chance to escape.

Soon, Lester does discover the gun. Frantic for Irene's safety, he looks for her in the apartment's other rooms. When he returns to the living room, he sees that the closet door and the apartment's front door are now both open. He goes to the closet and picks up a handkerchief that tips him off that Myra has been hiding there. He goes after her, chasing her relentlessly through the dark neighboring streets by foot, then in a car, then on foot again, then back in the car with a searchlight beside him.

Meanwhile, Irene, who, with a white dress and scarf and dark coat, is dressed very similarly to Myra, is tired of waiting for Lester, begins to walk back to her apartment. Lester, in the car, sees her from the back and, thinking it's Myra, plows into her, loses control of the car, and kills them both.

Myra, exhausted by the horror she has just experienced, manages to gather herself and walk up the street, away from the accident. Ahead of her, we see what appears to be the new day's first glimmer of light.

❖ ❖ ❖

Premiering in New York on August 7, 1952, *Sudden Fear* was an immediate commercial and critical hit. With audiences flocking to the theater, Crawford's gamble of foregoing a salary for a percentage of the profits paid off handsomely. Eventually, her cut of the spoils would come to approximately $1 million.[8] Critics were enthusiastic as well. In the *New York Times*, A.H. Weiler singled out Crawford for giving "a truly professional performance." Later in the review, Weiler also noted, "The entire production has been mounted in excellent taste and, it must be pointed out, that San Francisco, in which most of the action takes place, is an excitingly photogenic area. David Miller, the director, has taken full advantage of the city's steep streets and panoramic views. And, in his climactic scenes in a darkened apartment and a chase through its precipitous dark alleys and backyards, he has managed to project an authentically doom-filled atmosphere."[9] In the rival *New York Herald Tribune*, reviewer Otis Guernsey was quite complimentary as well, writing "The scenario ... is designed to allow Miss Crawford a wide range of quivering reactions to vicious events, as she passes through the stage of starry-eyed love, terrible disillusionment, fear, hatred, and finally hysteria. With her wide eyes and forceful bearing, she is the woman for the job."[10] Soon afterwards, French film critic and future director François Truffaut also wrote about *Sudden Fear*, enthusiastically proclaiming that, outside of two dream sequences, "there is not a shot in this film that isn't necessary to its dramatic progression. Not a shot, either, that isn't fascinating and doesn't make us think it's a masterpiece of cinema."[11]

The success of *Sudden Fear* with both audiences and critics soon turned into serious Oscar buzz. And, in early 1953, when the 1952 Academy Award nominations were announced, the film received four nods: Crawford for Best Actress, Palance for Best Supporting Actor, Lang for Best Cinematography (for a black-and-white film), and Sheila O'Brien for Best Costume Design (for a black-and-white film). In a year of many fine films that also included such other Oscar contenders as John Ford's *The Quiet Man*, Cecil B. DeMille's *The Greatest Show on Earth*, and Vincente Minelli's *The Bad and the Beautiful*, the competition was fierce, and, on awards night, *Sudden Fear* was passed over in all categories. Still, as a relatively low-budget independent production without a big-studio Oscar promotional campaign behind it, four Academy Award nominations was a major triumph. Crawford was again back on top, and Palance's film career soon took off like a rocket. The very next year, in fact, he received his second straight Academy nomination for Best Supporting Actor, this time for playing the villainous hired gun Jack Wilson in director George Stevens's classic western *Shane*.

❖　❖　❖

As the decades have passed, *Sudden Fear* has lost little, if any, of its luster. And today it is considered one of the outstanding examples of woman-in-distress noirs of the 1940s and 1950s.

The characters in *Sudden Fear* don't have the complexity of many of those in Crawford's best mid- and late 1940s films, but rich, nuanced personalities are not really the point here. This, after all, is a suspense film, a plot-driven thriller: we fear for the safety of our endangered heroine, and we wonder how she will get out of the mess she is in.

Although the film is not mainly character driven, it does contain some subtle glimpses into characters. One fascinating example is the speech from Myra's play that Lester delivers, first, on stage in New York and then later in Myra's home office:

> When I wake in the morning, when I go to sleep at night, I think of you. You are like the air which surrounds me, the sky which spreads above me, the earth beneath my feet. When I hear music, when I see beauty, when I breath in the sunlight, I think of you. You are the sister I never had, the mother I have almost forgotten, the wife I have always dreamed of. There isn't a relationship you can name which exists between a man and a woman of which I wouldn't say: let it be you. Oh, let it be you!

We hear about how accomplished and successful a playwright Myra is, yet what she writes sounds like it's straight out of a drugstore romance novel. She also seems to be a very strong, assertive, sophisticated woman, yet the suggestion in this speech is that she secretly longs for a man to see her in an idealized, almost worshipful way. Lester seems to sense instinctively that this longing is her Achilles heel, and— at the optimal moment, of course—he exploits what seems to be her starry-eyed naivete, seducing her with her own words.

Rich, complex characterizations aside, *Sudden Fear* is a very inventive, finely tuned, expertly executed piece of filmmaking, with all the elements seeming to work together with the precision of the clock featured in both the film's opening credits and in later scenes as Myra plans her revenge. In this film, everyone in a critical production role came through.

The script by Coffee and Smith (with additions by Crawford and Miller) is tightly written and constantly pushes the action forward. Among its more impressive qualities are the ways it maintains or enhances viewer engagement. For example, several of the scenes played with few or no words particularly stand out. Because virtually all the communicating is conveyed visually, we can't take our eyes off the screen for fear of missing something important. Another example is the script's use of deliberate mis-directions, such as Lester's mention of the absence of a hand railing on the steep stairway leading down from Myra's summer house and words of concern for her safety. We immediately wonder if this is a significant piece of exposition. It isn't, of course; it's a Hitchcock-style tease to keep us off-balance, guessing about what might or might not happen later, and, as a result, highly absorbed in the proceedings.

Together, Miller and Lang do a fine job of telling the story visually. The idea for the scene in which Myra imagines her deadly plot unfold in her head, for example, is usually credited to Miller. In it we see an extreme close-up of her eyes superimposed over a succession of very short scenes that dramatize the sequence of events she envisions. It's a classic moment of noir: expressionistic in nature, jarring to viewers, and quite effective. Lang's work is also impressive at enhancing the film's noir look and mood. Of special note, for example, are the scenes in which Myra waits for Lester in Irene's apartment and the street scenes (as Lester pursues Myra) that immediately follow. These scenes are enveloped in darkness, heightening Myra's terror and the viewers' anxiety, yet all the information that needs to be conveyed is, and often with great effectiveness. In fact, the very narrow slivers of light in some shots are handled with such pinpoint precision that they compel our undivided attention. An excellent example is the unnerving scene in Irene's apartment, in which Lester winds up a small mechanical toy dog and watches it as it waddles across the floor and, unknown to him (but not to us), toward the closet Myra is hiding in.

Another major contribution to *Sudden Fear* is Elmer Bernstein's musical score. It is excellent at heightening the mood of scenes throughout the film, humming with big-city vitality when introducing New York in the first scenes, swelling with romantic fervor as a love-struck Myra shows Lester San Francisco and other nearby sights, and pounding with fearful urgency as Lester pursues Myra through the streets in the film's final scenes. With its jazz-inspired sections and frequent use of horns, it is, as Crawford wanted, much more contemporary in tone (in this case, early 1950s) as well as fresher, more original than many of the hackneyed studio-manufactured scores of the period.

One of the often-cited strengths of *Sudden Fear* is the acting, particularly the performances of Crawford and Palance.

Crawford usually receives her highest praise for two stunning scenes in which she hardly utters a word. The first is the scene in which she listens to the playback of the conversation between Lester and Irene as they plot her murder. In it, she only listens and reacts, and we see her run the gamut of emotions from surprise to shock, hurt, sorrow, fear, and revulsion at all she is hearing. This would be an easy scene to overplay, but Crawford doesn't. As she reacts to the various revelations she hears, each of Myra's responses is painfully real. Commenting on this scene, film writer Sheila O'Malley has even gone so far as to say that Crawford's work here "should be studied by young actors as an example of the pinnacle of what film acting can be."[12] The other, of course, is the scene in Irene's apartment. The moments that Crawford herself referred to with great pride are those when she is in Irene's closet with only a sliver of light on her, and it is remarkable how much she conveys with so little screen space to work with. Before this, too, there is another moment, just prior to Lester's arrival, that is just as stunning. Myra steps out of the closet and inadvertently spots herself in a wall mirror. She is shocked to see herself holding a gun, presumably ready to use it to shoot Lester. This time the horror she feels is at what she is plotting to do: she is horrified to see what *she* has become. This moment of recognition triggers a complete change in her thinking. As much as she loathes Lester and Irene, she can't go through with her murderous plan. Again, Crawford doesn't overplay. With great specificity, she reveals her turnabout almost entirely with facial expressions and other gestures.

Although these scenes are standouts for Crawford, they still represent only a fraction of her overall performance. In the course of the film, her character goes through a significant transformational arc—in this case moving from confident playwright to enraptured lover and bride, to betrayed and endangered wife, to calculating avenger, to resourceful prey, and finally to deeply saddened but resolute survivor. As she had done in films ranging from *A Woman's Face* to *Flamingo Road*, she is in full command of her character at each phase in the character's journey. This is a polished, painstakingly prepared, and exquisitely executed portrayal. "It is," as O'Malley staunchly asserts, "world-class acting, period."[13]

As the villainous Lester, Palance turns in an admirable performance as well. In the film's early going, we have considerable empathy for this character. We see how frustrated and hurt this ambitious young actor is at being fired from a role because he isn't "romantic" looking enough. Then we see him seemingly warm to Myra, becoming fast friends with her as they ride the train to California. But is this *all* we are seeing? One fascinating moment that's easy to miss on a first-time viewing is when Myra first calls his name to ask him into her stateroom. For just an instant—literally a blink of an eye—we see a look on his face. He is unsurprised and perhaps somewhat pleased. For him, this isn't just a coincidental meeting. It is as if he had planned for this moment and now Myra has taken the bait. It's quite subtle, and Palance has many such revealing moments throughout the film that become more apparent with repeat viewings. Also, when Irene comes to town, it's interesting to see how he responds to her. In contrast to the ultra-polite, solicitous way he treats Myra, he reveals who he actually is: a feral, sexually charged, utterly amoral brute. From these scenes on, Lester needs to appear quite menacing, and Palance—with his imposing physical frame, almost-hypnotic voice, and capacity to convey simmering rage—is absolutely up to the task. His Lester is exactly what the role calls for: one scary fellow.

It's curious that, relative to her two main co-stars, Grahame hasn't received nearly as much attention or praise for her portrayal of Irene.

One reason may simply be her relative lack of screen time. Of the film's three main roles, hers, of course, is by far the smallest. Another reason may be that, by 1952, audiences had become so accustomed to seeing her in noir bad-girl roles that her Irene might not have seemed that special. Whatever the case, Grahame nevertheless does a fine job with the character as Irene uses her sex appeal to manipulate both Lester and Junior Kearney, coldly conspires with Lester to plot Myra's murder, and yet still manages to maintain a small degree of vulnerability. "[Grahame] made this movie the same year as her Oscar for *The Bad and the Beautiful*," film writer Farran Smith Nehme has noted, "but *Sudden Fear* gives [her] the more substantial part—scheming, venal, but inspiring some pity by the end."[14]

Although it is a very polished and enjoyable film to watch, *Sudden Fear* does have some shortcomings. One is an occasional tendency to overemphasize certain points. A prime example is a series of possible murder scenarios Myra envisions soon after she learns that Lester and Irene are planning to kill her. (This may be one of the unnecessary dream sequences that François Truffaut mentions in his review of the film.) When we see these scenarios, Myra's fears are already quite well established, and the scenes simply repeat the obvious. Also appearing now and then are small continuity issues. A good example comes at the very end of the film, as Myra walks up the street and away from the wreckage of the car and bodies of Lester and Irene. Most likely, it is about 1:00 in the morning. Yet, it appears as if the sun is rising and, just as audiences did at the very end of *Mildred Pierce*, viewers of *Sudden Fear* see the first glimmers of the new day. In the earlier film, this effect, the new day suggesting a new beginning for the heroine, works nicely because Mildred really has spent the entire night inside the police station. Here, the visual effect also works, but the timing is way off: the sun is rising about five hours earlier than it ought to be.

Overall, though, *Sudden Fear's* shortcomings are minuscule compared to its strengths. It is little wonder that this brilliant film remains as fresh and riveting today as it was when audiences first saw it in 1952. Many people, of course, are responsible for its enduring success but none more so than its star, prime mover, and de facto producer. Crawford's fine performance in *Mildred Pierce* earned her an Oscar, but, in many ways, her multi-faceted contribution to *Sudden Fear* may be her most impressive career achievement. This risky, independent effort was all on her shoulders, and she bore the burden in grand style.

Yes, the "Miss Crawford's Wardrobe" slide in the opening credits of *Sudden Fear* is an indulgence. But, if anyone connected with this film earned the right to be a little self-indulgent, it was Crawford.

◆ ◆ ◆

With her career revitalized after the success of *Sudden Fear*, Crawford opted for a major change of pace from the dark, noirish films she had come to specialize in, and the level of production control she had routinely insisted upon, over much of the previous decade. She accepted an offer to act in a musical—her first since MGM's *Dancing Lady* twenty years earlier—that would be produced at, of all places, MGM. Released in October 1953, the film, *Torch Song*, is widely considered to be one of the usually shrewd actress's major career miscalculations. As well as losing money and receiving largely negative reviews, it has since become one of the prime examples of "Crawford camp," the kind of overwrought, poorly executed effort that some modern audiences love to watch and laugh at simply because it is so bad.

After *Torch Song*, Crawford, undeterred, briefly helped develop a noir thriller called *Lisbon* for Paramount, which would star her and be directed by the brilliant, eccentric Nicholas Ray. When this project was delayed indefinitely because of cost concerns, she then pivoted in an entirely different direction: she would produce and star in a western. She had a property in mind, an unpublished novel called *Johnny Guitar* written by an old friend of hers, Roy Chanslor, and she took both the property and her A-list name to Republic Pictures, a low-prestige studio that had long specialized in westerns, cliffhanger serials, and budget mystery and action films. Ray would direct.

The result is the screen version of *Johnny Guitar*. A very stylized film, and unabashedly operatic in nature, it appears to be a western, but, as film director Martin Scorsese has pointed out, one that "deviates from all the conventions of traditional westerns."[15] Crawford intensely hated both the experience of making the film and the finished product, once saying "I should have had my head examined for doing it" and then adding that there was "no excuse for a picture being this bad."[16] Yet, largely due to the film's very modern, subversive sensibility and its highly original presentation treatment, it has since become a cult classic that is often written about in film journals and blogs, shown at film revival festivals, and studied in university film classes.

Perhaps because of its uniqueness and subversive sensibility, it is also—and often—referred to as a "noir western"[17] and grouped with scores of post–World War II westerns that incorporate elements of classic noir into the genre's traditional "wild west" settings, storylines, and themes. Seeing *Johnny Guitar* in this way, however, might be a bit more than a bit of a stretch. In terms of style, for example, an undisputed noir western such as Raoul Walsh's *Pursued* (1947)—with its brooding black-and-white cinematography, flashbacks, voice-over narration, off-kilter camera angles, traumatized protagonist, and other signature noir elements—fits the classic noir mold much better. The same can also be said of other dark westerns of the era such as Andre De Toth's *Ramrod* (1947) with its manipulative femme fatale (played by noir bad girl Veronica Lake) or Walsh's *Colorado Territory* (1949) and Anthony Mann's *Devil's Doorway* (1950) with their grimly fatalistic endings. In fact, *Johnny Guitar* lacks all of these significant noir elements.

While a vague case can be made for calling *Johnny Guitar* a noir—its downbeat tone, sharp-edged dialogue, pessimistic takes on human behavior, etc.—this has never been a convincing case. When asked about this subject, noir historian Eddie Muller simply stated, "I'm not going to include *Johnny Guitar* in the [noir] canon."[18] And this noir chronicler heartily concurs. We may admire *Johnny Guitar* as much as Martin Scorsese does, or we may dislike it was much as Crawford did, but, despite how we may feel about it, and despite the noir label that many people attach to it, it is not a noir. If it were, it would, of course, be the subject of the next chapter of this book. But, since it isn't, it won't be.

◆ ◆ ◆

Instead, we'll move to Crawford's next two noir-tinged films, both released in 1955 and both contributors, along with *Torch Song*, to one of the unfortunate outcomes of Crawford's otherwise very rich noir period: her emergence as a camp figure.

10

"Aren't I wicked?"

Female on the Beach
and *Queen Bee* (Both 1955)

Today, many people refer to Crawford's next two films, *Female on the Beach* and *Queen Bee*, as noirs or, if they tend to be a bit more cautious, noirish melodramas. In many respects, the noir designation seems appropriate. *Female on the Beach* has many familiar noir elements, including a murder, a wise-cracking police detective, flashbacks that provide details of the murder, and a sexy homme fatale who may also be the killer. *Queen Bee* has its share, too: emotional manipulation, dysfunctional relationships, a vile femme fatale, a suicide, and, for a finale, a car crash murder/second suicide that echoes the shocking ending of Otto Preminger's noir *Angel Face* (1952). Both also feature the beautiful noir-style camerawork of Crawford's favorite 1950s cinematographer, the talented Charles Lang.

Many people also consider these efforts to be classic examples of "Crawford camp," films they'll see to hoot and howl at the mean-girl characters Crawford plays as well as the bad dialogue, contrived plots, and other dated or just-not-very-good-to-begin-with elements. Starting in the early 1950s, these kinds of films regularly appeared for several years and ushered in both Crawford's long career decline and her rise as a camp icon. Along with *Mommie Dearest*—the still-controversial 1978 tell-all memoir by Crawford's adopted daughter Christina and the follow-on 1981 bio-pic starring Faye Dunaway—they've also been instrumental in shaping popular contemporary attitudes about Crawford and what film writer Angelica Jade Bastien has called the actress's "warped legacy."[1] In fact, just by watching Dunaway in *Mommie Dearest* and then the real Crawford in *Female on the Beach* and especially in *Queen Bee* (performances that clearly influenced Dunaway's cartoonish portrayal), it's easy to see how this legacy has become so thoroughly distorted.

The intriguing story here, however, isn't whether or not two these films are sufficiently noir or why they've become irresistible camp for certain contemporary audiences. There is clearly enough noir content to call them noir or noirish, and—outside of Jeff Chandler's creditable acting in *Female on the Beach*, designer Jean Louis' elegant costumes in *Queen Bee*, and Lang's fine noir cinematography in both films—there isn't much in them that isn't ripe material for camp, anyway. These are both bad films, and going into greater detail about what makes them bad only belabors the obvious.

Instead, the intriguing story here is why these two films ever came to be. Why would Crawford, now a freelancer with greater artistic control and more options than ever before in her career, agree to star in either of them and then settle for such bad scripts? Why did she now select, and even seem to prefer to play, such harsh, unsympathetic roles? Finally, why did she play these roles with such scene-chewing relish, delivering the kinds of over-the-top performances she roundly criticized, especially in her own work?

❖ ❖ ❖

Let's begin with the first of these films, *Female on the Beach*.

The screenplay is based on an unproduced play called *The Besieged Heart* by Robert Hill. Film producer Albert Zugsmith, then with Universal Pictures, purchased the rights to the play in 1954, and he and Hill immediately began to work on the adaptation. (Another writer, Richard Alan Simmons, also contributed to the script.)

Both Zugsmith and Hill, incidentally, have interesting resumes. Zugsmith (1910–1993), who had worked with Howard Hughes at RKO, moved to Universal in the 1950s, where he produced a string of genre masterpieces including Douglas Sirk's sumptuous melodrama *Written on the Wind* (1956), the science-fiction classic *The Incredible Shrinking Man* (1957), and Orson Welles' highly praised crime noir *Touch of Evil.* (1958). Hill, on the other hand, went on to an inauspicious screenwriting career that included such exploitation films as *She Gods of Shark Reef* (1958) and *Sex Kittens Go to College* (1960).

The true genesis of *Female on the Beach*, however, was probably an affair Crawford had had or was still having (accounts vary) with Milton Rackmil, a co-founder of Decca Records who went into the film industry and became Universal's president in 1952. Once at Universal, he shifted the studio's strategy from an emphasis on low-budget films with second- and third-tier actors to larger, more lavish productions with top stars. In the next few years, his films would feature such major Hollywood figures as Cary Grant, Rock Hudson, Doris Day, Kirk Douglas, and James Stewart.

Crawford, still riding high after her success with *Sudden Fear* and subsequent Academy Award nomination, fit into this strategy quite nicely. Rackmil offered her an attractive financial deal, approval of cast and other contributors to the film, and a juicy romantic role. She agreed and soon asked for hunky Universal contract player Jeff Chandler (another former amour) to play her leading man/love interest. The filming took place in the autumn of 1954, and, by all accounts, the production went smoothly.

◆　◆　◆

The story of *Female on the Beach*, which is a murder mystery as well as a melodrama with the noir elements, takes place in and around a Southern California beach house owned by the recently widowed Lynn Markham (Crawford). Lynn, who is simply referred to as a former

Crawford's Lynn Markham and her beach bum lover, Jeff Chandler's Drummand "Drummy" Hall (right), struggle through a troubled relationship made even more unsettling by her suspicions that Drummy may, in fact, be a murderer in Joseph Pevney's *Female on the Beach* (1955) (Universal Pictures/Photofest).

"specialty dancer" from Las Vegas, has been renting the house and now plans to stay in it for a while. Soon, she meets an array of characters, including a less-than-forthright real estate agent Amy Rawlinson (Jan Sterling); Drummond "Drummy" Hall (Chandler), an attractive beach bum/gigolo who wanders in and out of the house as if he lives there; and a diligent police investigator, Lieutenant Galley (Charles Drake). She also learns quite a bit more. First, the house's previous tenant, a middle-aged woman named Eloise Crandall, has recently died by falling from a faulty deck railing. Second, the cause of death, which hasn't yet been determined, could be an accident, suicide, or even murder. And third, Drummy has been in cahoots with next-door neighbors and card sharks Osbert and Queenie Sorenson (Cecil Kellaway and Natalie Schafer) to scam Eloise. Specifically, Drummy romanced Eloise in order to lure her into high-stakes card games with the Sorensons, who regularly cheated her, raking in significant winnings for themselves and then giving Drummy a cut.

Despite Drummy's dubious lifestyle and Lynn's growing suspicions that he may have murdered Eloise, she finds him irresistible and falls passionately in love with him. Soon, he extricates himself from the Sorensons, the two get married, and they plan to honeymoon on Drummy's boat. That night, Drummy runs into Amy near the boat dock. She now seems crazed, admitting that, because she loves Drummy and wants him for herself, she killed Eloise and has plotted to do away with Lynn as well.

Luckily, Lieutenant Galley happens to show up just in time to overhear Amy's confession and subdue her as she yells, "I did it for you, Drummy!"

Now, Lynn and Drummy can be together.

❖ ❖ ❖

"The only thing wrong with it was lack of credibility," Crawford later said about *Female on the Beach*.[2] She was correct, but she may have also been trying to minimize the damage. Without a core of credibility, any story is doomed from the outset, and such is the case with this film.

Much like *This Woman Is Dangerous*, the main culprits here are, as *New York Times* film critic Bosley Crowther noted in 1955, "the inanities of a hackneyed script."[3] Unlike that film, which does have honest, believable moments here and there, however, this film has next to none. The character of Lynn has a hard, brittle edge, and it's fun, for example, to hear Crawford deliver testy lines such as "I'd like to ask you to stay for a drink, but I'm afraid you might accept." Overall, though, the writing is pedestrian, characterizations shallow, and plotting contrived. Without the saving grace of Lang's artful noir cinematography and a few good acting moments by Chandler in scenes when Drummy shows his more vulnerable side, the film has little to offer.

◈ ◈ ◈

Two of the highlights in Ranald MacDougall's *Queen Bee* (1955)—designer Jean Louis' elegant costumes and Charles Lang's fine noir cinematography—are on full display here as Crawford's Eva stands center stage with her butler, played by Marvin Lindsay (right). Both Jean Louis and Lang received Academy Award nominations for their work on this film (Columbia Pictures/Photofest).

From *Female on the Beach,* Crawford quickly went into production on *Queen Bee.*

In this film, she worked as de facto producer, much as she had done on *Sudden Fear.* She was fascinated by a 1949 novel by Edna Lee called *The Queen Bee,* whose main character is, as the title suggests, a manipulative, domineering matriarch whose venomous stings eliminate any and all competitors, leaving only subservient male drones to attend her. Paying Lee $15,000 for the film rights in late 1954, Crawford sold the property to Columbia Pictures as part of three-picture deal that was negotiated pretty much on her terms. Trusted colleagues who'd made important contributions to past Crawford hits would also participate: Jerry Wald as producer, Ranald MacDougall as the writer and director, and Charles Lang as the cinematographer. In addition, she would have input into casting decisions and be able to choose her hair, make-up, and costume designers. Filming was completed in the spring of 1955, and the film was released that November.

◆ ◆ ◆

The story in many ways plays like a combination of a bad Tennessee Williams melodrama and a monster movie, with Crawford as the monster.

The Phillips family lives in a grand Georgia mansion. The titular head of the family is Avery (Barry Sullivan), a mill owner who spends much of his time cloistered in his room drinking. As everyone including Avery knows, however, the person who really rules the roost is his wife Eva (Crawford), who he hates and everyone else fears. "Aren't I wicked?" Eva coquettishly tells the family firm's lawyer Jud Prentiss (John Ireland) at one point after lying to get out of a dinner engagement. Jud reacts with great discomfort, taking this not merely as a flippant or cute remark but as the literal, terrifying truth.

As the film begins, a cousin, Jennifer Stewart (Lucy Marlow), moves in with the family and watches in disbelief as Eva maneuvers to prevent the marriage of Jud to Avery's sister Carol (Betsy Palmer).

That night, Eva and Jud secretly meet. We learn that they have had an affair and that he wants to emphasize that it's over and that he is definitely marrying Carol. Eva refuses to accept this and begins kissing him. He pulls away. From another camera angle, we now learn that Jennifer has seen this and is duly shocked. Soon, Eva makes certain that Carol learns about her affair with Jud. Carol then confronts Jud, he acknowledges it, and a distraught Carol hangs herself in the barn.

Meanwhile, Jennifer and Avery become close and at one point share a brief, spontaneous kiss. Eva senses their developing relationship and increases her malevolent actions, telling Avery not to spend time with Jennifer any more. When he refuses, she threatens to drag his name through the mud in divorce court.

Jud, guilt-ridden and haunted by Carol's death, leaves the house for a few weeks but then returns one day for work. He learns that Eva had told Carol about the earlier affair, precipitating the events that led to Carol's suicide.

Then, in what appears to be a new strategy, Avery acts as though he is again in love with Eva. This, it seems, has an effect on her, and she says that she is done being controlling and manipulative because she and Avery have rekindled their love. Jud, however, sees through Avery's charade and confronts him, declaring that his real reason for being nice to Eva is to get closer to her and then to kill her and, in the process, himself.

That night, Jud preempts Avery's plan when, without Avery's knowledge, he steps in for him to drive Eva to a social event. In the car, she sees that Jud is planning to kill them both and frantically tries to stop him. He loses control of the wheel, the car careens over a cliff, and they both die in a fiery wreck.

Now, Avery and Jennifer are free to be together.

◆ ◆ ◆

Again, we have to wonder what's going on here.

"I ended up hating myself [when playing Eva]," Crawford once recalled, "honestly feeling that in my death scene I was getting precisely what I deserved."[4]

Crawford was by no means the only one who felt this way. In his review of the film for the *New York Times*, Bosley Crowther went apoplectic not only about Eva but also about Crawford's portrayal and the entire film:

> When she is killed at the end, as she should be, it is a genuine pleasure and relief. The one blatant trouble with this picture, for which Ranald MacDougall is to blame, since he was the writer and director, is that the killing is too long postponed. Five minutes after Miss Crawford appears on the luxurious scene, acting the queen bee like a buzz saw and oozing her unctuous poison from every cell, it is evident—no, it is mandatory—that she should be taken out and shot or run off a cliff in an automobile, which is how it is finally done.[5]

While the cinematography by Lang and the costumes by Jean Louis (both of whom received Academy Award nominations for their work on this film) are excellent, the rest of the film is—by all conventional criteria—beyond dreadful. As Crowther noted, the main person to blame here is writer-director MacDougall and his terrible script. The actors gamely tried to work with what they had (which is nothing), but none of them, even the consistently reliable Barry Sullivan, came out of this well. It's little wonder that *Queen Bee*, perhaps even more than *Female on the Beach*, has become a camp classic—one of those "it's-so-bad-it's-irresistible" movie experiences that, much like the proverbial train-wreck, is painful to look at but impossible to turn away from.

❖ ❖ ❖

Although both *Female on the Beach* and *Queen Bee* are little more than curiosities for fans of Crawford and/or camp these days, it's fascinating to speculate about Crawford's participation in both efforts. Why commit to them, especially when the scripts were so bad, and not insist on major rewrites? Why play such unsympathetic characters? Then why overplay the parts in such broad, exaggerated ways?

Crawford seems to have had somewhat different reasons for committing to the two projects. In the case of *Female on the Beach*, her friend Milton Rackmil, according to several accounts, presented the film package to her as a gift.[6] This flattering gesture (with its generous financial terms) certainly accounts for why Crawford signed on, but, once on board, why didn't she insist, as she so often did, on serious script changes? Perhaps she saw the project as simply a lark, a film in which she, now about fifty, could satisfy her vanity by showing off how trim and attractive she still looked in beach clothes and occasionally exchanging long, passionate screen kisses with the ruggedly handsome, and much younger, Jeff Chandler. Perhaps she had entirely different reasons. It's hard to tell. In the case of *Queen Bee*, however, Crawford was the prime mover. She'd read the novel upon which the film was based, clearly wanted to play evil Eva, and then, much as she'd done in other film projects, made the whole thing happen. It is a mystery, though, why she didn't insist on major script changes here, too. Ranald MacDougall, who had worked on the adaptations of both *Mildred Pierce* and 1947's *Possessed*, was certainly capable of much better work. Perhaps the fact that he was also directing *Queen Bee* made matters more complicated. Again, it's hard to tell.

This, of course, begs the question: At this juncture in her career—a time film writer David Krauss has called, Crawford's "ball-breaking butch period, [when her characters delight] in castrating weaker, usually younger men and reveling in their subsequent servitude"[7]—why did she want to play such roles?

Again, it's fascinating to speculate about but fruitless to think that we can find solid answers. Some people have noted that better-written and more sympathetic female roles, especially for middle-age actresses, were hard to come by during that period. That may be true, but Crawford was also up for several of these roles, and, in some cases, withdrew herself from consideration.[8] Another reason might be her ongoing campaign to prove her range as an actress. She had taken roles in *A Woman's Face, Mildred Pierce, Humoresque,* and *Possessed* to stretch herself and continue to demonstrate that, yes, she could do much more than the nice-girl-Joan roles she'd played throughout the 1930s. Perhaps she was still trying to prove herself by now playing a succession of mean-girl roles. Still another reason may be personal. During these years, she was between marriages and having a string of transient affairs and flings. Perhaps these particular choices of roles reflected (at least in part) a bitterness or anger toward men and romantic relationships at the time. Curiously, after her 1955 marriage to Pepsi-Cola Company CEO Alfred Steele, a man she greatly admired, she was much less inclined to go the mean-girl route.

Finally, why did Crawford, who truly believed in the power of understatement in film acting, play these roles, as film writer Ken Anderson aptly put it, "in such boldface type?"[9] One reason might be the deadly combination of a weak script and a weak director. When Crawford felt insecure with her material, her instinct was simply to try harder by amping it up and putting more "oomph" into her performance. Throughout her career, she also appreciated strong, intelligent directors such as Clarence Brown and George Cukor at MGM, Michael Curtiz at Warner Brothers, and later on Robert Aldridge, all of whom could call her on her bad habits and elicit more restrained, subtle, honest, and moving performances from her. Unfortunately, in neither *Female on the Beach* nor *Queen Bee* did she have a good script or a strong director. She'd been in this situation before. *This Woman Is Dangerous* is a good example. In that film, however, she was able to overcome her own tendencies toward excessiveness and underplay her role. The result wasn't great art, but it wasn't as embarrassing as her work in these two films.

Some of the more enthusiastic fans of Crawford camp have wondered whether the actress was actually pulling off brilliant self-parodies in these films, particularly in *Queen Bee.* It seems far more likely, though, that the results were simply misfires. Crawford took herself very seriously and worked hard at every role she ever played, even if she didn't have much of a role or a strong director to call her on her excesses. She was fiercely proud of her own work ethic and perfectionist drive, and, even after she was a firmly established star, she longed to be acknowledged as a first-rate actress as well. Ironically, it could just be a strained intensity that she brought to her performances in these two films, an intensity born out of a desperate desire to make silk purses out of sow's ears, that give the films and her work in them their bizarre but still alluring camp appeal.

✦ ✦ ✦

Sadly, the birth of what would become the Crawford-as-camp phenomenon is one outcome of the actress's later noir period. For whatever reasons, she made several bad choices in film roles, some of which—when later mingled in with the images of her presented in both the book and film versions of *Mommie Dearest*—helped to turn the name "Joan Crawford" into a punchline. While some Crawford partisans blame daughter Christina solely for the actress's catastrophic post-mortem public image problems, we must acknowledge that performances in films such as *Female on the Beach* and *Queen Bee* also factor in.

It's important to emphasize, too, that these films represent only a small part of Crawford's overall contribution to noir and an even smaller part of her total contribution to film going back to the silent era. By the time she made them, she had already played significant roles in more than seventy films dating back to the late 1920s, and, in dozens of those films, had delivered performances ranging from good to excellent, to great.

By 1955, Crawford's best filmmaking years were clearly behind her, but, despite the paucity of good roles for older actresses, changing audience tastes, and numerous other challenges, she was determined to press on and add at least a few more excellent or even great performances to her resume. In fact, when *Queen Bee* opened in theaters in November 1955, she had just finished work on one of these—a performance that would also provide a fitting and dignified conclusion to her own noir cycle in films.

11

"Your filthy souls are too evil for Hell itself"

Autumn Leaves (1956)

Among Joan Crawford's films in the 1950s, one of the best and per-haps the most tragically underappreciated is the 1956 noir-tinged melo-drama *Autumn Leaves*. After a succession of mean-girl roles in films such as *Harriet Craig, Torch Song, Female on the Beach,* and *Queen Bee,* the actress returned to the kind of film more reminiscent of the Joan Crawford pictures of the 1930s. Here, as in many of those films, she plays a smart, good-hearted working woman who comes to the aid of a troubled man in her life. This time, however, several noirish features, combined with a post–World War II sensibility, give the story a much darker and more complex character.

Overall, *Autumn Leaves* is quite a remarkable effort. Bolstered by an intelligent and poignant script written mostly by Jean Rouverol and Hugo Butler, the skilled and sensitive direction of the talented Robert Aldrich, the expert camerawork of Charles Lang, and the contributions of other film artists and artisans, Crawford and her fellow actors do excellent jobs. Her work here is certainly one of the best five or six per-formances of her career. As the troubled man in the Crawford charac-ter's life, co-star Cliff Robertson delivers one of his finest performances in a film career that would continue for another half-century. Both stars are also ably supported by veteran actors Lorne Greene and Ruth Don-nelly and the up-and-coming Vera Miles. All those involved, it seems, had considerable regard for the story and invested a great deal of them-selves and their talents into its telling.

In addition to being an excellent film, *Autumn Leaves* is significant for Crawford in at least three respects. First, it marks the first time she worked with Aldrich, a director whose impact on her work and career rivaled such earlier mentors as George Cukor and Michael Curtiz.[1] Aldrich, of course, was instrumental in pulling off the last of the actress's legendary career comebacks when he directed her in the 1962 horror-thriller *Whatever Happened to Baby Jane?* He was also, and perhaps more important, a strong personality with a clear directorial vision who knew exactly how to get the best possible work from her. Second, *Autumn Leaves* is the last Crawford film with enough noir content in it to credibly count as part of her contribution to the classic noir cycle. Its story deals with common noir themes such as loneliness, betrayal, and mental illness, and its "look" is filled with the familiar noir visual trimmings. Also, the film falls squarely into "Crawford noir," which includes, along with the more conventional noir elements, a complex female protagonist, an emphasis on troubled family and/or romantic relationships, and melodramatic content. Third, much like *A Woman's Face* had done a decade and a half before, *Autumn Leaves* serves as a kind of bridge film to a new chapter in Crawford's career. After an impressive string of critical and commercial hits, mostly in noir and noirish melodramas, she was now moving into the final phase of her professional life, a decade and a half which would include one more stunning comeback and a few solid performances but also many more misses than hits. As a bridge film—especially at this later point in the actress's career—it also has a special poignancy about it that's reflected both in the film's sometimes wistful, melancholy tone and in the popular song, "Autumn Leaves," which plays during the film's opening credits and inspires its title. There is a sense as we see the film today that—like the speaker in the song and the character Crawford plays in the story—we are also seeing the actress as she passes from the summer into the autumn of her career, with, as the song's lyrics tell us, "old winter's song"[2] just ahead.

❖ ❖ ❖

In a departure from her active production involvement in her recent films such as *Sudden Fear, Johnny Guitar,* and *Queen Bee,* Crawford was not the prime mover behind *Autumn Leaves.* That task fell to its director, Robert Aldrich (1918–1983), a fascinating film industry figure whose up-and-down career spanned forty years, from the early 1940s to the early 1980s.

Aldrich was born into one of Rhode Island's most prominent families. Among his distinguished ancestors were Roger Williams, the founder of the Rhode Island Colony, and Nathanael Greene, one of George Washington's most respected Revolutionary War generals. His grandfather, Nelson Aldridge, was, for thirty years, a prominent U.S. senator, earning the nickname "General Manager of the Nation" for his

Cliff Robertson (left) and Crawford discuss the date-at-the-beach scene in *Autumn Leaves* (1956) with director Robert Aldrich (right), who would work with her again six years later in the hit *Whatever Happened to Baby Jane?* (Columbia Pictures/Photofest).

role in setting federal monetary policy. His Aunt Abby married John D. Rockefeller, Jr. One of their sons—and Robert's first cousin—was Nelson A. (for Aldrich) Rockefeller, the four-term Governor of New York, three-time Presidential candidate, and U.S. Vice President under President Gerald Ford. Two other first cousins, Nelson's brothers David and

Winthrop, went on to become, respectively, the Chairman of Chase Manhattan Bank and the Governor of Arkansas.

As the only male heir from his side of the Aldrich family, Robert was under great pressure to compete in a clan of establishment high achievers. Instead, in 1941, soon after dropping out of college, which infuriated his father, he went to work as a film production clerk at RKO Pictures for twenty-five dollars a week, which infuriated his father even more. A relative had offered to pull some strings and have Robert start instead as an associate producer, but Robert declined, saying he wanted to get ahead on his own. Consequently, his father disinherited him and Robert rarely spoke of his family again.

Gradually, Aldrich worked his way up the film industry ranks and, between 1944 and 1952, served as an assistant director under an array of master filmmakers including Jean Renoir, William Wellman, Louis Milestone, Joseph Losey, and Charlie Chaplin. Making the most of these opportunities, he concentrated on learning as much as he could from all of their directorial strengths and weaknesses. From Wellman, for example, he learned how to stage action scenes. From Milestone, he learned techniques to successfully pre-plan shots. And from Chaplin, he learned how to forge an emotional connection between what the camera records and what the audience sees.[3]

After a brief stint directing for television in the early 1950s, Aldrich moved to directing films and immediately distinguished himself in some critical circles as a "macho auteur"[4] who brought new levels of cruelty, cynicism, and violence to such male-oriented genres as westerns, crime noirs, and war films. Among his noirs is the film widely considered to be his masterpiece, the grimly pessimistic *Kiss Me Deadly* (1955). Then, after completing *Kiss Me Deadly* and a scathing look at Hollywood, *The Big Knife* (1955), he did a totally unexpected turnabout and began work on the very un-macho *Autumn Leaves*. The reasoning behind this decision is quite intriguing. "I guess self-survival made me do that one," he once confided in an interview. "People were getting pretty collective in their criticism of the violence and anger and wrath in my pictures, although these things were intentional, and I thought it was about time I made a soap opera.[5] I was also a great fan of the Butlers—Jean Rouverol and Hugo Butler—and this was her original story."[6]

Jean Rouverol Butler (1916–2017) and Hugo Butler (1914–1968) are an interesting story in their own right. Both were film writers who, in 1943, became members of the American Communist Party. Then, in 1951, at the height of the U.S. House of Representatives Un-American Activities Committee (HUAC) hearings investigating Communism in the film industry and elsewhere,[7] they moved with their four children to Mexico rather than risk getting subpoenas to appear before the committee and possible jail sentences. While in Mexico, the two were "blacklisted" by the film studios, or unofficially banned from working for them because of their Communist sympathies. They still continued to write scripts, however, and one of their joint efforts was the screenplay for the story that eventually became *Autumn Leaves*, a story based on a novella Jean had written. Since they couldn't sell their work under their own names, they asked another writer, Jack Javne, to "front" for them, or to officially present the work as his own and then split the screenwriting fee with the Butlers. (This was a common practice among blacklisted screenwriters during this period.) Javne, not the Butlers, also received screen credit.

In 1964, the Butlers were finally able to return to the U.S. Hugo died in just four years later, but Jean lived to be a hundred years old, passing away nearly forty years after he did. During the succeeding years, she wrote for daytime television dramas as well as for the popular primetime show *Little House on the Prairie*. She also taught screenplay writing and wrote books, including one she published in 2000 (when she was eighty-four) that tells her family's story during the years when she and Hugo were blacklisted.[8]

With the Butlers' script in hand, Aldrich approached Crawford, whose work he admired. She expressed interest, and they sold the project to producer William Goetz, who, like Crawford at the time, was under contract with Columbia. Filming began in late August 1955 and was completed that October.

By all accounts, the filming generally went well. Crawford, who, according to some reports, had initially expressed an interest in approaching Marlon Brando to co-star, was thrilled with Robertson's portrayal. "I really think Cliff did a stupendous job," she said years later. "Another actor might have been spitting out his lines and chewing the scenery, but he avoided that trap."[9] She also had high praise for the young Vera Miles, whose work had particularly struck her. Robertson, too, was similarly impressed with Crawford. "She was able to summon up some very real emotions," he said. "She was ... a damn fine actress."[10] Robertson was also fascinated by how Crawford could use her body almost like a musician uses an instrument to get a desired effect, once recounting that, when Aldrich asked her to shed a tear in a scene, she responded by asking which eye he wanted the tear to fall from.

Aldrich did note, though, that he did initially have an issue with Crawford who insisted on bringing in "her own writer"[11] (Ranald Mac-Dougall) to make some script changes. When Aldrich refused the request, she then gave him an ultimatum: no writer, no star. Then, when he stood his ground, she relented, reporting to work the next day without her writer. "But she didn't talk to me for about four or five days," Aldrich later said. "She took direction, she did what she was supposed to do, but there was no personal communication. Then one day she was doing a scene terribly effectively. I forget which one. I was really touched, and, when she looked up after finishing it, I tried not to be obvious in wiping away a tear. That broke the ice, and from then on we were good friends for a long time."[12]

❖ ❖ ❖

Autumn Leaves tells the story of Millicent "Millie" Wetherby (Crawford), a lonely, middle-aged spinster who supports herself as a freelance typist. She works out of her modest Los Angeles area bungalow, and except for occasional visits from her landlady Liz (Ruth Donnelly), she seems to have a non-existent social life.

One day, a client gives Millie two tickets to a classical music concert and she asks Liz if she would like to go with her. Liz says she "can't stand that kind of music," so Millie goes alone. Listening to one Chopin piece in the concert hall, she recalls listening to the same piece years before when she took care of her ailing father and, out of concern for him, kept male suitors at a distance.

After the concert, she stops at a coffee shop for a bite to eat, and a young man named Burt Hanson (Robertson), also alone, asks to join her. After she initially refusing him, he is persistent and she agrees. He is quite charming, and eventually he gets her to relax and enjoy herself. Afterwards, he accompanies her back to her bungalow and they make a date to go to the beach the following afternoon. At the beach, they kiss passionately in the surf, and, being conscious of the significant age difference between them, she tells Burt afterwards that they shouldn't see each other anymore, that he should go out with women his own age. He is saddened but agrees to comply with her wishes.

A month goes by, and Millie seems lonelier than ever. Then one day Burt shows up unexpectedly, tells Millie that he's received a promotion at work in a local department store, and begs her to go out and celebrate with him. He says that he has gone out with younger women but that he doesn't connect with them the way he does with Millie. Later, he tells Millie he wants to marry her. She tries repeatedly to convince him that this would not be a good idea, but, overcome by her growing feelings for him, she agrees. The next morning, they drive to Mexico and are married. As they drive back from Mexico, however, Millie asks Burt why he put his birthplace down on the marriage form as Chicago rather than as Racine, Wisconsin, which he had originally told her. Burt simply shrugs her question off, saying that she must be mistaken, that he was born in Chicago, not Racine.

For a brief time, all seems to be well. Millie asks Burt not to spend so much money on presents for her, but otherwise the two seem very happy. Then one day Millie is shocked when Burt's former wife Virginia (Vera Miles) appears at the front door. Burt had said that he'd never been married, and Virginia says that their divorce has only been final for about a month and that she has come by to get Burt's signature on a property settlement she would like finalized. Virginia also mentions that Burt's father, who Burt said had died, happened to be in Los Angeles and, if Burt were agreeable, would like to see him. As she leaves, Virginia looks at Millie with what appears to be genuine sympathy, saying that Burt "just lies."

When Millie confronts Burt with these revelations, he is evasive and dismissive, saying that nothing that happened in the past really matters, that all that matters is their happiness now and in the future. Millie continues to probe, however, and learns both that Burt has been stealing the items he's given to Millie as presents and that he suffers from a severe psychological trauma caused at least in part by an experience when he inadvertently walked in on his father and Virginia having sex.

Rather than distancing herself from Burt, Millie becomes his fierce protector. When Virginia and Burt's father, known only as Mr. Hanson (Lorne Greene), come to the bungalow to insist on getting Burt's signature on the property settlement, she tells them that Burt is emotionally sick and can't see them now. But Mr. Hanson and Virginia keep pressing her:

> HANSON: You're his wife. Authorize some kind of headshrinker to go to work on him. Get it over with.
> VIRGINIA: Sure, he should be committed.
> MILLIE: Of course. You want me to commit him, get him out of your life permanently someplace where he can never remind either of you of your horrible guilt: how you and you committed the ugliest of all possible sins, so ugly that it drove him into the state he's in now.
> HANSON: What kind of a woman are you to be satisfied with only half a man? There must be something wrong with you.
> MILLIE: Even when he doesn't know what he's doing, he's a saner man than you are. He's decent and proud. Can you say the same for yourselves? Where's your decency? In what garbage dump, Mr. Hanson? (to Virginia) And where's yours, you tramp ...?
> VIRGINIA: She's the one who's crazy.
> HANSON: She's got to be crazy to put up with that weakling.
> MILLIE: (to Hanson) You, you doting fraud of a father! (to Virginia) And

you, you slut! You're both so consumed with evil, so rotten, your filthy souls are too evil for Hell itself!

Despite Millie's efforts, however, Burt slips more deeply into mental illness, at one point assaulting her in a paranoid rage and seriously injuring her hand by throwing her own typewriter down on her. Soon, she consults a psychiatrist. Following his advice, she commits Burt to a sanitarium for several months to undergo various forms of therapy, including drugs and shock treatments. Although it appears that Burt is making progress, Millie is preoccupied by the thought that, all along, she has been more of a mother to him than a wife, someone Burt has been drawn to out of need rather than love.

On the day he is scheduled to be released, she visits him and says that he doesn't owe her anything, that he is free to leave her and start a new life, if that's his wish, and that she is fine with this. He listens to her short speech without saying a word. Then, as she turns to leave, he follows. At first, he asks to look at the hand he'd injured with the typewriter. He kisses it tenderly, and says that the scar is nearly healed. Then he looks at her:

BURT: You didn't even give me a chance to say "Hello."
MILLIE: Did you want a chance?
BURT: (nods) Hello, Millie.
They kiss.

◆ ◆ ◆

When it premiered in August 1956, *Autumn Leaves* became a modest hit with audiences and received generally positive reviews. Lawrence Quirk of the *Motion Picture Herald* praised the film's "moving eloquence," a result largely due, he notes, to "Robert Aldrich's control over a taut, well-knit, extremely literate script." He also praised Crawford for bringing to the role of Millie "all the acting resources she has cultivated so successfully in thirty-one years of picture-making."[13] William K. Zinsser of the *New York Herald Tribune* also lauded the actress, saying "The strength of Miss Crawford's performance is that it is natural and controlled. A lesser actress would bring more than a tinge of ham to such a juicy role."[14] For his efforts, Aldrich also won the Silver Bear Award for Best Director at the 1956 Berlin International Film Festival.

Well into the new millennium, *Autumn Leaves* and its principal contributors still receive high marks. Film writer Dan Callahan has dubbed *Autumn Leaves* Aldrich's "secret gem"[15] in a decade in which the director made several fine films. In addition, he has been especially complimentary toward its two stars. "Crawford is sensitive, operatic, and quite touching, especially when Millie first lets her guard down," he writes. "This is arguably her best performance. As far as Robertson goes, there can be no argument that this is his best work."[16] Film writer Nathanael Hood has also noted, "Crawford particularly stuns" as she "brilliantly realizes" Millie throughout the film.[17]

Curiously, Hood also speculates on why, despite Crawford's excellent performance and the quality of the film overall, *Autumn Leaves* is not better known or more widely appreciated today. While emphasizing that "there is no 'camp' in *Autumn Leaves*, just genuine gut-wrenching agony," he also posits: "Crawford's casting doomed the film in many circles, especially after the release of Frank Perry's *Mommie Dearest* (1981), a film which retroactively reframed [her] as a camp icon. Aldrich's own ... *What Ever Happened to Baby Jane?* further exacerbated attempts to appreciate Crawford's films outside a camp context."[18] Other factors— such as the decline of the female-centered melodrama in the 1950s and 1960s and *Autumn Leaves'* standing as an anomaly in work of macho auteur Aldrich—may be in play here, too, but the widespread trivialization of Crawford into little more than a camp figure is certainly a contributor.

◆ ◆ ◆

Although Aldrich backhandedly called *Autumn Leaves* a "soap opera" when discussing his decision to make the film, anyone familiar with the result has to be impressed by the level of respect those involved had for the story and characters and the level of commitment and talent they put into the effort. While similar to a soap opera in some respects, the film also, and often, rises to the level of art.

Much of the credit, of course, goes to the script and to Aldrich, who, working closely with cinematographer Lang, complements the thoughtful and heartfelt story with numerous visual images that reinforce meaning and give the story's themes greater resonance. Some of the most compelling are the images of loneliness early on: as the camera leads us in to the group of forlorn-looking bungalow apartments where Millie lives, as we see Millie's empty bed behind her as she works, as we see Millie sitting alone at the beach after her break-up with Burt, and elsewhere. One of the most effective of these touches occurs when Millie sits in the middle of a crowded audience at the concert. As she listens to the Chopin, Aldrich isolates her visually from others by literally making them disappear into black and then transporting her back to an evening years before when she and her sick father had listened to the same piece. This is a wonderful way of showing both how disconnected she seems with the world in which she currently lives and why she is in this situation.

Loneliness, however, is by no means the only story element that Aldrich and Lang visually reinforce to great effect. Throughout the film, lighting and camera placement are skillfully used to make various dramatic points. One emotionally charged moment, for example, begins with a long-shot of Burt alone, his head drooped in complete desolation. He is leaning against a wall in the hotel where (we presume) he has just had a disastrous encounter with his father and Virginia. Millie rushes to him, and behind them we see a disheveled bed that clearly has just been used for sex. Another very well-executed scene is when Burt rages against Millie and then attacks her, hurling her typewriter down on her hand. Throughout, the camera is nearly always below Burt's face and above Millie's to emphasize the danger he poses to her as well as her relative vulnerability. But, in a scene where the camera angles could be much more exaggerated for greater melodramatic effect, they are carefully moderated. This both reduces the potential for overwrought melodrama and reinforces the truth of the situation, making the moment all the more real and horrifying.

Another major Aldrich contribution was to give *Autumn Leaves* additional tension and complexity by mixing some of the more modern hard-edged violence and straight-up nastiness central to his tough-guy films with the more traditional and genteel female-centered melodrama. One example, of course, is Burt's slapping Millie and then throwing her typewriter down on her arm. Another is the presence of truly vile people such as Burt's father and Virginia. After we understand them as fully as we need to, Millie's scolding words, "your filthy souls are too evil for Hell itself," seem like a relatively mild rebuke. Far removed from the type of people we would see in a 1930s or even 1940s female-centered melodrama, these two seem far better suited for the darkest kinds of mid–1950s noir—a much better fit for the world of *Kiss Me Deadly* or *Sweet Smell of Success* (1957) than, say, the world of *Stella Dallas* (1937) or *Now, Voyager* (1942).

Still another fascinating component to *Autumn Leaves*, which may be the contribution of the Butlers as well as Aldrich, is some fairly subtle and ambiguous content that may (or may not) give us added perspective on what might be going on beneath the surface in this story. Dan Callahan, for example, points to an odd line that Millie's landlady Liz drops offhandedly early in the film when she describes her brother as "tall and skinny and all muscle."[19] Here, there is clearly a suggestion of a forbidden sexual attraction. Could this, Callahan poses, foreshadow Millie's attraction to the much younger Burt, something also deemed inappropriate by much of society in the 1950s? Or could it suggest something else? Callahan then proposes an intriguing reading of the film. "The real theme of *Autumn Leaves* isn't loneliness, but incest," he writes. "Liz wants her brother, Millie wanted her father, and Burt wants a mother to protect him from his father."[20] Likewise, in his article on the film, Nathanael Hood offers another interesting thought related to one of the lies Burt tells. At first, Millie hears that, during the Korean War, Burt had never seen combat. Later, however, she overhears Burt telling another character that, in Korea, he had been part of a combat unit that suffered a forty-percent casualty rate, an appalling statistic from any perspective. So, which is the lie and which is true? Or are they both lies? We, of course, don't know for sure, but, if the combat unit story is true, then, Hood suggests, Burt could also be suffering from an extreme case of PTSD, and this could shed additional light on his extreme behavior. As Hood adds:

> [How] sane could a man expect to be after coming home from the hell of war to find his wife cheating on him with his dad? What faith in the world could he have left? What faith in himself to make any sense of it? So why not lie and lie and lie until you trick yourself into living in whatever reality the world demands at any given moment?[21]

These are only speculations based on what may or may not be hints sprinkled into the script. Still, both these film writers found these lines curious enough to mull over and discuss in print. The rest of us can accept or reject what they suggest, but, at the very least, their speculation encourages us to think more about other ambiguities in the story and perhaps acquire a fuller understanding of, and appreciation for, the artistry behind it.

Although Aldrich noted that his reason for doing *Autumn Leaves* was "self-survival," a way to soften his image as a director, both the choice of story and the great creative investment he put into the film's making are worth noting. Considering the kinds of subjects he was typically drawn to, the idea of his directing *Autumn Leaves* seems about as far-fetched as Alfred Hitchcock directing a western. Yet, a part of him also admired the work of Jean Rouverol and Hugo Butler, appreciated Crawford's acting, and was open to the possibility that, at least sometimes in life, characters can face and overcome serious problems and that love can triumph. We have to admire his willingness to be open to a fairly wide spectrum of human experience. Also, in virtually every aspect of his work on *Autumn Leaves*, from the very creative shot selection to the expert handling of actors, Aldrich put an extremely high level of personal commitment into the effort. He may have seen this film merely as a project that might help soften his professional image, but by no means did he approach it in a half-hearted or slap-dash way. Again, we have to admire him—this time for his willingness to take (for him) unusual material and invest so much of himself into conveying it with such intelligence and conviction.

◆ ◆ ◆

Along with Aldrich, the Butlers, Charles Lang, and other behind-the-scenes contributors, Crawford and the other actors add substantially to the overall quality and effectiveness of *Autumn Leaves*.

Crawford certainly deserves the very positive notices she received, and continues to receive, for her work. As she takes us through Millie's personal journey from resigned spinster to hesitant lover, to blissful wife, to terrified victim, to committed protector, to resigned stoic who has accepted that she might have to let her beloved husband go, and finally to joyously reconciled wife, she channels the character in virtuoso fashion. In her first scene, for example, she is absolutely convincing

Crawford's Millicent Wetherby finds it difficult to accept the disturbing news that her new husband's former wife, Vera Miles's Virginia (right), delivers in a scene from *Autumn Leaves*. The film featured one of three exceptional supporting roles Miles played in films released in 1956. The other two were in John Ford's classic western *The Searchers* and Alfred Hitchcock's noirish *The Wrong Man* (Columbia Pictures/Photofest).

as an unassuming but highly competent typist in both her demeanor and her seeming mastery of Millie's work tools and environment. When Millie and Burt go to the beach, she excellently captures Millie's anxiety both at being out on a rare date and at also being out with a man who is much younger than she is. When Millie better understands Burt's problems, the actress is wonderful at showing both Millie's growing concern for his welfare and a growing confidence in her ability to help and, if necessary, defend him. By the end of the film, Millie is a very different person from who she was at the beginning: stronger, more self-assured, and clearer about who she is and what she wants from life. To Crawford's great credit, she portrays this complex, dynamic character in a very clear, focused, precise, and disciplined way throughout. As noted earlier, this really is one of her best performances.

In an interview, Aldrich once said that he had been frustrated by not getting Crawford "to be a drab, aging woman, which threw off the balance of the picture."[22] While Aldrich's instincts about what was right for the story were usually excellent, he may not have been correct here. Even though Millie is significantly older than Burt, he still needs to find her sufficiently attractive for the relationship to take hold. Crawford's Millie is attractive, but in the way a fit, appealing middle-age woman—and not a glamorous Joan Crawford–like movie star—would be. Her Millie also dresses fairly plainly and primly, in a style that is much more consistent with Millie's, not Crawford's, character.

In only his second film, Cliff Robertson (1923–2011), who had come to Hollywood by way of Broadway, is exceptional as Burt. This is a particularly difficult role, in which an actor has to be convincing, first, as a charming and affable suitor; later, as a profoundly disturbed man descending into infantilism and capable of delusional rages; and finally, as a man who has successfully recovered his sanity. The script treats some of these steps in very cursory fashion, too. His several-months-long sanitorium recovery, for example, is covered in a two-and-a-half-minute montage. Despite such challenges, Robertson convinces throughout by underplaying a role that could easily have been overplayed to the hilt. Twelve years after *Autumn Leaves*, he would star in Ralph Nelson's *Charly*, a film in which an intellectually disabled man undergoes a surgical procedure that triples his IQ. He learns afterwards, however, that the impact of the procedure will soon wear off and that he will regress back to his original intellectual level. It's an emotionally gripping film, and Robertson, quite moving in the role, went on to win a Best Actor Academy Award for his work in it. When watching Burt's equally convincing transformation from charming suitor to delusional abuser, to recovered patient, it's fascinating to think about the similarities between the two roles and Robertson's extraordinary ability to pull them both off so well.

In the supporting roles, Ruth Donnelly, Lorne Greene, and Vera Miles all deliver fine performances. Donnelly (1896–1982), nearing the end of a long film career that began in the 1910s, brings charm and depth to the small role of Liz, Millie's dowdy but caring landlady. Greene (1915–1987), best known today for playing Ben Cartwright, the kindly patriarch on the long-running television western series *Bonanza*, is quite effective playing against type as the despicable—and very intimidating—Mr. Hanson. Finally, the young Vera Miles (1929–) is especially good in the scene when she first visits Millie, introduces herself as Burt's ex-wife, says she's come to ask Burt to sign some legal papers, and shares several bits of disturbing information about him. Here, Miles's Virginia is quite low-key and composed and seems extremely respectful and empathetic toward Millie, especially as Millie tries to cope with what she is hearing. "I know how you feel," Virginia says very gently. "I was married to him, too." This is Miles's scene and she delivers a superb piece of acting, a turn we appreciate all when more later in the film when we learn what a ruthless, scheming person Virginia actually is.

❖ ❖ ❖

Despite a bit of friction at the beginning of filming *Autumn Leaves*, Crawford and Aldrich were both sufficiently impressed with each other's talents to quickly make plans to work together again. They proposed a film adaptation of a stage play, *Storm in the Sun*, starring Crawford. Columbia, apparently, gave the go-ahead to the effort and then reneged. In response, Aldrich sued, and, although the case was soon settled, relations between him and the studio had soured.

Crawford and Aldrich eventually—and quite famously—did work together again six years later on *Whatever Happened to Baby Jane?*, and Crawford began work on (and then left) a follow-on Aldrich film, *Hush, Hush, Sweet Charlotte* (1964).[23] *Baby Jane*, of course, became an enormous hit, inspiring a whole series of horror-thrillers condescendingly nicknamed "psycho-biddy" or "hagsploitation" films because they starred aging actresses.[24]

Aldrich continued to make films regularly throughout the 1960s and 1970s. Although he worked in a variety of genres, he is probably best known today for *Kiss Me Deadly* and *Baby Jane* and for his later male-centered efforts (and two biggest box office hits), the war film, *The Dirty Dozen* (1967) and the football film, *The Longest Yard* (1974). Along the way, he made many concessions to studio meddling that compromised his films, but he never lost the rough, obstinate, rebellious streak that had once led to his banishment from Rhode Island royalty and then inspired the in-your-face immediacy and vitality of his best directing work.

Aldrich died of kidney failure in December 1983. He was sixty-five years old and, according to film historian David Thomson, "not too far from broke."[25]

❖ ❖ ❖

In August 1956, the same month that *Autumn Leaves* premiered in U.S. theaters, Crawford went to the U.K. to begin production on the third and final film on the Columbia Pictures contract that had begun with *Queen Bee*. This was a conventional drama/melodrama called *The Story of Esther Costello*, and it was about, among other subjects, corruption in large-scale fundraising. To direct, she was able to get David Miller, who had, just five years earlier, done such excellent work with her in *Sudden Fear*. "This was my last really top picture," she later noted in an interview[26] in what appears to be a backhanded slap at *Baby Jane*. Although she seemed pleased with the results, *The Story of Esther Costello* received tepid reviews and failed to attract any sizable audience.

By this time, too, it was becoming evident that Crawford's reign as queen of the Joan Crawford noir-melodrama, which had so closely tracked with the classic noir cycle of the 1940s and 1950s, was, like the cycle itself, clearly coming to an end.

12

"If you don't give me a divorce, we'll kill you"

Television Noirs
"The Road to Edinburgh" (1954)
and "Strange Witness" (1958)

Although Crawford's principal career focus was her film work, she, like many other established stars, occasionally acted for both radio and television. Her radio acting began in 1935 and extended into the early 1950s. Her television appearances spanned from 1953, when she starred in a half-hour tearjerker called "Because I Love Him" for the NBC anthology series the *Revlon Mirror Theater*, to 1972, when she made her last-ever acting appearance on an episode of *The Sixth Sense*, a series of hour-long dramas that dealt with the paranormal.

Among the radio and television dramas she acted in, several clearly qualify as noir or noirish. This was especially true during the 1950s, when interest in noir entertainments was high; radio dramas, though in decline, were still around; and television viewership was growing in leaps and bounds. On the radio program *Screen Directors Playhouse*, for example, she starred in reenactments of two of her recent noir films, one of *Flamingo Road* in 1950 and the other of *The Damned Don't* Cry in 1951. Then, soon after her television acting debut, she also showed a penchant for noir-infused content in this medium, starring in a pair of darkly suspenseful half-hour dramas aired on the CBS anthology series *General Electric Theater*: "The Road to Edinburgh" (1954) and "Strange Witness" (1958).

In this chapter, we will focus on these two little-known, and under-appreciated, efforts. Before we do, however, it may be useful to provide some context about television noir at that time.

❖ ❖ ❖

One of the ironies associated with the study of classic-cycle noir in the late–1940s and 1950s is the relative lack of attention the era's television noir has received compared to the era's feature-length noir movies. Today, as it has been for several decades, interest in noir feature films remains high. Writers continue to churn out books and articles about various facets of the subject. Noir-themed film festivals in major cities across the U.S. consistently attract large audiences. And social media groups and other online societies focused on the subject are numerous and thriving. In contrast, early television noir is, outside of a few books on some of the series and some social media interest, largely overlooked. This is fascinating because, during much of the 1950s, tens of millions more people were most likely watching noir on their television screens each week than on the screens at their neighborhood movie theaters.[1] Given television noir's widespread popularity as well as abundant output (some series at the time aired as many as thirty-nine episodes a year), it's difficult to dismiss the huge cultural impact it must have had both during the 1950s and in the decades that followed. It's unfortunate that more attention isn't paid to it today.

One reason for the relative neglect of early television noir, of course, is the tendency of film historians, scholars, and aficionados to dismiss it as inferior to the higher-quality feature-length noir films and, therefore, not worth their time.

There is, of course, a logic to this point of view. Very little, if any, noir developed for 1950s television can compare with such classic film noirs as Joseph L. Lewis's riveting *Gun Crazy* (1950) or Stanley Kubrick's brilliantly orchestrated *The Killing* (1956). Yet, much of this television noir is engaging, entertaining, and clearly superior to many of the low-budget noir films being cranked out as second features for movie houses. Watching just a few episodes of such now-classic television noirs as *Dragnet* (NBC, 1951–1959), *M Squad* (NBC, 1957–1960), *Peter Gunn* (NBC/ABC, 1958–1961), or *Johnny Staccato* (NBC, 1959–1960) will easily support this contention. All these series inhabit dark, troubled worlds; are written in terse, Hammett-like hard-boiled prose; and emphasize direct, understated acting. One intriguing feature of *Dragnet* is its occasional noirish dark humor, especially in its depiction of people who think they can outsmart the law. Very appealing features of *M Squad*, *Peter Gunn*, and *Johnny Staccato* are these shows' moody, often brooding jazz soundtracks, which, in nearly all their episodes, stylishly underscore noirish life-is-hard themes.

Those who contributed to many of these television series also

Heavily influenced by the documentary style and understated acting of the police procedural film noirs of the late 1940s, the popular television series, *Dragnet*, starring Jack Webb (left) and Ben Alexander (right) as Los Angeles police officers, ran on NBC between 1951 and 1959, a total of 276 episodes. In the late 1960s, the show was revived for four more seasons (NBC/Photofest).

deserve great credit for delivering solid entertainment while working under major constraints filmmakers usually didn't have to worry
about. Scripts, for example, had to be written to accommodate strict
twenty-nine- or fifty-nine-minute time formats that included opening and closing credits as well as periodic commercial breaks so spon-
sors could pitch their products. Production budgets were usually tight.
Shooting schedules, too, were almost always short and grueling. Many
of these people, however, soon learned how to work with, and sometimes thrive because of, these constraints. By working with less, they
discovered, they could sometimes deliver more. One excellent example
is the efficiency with which television writers could compress exposition at the beginning of episodes, sometimes setting up the characters,
conflicts, and other key story ingredients in a matter of seconds. Not
only did this get to the action much more quickly, but it also helped
to "hook" viewers, sufficiently intriguing them so they wouldn't simply turn the dial to see what a rival television network might be offering.

It was into this vibrant, and turbulent, production environment
that Crawford first ventured in 1953. Over the next two decades, she
made more than a dozen acting appearances in prime-time television
series ranging from the drama *Route 66* to the comedy *The Lucy Show*,
to the western *The Virginian.* In addition, she made more than a hundred appearances on television variety, awards, game, and talk shows.
Her contribution to television noir is quite small, certainly not nearly
as large as her contribution to feature-length noir and noir-melodrama
hybrid films. Still, adaptable professional that she was, she knew by the
early 1950s that, if most film actors wished to remain relevant, they
must reckon with the reality of television, and she embraced the new
medium.

Of Crawford's television acting appearances during the 1950s,
three were for *General Electric Theater,* one of the most popular and
highly regarded of the era's many television anthology series. Running
on CBS from February 1953 until June 1962, comprising more than
200 self-contained twenty-nine-minute episodes, and hosted for most
of its run by actor and future U.S. president Ronald Reagan, the series
focused mainly on presenting adaptations of novels, short stories, plays,
films, or magazine fiction. Its consistently good scripts and high ratings
also attracted top directing and acting talent. For example, the highly
respected Jacques Tourneur (1904–1977), who had directed the classic
1947 film noir *Out of the Past,* directed four episodes. And, in addition
to Crawford, scores of major Hollywood stars appeared on the show.
Just a few include Fred Astaire, Jack Benny, Claudette Colbert, Ronald
Colman, Joseph Cotten, Bette Davis, James Dean, Judy Garland, Charles

Laughton, Myrna Loy, George Sanders, James Stewart, and Natalie Wood.

The first of Crawford's three appearances on *General Electric Theater* was in *The Road to Edinburgh*, a drama with a decided noir bent, which first aired on October 31, 1954.

◆ ◆ ◆

"The Road to Edinburgh" has what appears to be a fascinating backstory. While produced specifically for television, it was likely not produced specifically for *General Electric Theater*.

In September 1953, after her television debut for *Revlon Mirror Theater*, Crawford—once again initiating a major project—hired Andrew Solt (1916–1990), a screenwriter whose impressive credits include work on such notable noirs as Otto Preminger's *Whirlpool* (1950) and Nicholas Ray's *In a Lonely Place* (1950). Solt's assignment was to write scripts for twenty-six episodes for a proposed new television series called *The World and I*. In it, Crawford, who was probably also eyeing a producing role, would star as a globe-trotting newspaper columnist. A pilot for the prospective series was filmed in January 1954, with director Rod Amateau (1923–2003)—who would later work on such hit television series as *The Many Loves of Dobie Gillis*, *Mr. Ed*, and *Gilligan's Island*—helming. By June, however, Crawford hadn't been able to find any takers among the major television networks and apparently forfeited the pilot to CBS to use on *General Electric Theater*. The likely result is "The Road to Edinburgh," on which Crawford starred as the globe-trotting reporter, and Amateau and Solt received the credits for, respectively, directing and writing the teleplay.[2]

Further evidence that Crawford was working in some kind of producing capacity on the project is the participation of two other major contributors, cinematographer Charles Lang and costume designer Sheila O'Brien. Both had greatly impressed her two years earlier with their Academy Award nominated work on *Sudden Fear*, and, especially during the 1950s, the star, whenever she could, would recruit them to assist in her various ventures.

◆ ◆ ◆

"The Road to Edinburgh" opens in London, where syndicated newspaper columnist and recent Korean War widow Mary Andrews (Crawford) prepares to leave for Scotland to cover the Edinburgh Art Festival. Her boss strongly prefers that, for her own safety, she travel by train, but Mary, both fiercely independent and stubborn, insists on driving.

Early in her journey, she gets a flat tire and, with her can-do attitude, begins to replace the flat with her rental car's spare. As she tries (not very successfully), a man (John Sutton), who has been walking along the road, approaches her and offers to help. At this point, we see him only from the back or side: his face is a mystery to us. She looks at him, though, and, ever the newswoman, she assesses him. "An unusual face, stern, hard," we hear in her voiceover. "Yet, his eyes and mouth are kind, gentle." As he works, she notices that he is carrying in his coat pocket a newspaper from 1937. Appreciating his help, she tells him she is going to Edinburgh and asks if he would like a ride. He accepts, and they introduce themselves. His name is Tom Wickers, and, when he hears that Mary is a widow, he mentions that he is a widower.

Now on the road, Mary asks about the 1937 newspaper. He seems upset by the question and throws the newspaper out the car window. She asks if he can get her a cigarette from her purse. When he opens it, he notices that she is carrying a considerable amount of money with her. "You really shouldn't carry that much money around with you," he says. "It isn't wise."

In a voiceover, she says, "Why did he say 'it's not wise?' Why are my knees shaking? Maybe I shouldn't have offered him a ride. After all, he is a complete stranger."

She asks him if he would accept some money for changing her tire. He declines, but adds with bitterness in his voice, "Money, it's always been highly overrated to me, but I feel differently now. I have to have it—a great deal of it."

A bit later, he shares with her that he was just released from prison a couple of hours earlier with just a five-pound note to his name and that she is the first person he has talked to in seventeen years without a guard standing watch. "I killed a woman," he adds. He tells Mary a few of the details. The woman was his wife's aunt. She had money his wife wanted, and his wife, who was pregnant, presented him with a very unpleasant choice: if he didn't kill her aunt, she would abort their unborn child. He was desperate, got drunk, and did the deed. Both he and his wife were convicted and imprisoned. His wife was killed during the Blitz, the German bombing campaign on London in World War II, but the baby, a daughter, was evacuated to Canada. It's his wish to join her there.

Then, the music they are listening to on the car radio is interrupted to deliver an urgent police message: a man, whose physical description closely matches Tom's, has escaped from a local prison and is at large. Tom quickly turns off the radio. Mary is quite upset, and Tom tells her that, if he makes her uncomfortable, all she needs to do is stop and he will get out. Mary dismisses the suggestion, saying she wouldn't think of doing that. In voiceover, however, we learn that Mary is quite upset and figures that, as long as she is behind the wheel and driving, she is safe. But, as she adds in voiceover, "I must find help. I must."

Later, she sees a small village and says that she needs to stop for petrol. She enters the store behind the petrol pump alone and calls the police. Tom soon follows, and she hangs up the phone without being able to tell an officer about her suspicious passenger. The two continue on.

Soon, she stops to pick up a hitchhiker, an American serviceman (Chuck Connors) enroute to his wedding with an Englishwoman, who lives locally. He offers Tom some whiskey, and, after Tom takes a couple of swigs, tells him to keep the flask. Tom continues to sip from it. A little later, the serviceman, now at his destination, asks to be dropped off. Reluctantly, Mary stops the car and lets him out. She and Tom drive on.

Later that night, it is clear that the whiskey has had an effect on Tom. Looking flushed and drunk, he begins to rhapsodize, "The first drink, the first time being close to a woman in seventeen years—I wondered what it would be like." He moves closer to Mary and puts his arm around her. "You know," he continues, "you have a beautiful figure. I noticed it the first time I saw you. You have beautiful hair ... high cheekbones ... lovely blue eyes."

Just then, they hear the siren from a police car coming up behind them. Instead of pulling them over as Mary hoped, however, the police pass them by, clearly on other business. Now frightened by Tom's advances, as well as all the other disturbing information she has heard, Mary, feeling quite desperate, decides to chase the police car in a quest for help. In her pursuit, she drives well over the speed limit and quite recklessly. Noticing this, the police pull her over. Delighted, Mary runs out to tell one of the officers that she thinks she has the escaped prisoner in her car. The officer says that her passenger can't be the escaped prisoner because he has just been caught and that they were on their way to collect him. The officer then gives Mary a ticket with a five-pound fine and a scolding about her reckless driving. Tom joins them, and the officer asks to see his release papers, which are in order.

At this point, Tom thinks that it will be better for Mary to continue on without him. Before he leaves, though, he asks her for a cigarette. She hands him a pack, he takes one, she lights it for him, and he returns the pack. They both wish each other well and he leaves. She reaches in the pack for a cigarette for herself and realizes that he has left her his five-pound note, all the money he had on him and just enough to pay the fine for her speeding ticket. "I've never," she says in voiceover, "been so ashamed in my life."

❖ ❖ ❖

Although "The Road to Edinburgh" might strike some as more of a simple suspense story than a noir, it is, especially after the mysterious Tom appears, filled with elements of a woman-in-distress noir. Throughout, the tension builds and Mary's fear mounts. In the end, however, we learn that her fear is unfounded. While not a pure noir ending, the story doesn't really end happily, either. Mary isn't robbed, raped, and/or killed, but she is mortified by the way she has acted towards this man.

Another noirish element in "The Road to Edinburgh" is Tom's own backstory. His wife's plan for him to kill her aunt for money, her threat to abort their unborn child if he doesn't, his decision to follow through with the deed, and the ultimate futility of the entire scheme is a story that goes about as deep into noir darkness as a story can go.

Finally, "The Road to Edinburgh" is peppered with several effective noir stylistic touches. One is voice-over narration we hear from Mary's point of view, which concisely tells us what she is thinking and why she is taking certain actions and, in the process, highlights her feelings of vulnerability and adds to the viewers' anxiety. A second is the decision to set the second half of the story at night, when Mary stops for petrol, picks up the hitchhiker, endures Tom's half-drunken advances, and recklessly chases the fast-moving police car. Because it's night, and darkness is pervasive, all of these scenes play with a greater intensity than they would if set during the day, further adding to viewer anxiety. A third, which Charles Lang may have influenced, is the way the character of Tom is filmed, especially in his initial scenes. At first, we only see him from the back, which gives him an aura of mystery. Then, when he is riding beside Mary in the car, he is much more dimly lit than she, adding to this aura. As viewers, we have to wonder about his man: is he someone who might present a threat to Mary, or not?

Overall, "The Road to Edinburgh," while not exceptional, is solidly crafted and engaging. Solt's original story is well-plotted and consistently suspenseful. Amateau, Lang, and their production teams, get the most out of the material. And both Crawford and British actor John Sutton (1908–1963), who had a prolific career in character parts for films and television from 1935 until his death, ably handle their key roles. Much as she had done in *Sudden Fear*, Crawford is excellent at portraying a so-called confident, world-wise woman who is actually more naïve and vulnerable than she realizes. Sutton, too, does a fine job of portraying a sad, haunted man who may also be dangerous.

❖ ❖ ❖

Unlike "The Road to Edinburgh," which had a much more involved backstory, the lead-up to Crawford's next effort for *General Electric Theater,* the deeply noir "Strange Witness," appears to be much simpler and more straightforward.

Tom Tryon's David (left) and Crawford's Ruth are adulterous lovers who confront Ruth's husband in "Strange Witness," a very dark noir story that first aired on CBS's *General Electric Theater* on March 23, 1958 (CBS/Photofest).

The story, originally titled "Eyewitness," is the work of Englishman John Whiting (1917–1963), who, while spending much of his professional life writing plays, television and film scripts, and criticism, was also an actor, who for a time worked in the legendary John Gielgud's stage company. The story was then adapted into a teleplay by another native Englishman, Gavin Lambert (1924–2005), who spent many years in Hollywood writing screen- and teleplays as well as fiction and non-fiction books, often about the film industry. A highlight of his screenwriting career came in 1962, when he received an Academy Award nomination for adapting Tennessee Williams' novella *The Roman Spring of Mrs. Stone* into the screenplay for the 1961 film of the same name starring Vivien Leigh.

Moving to production, Herschel Daugherty (1910–1993), a dialogue director and actor in movies who, in the 1950s, went on to specialize in directing for television, was assigned to direct the episode for Revue Productions, which produced *General Electric Playhouse.* "Strange Witness" was one of thirty-six episodes he directed for the series between 1955 and 1962. True to form, Crawford requested, and received, the services of cinematographer Charles Lang for the episode.

Rehearsals and filming took place in late February and early March 1958, and the episode was first aired on Crawford's birthday that year, March 23.

❖ ❖ ❖

"Strange Witness" opens in a darkened living room in a well-adorned New York City home as a mid-afternoon rain pours down outside. The camera pans around the room revealing, first, a fire burning in the fireplace and then a couple lying on the floor tightly embraced and kissing. Between kisses, the woman, Ruth (Crawford), and the man, David (Tom Tryon), discuss Ruth's husband John. David asks if she's ever asked John for a divorce outright. Ruth insists that John would never agree. When David presses her about this, Ruth tells him that if he isn't fully committed to the course of action the two have planned, then he should leave. "Hey, wait a minute," David says. He again begins to kiss her passionately.

A little later, and much to their surprise, they hear John (John McIntire) entering the house. Ruth immediately goes to another room to fix her makeup, and David remains. As John enters the room, David tells him that he's just dropped by to return some the books that he's borrowed. Ruth returns, and John, who clearly knows what's been going on, confronts the two about their affair. Ruth says she wants a divorce. When John mocks her, she counters, "If you don't give me a divorce, we'll kill you."

After John belittles David as well, David suddenly pulls a gun out of his pocket. When John smugly tells him to put the gun away, David shoots him. John falls to the floor dead, and, in the process, his drinking glass shatters.

Ruth is shocked and aghast, saying that she never knew that killing John would be like this and that she never really meant for it to happen. David tells her that that isn't what she had said only an hour before. The two agree, as they had originally planned, to wait until dark in order to remove and dispose of John's body without being noticed.

As Ruth fixes herself a drink, David goes through John's wallet for money and finds quite a bit. Ruth wonders if he will just take the money and leave her.

In the midst of this, a visitor comes calling. He is Chris Siddon (Sidney Blackmer), a lawyer friend of John's who is blind. Ruth and David don't answer the front door. Chris, however, notices that it is unlocked and comes in to get out of the rain. Ruth realizes that she will have to talk to him. Chris mentions that John had invited him over for a drink that afternoon, but Ruth says that John had been delayed. At the very least, she says, she can give him that drink.

She leads Chris into the living room and sits him in his favorite chair, which, coincidentally, is just a few feet away from John's body and the drinking glass that broke when David shot John. Then, for the next few minutes, Chris, notices things that aren't quite right: the sound of broken glass as Ruth steps on it when she goes to fix his drink; the smell of a cigarette that David, who is across the room, has lit; inconsistencies in Ruth's statements; and so on. Finally, though, he finishes his drink and leaves, seemingly satisfied with Ruth's explanations.

Several minutes later, however, Ruth's phone rings. It is Chris. He tells Ruth that John had lent him money to have an operation that would enable him to see again and that it was successful. (Apparently, he had intended to surprise John and Ruth with this news during their drink, but, because he could now see, he noticed both John's body and David in the room. Realizing that, if they knew that he was aware of John's murder, he might be murdered as well, he simply continued with his ruse.)

The scene cuts to a police station where Chris has just made the call. Chris tells an officer that Ruth and David are still at the murder scene. An officer immediately dispatches a patrol car to pick them up.

On the other end of the line an anxious David wants to know what Ruth has learned. Devastated, she tells him, "He can see! He can see!"

◆ ◆ ◆

While "The Road to Edinburgh" might be called noir-infused, "Strange Witness" is a thoroughbred noir whose credentials not even the most fanatical noir purist would question. The story, of course, is a riff on the familiar *Double Indemnity/The Postman Always Rings Twice* plotline, in which an adulterous couple scheme to kill the woman's husband to get his money, do the deed, and face the consequences. The twist is that Chris, the blind guest, is no longer blind and uses Ruth and David's ignorance of this both to assure his safety and possibly to get additional pertinent information on the situation before he goes to the police. It's a captivating mini-morality play.

Of special note, are several of its key elements.

One is the Whiting/Lambert dialogue, especially many of the testy (as well as astute and revealing) lines the embittered John delivers during his confrontation with Ruth and David. When David declares that he wants to marry Ruth, for example, John laughs and says, "Unfortunately, for you, that's impossible—at least not while she's married to me. You have a long wait, and stolen love dies early on the vine." A little later, he tells David, "Do you want to know how extravagant [Ruth] is? Every time we go on a trip, she buys up whatever country we're in." When Ruth demands a divorce, he fires back, "On what grounds? *Your* infidelity?" Then, focusing on what he sees as David's shortcomings, he says, "[Y]ou might try getting a job. You know, there are some men who work for their money. Or maybe that would be an insult to a skillful parasite like you."

A second key element that's quite well handled is the acting. After the murder, for example, Crawford does a fine job of showing how Ruth is truly struggling to cope both with the enormity and potential consequences of what she and David have done as well as with her growing doubts about David's love for, confidence in, and loyalty towards her. Warranting special mention, too, are superb performances by John McIntire as John and Sidney Blackmer as Chris. Both are on screen only briefly (McIntire for only five minutes and Blackmer for just six and a half), but both make the most of their moments, dominating the back-and-forth between the characters and providing formidable opposition to Ruth and David. Blackmer is especially fun to watch on a second viewing, once we know that Chris had been leading Ruth and David on all along. We see what we likely didn't see the first time—that Chris is getting a genuine sadistic thrill by watching Ruth and David squirm as he, supposedly ignorant of what's occurred, catches Ruth in lies, walks extremely close to John's body, and so on. The only weakness in the casting is Tom Tryon's David, the story's homme fatale. While the actor certainly has the looks to play the handsome gigolo, his wooden performance contributes to making David the least interesting of the drama's four characters.

Still another standout element is Charles Lang's noir cinematography. It cleverly creates a gloomy, foreboding, almost gothic-novel atmosphere in the darkened living room while simultaneously lighting Crawford (here in her early fifties) in ways that accentuate her allure.

"Strange Witness" is clearly no *Double Indemnity* or *The Postman Always Rings Twice*. Yet, more than six decades after it first aired on television, its solid crafting makes it quite entertaining and, for those who would like to know more about Crawford's overall contribution to noir, well worth watching.

◆ ◆ ◆

While many noir historians point to 1958, the year of Orson Welles' *Touch of Evil*, as the official close of the classic noir cycle, noir on television, unlike its big-screen counterpart, lost none of its momentum. In fact, it immediately began to grow and evolve. New shows took it in different directions and often brought greater sophistication to the presentation of noirish stories. The crime series *The Untouchables* (ABC, 1959–1963), for example, gave television noir a darker, grittier, more violent character. The detective series *77 Sunset Strip* (ABC, 1958–1963) gave it a certain "cool," and, according to television historian Allen Glover, excelled in its "melding of the sunshine and seediness" that, for many, excellently characterizes noir's favorite city, Los Angeles.[3] *The Twilight Zone* (CBS, 1959–1964), one of the most striking and innovative shows of the era, literally took television noir, as host Rod Serling said at the beginning of many episodes, into "another dimension: a dimension of sound, a dimension of sight, a dimension of mind."[4] The drama *The Fugitive* (ABC, 1963–1967), one of the outstanding drama series of the 1960s, gave the noir hero a more sympathetic, Job-like quality. And the quirky British import, *The Prisoner* (CBS, 1968), gave television noir decidedly Orwellian overtones.

If any of Crawford's television acting after "Strange Witness" qualifies as noir, it is perhaps her 1969 appearance on the pilot of Rod Serling's follow-up to *The Twilight Zone*, the often-macabre *Night Gallery* (NBC, 1969–1973). Directed by a twenty-two-year-old Steven Spielberg, the episode is called "Eyes." In it, Crawford plays Claudia Menlo, a

In "Eyes," one of three half-hour stories that made up the premiere episode of Rod Serling's *Night Gallery* series on November 8, 1969, Crawford plays Claudia Menlo, a blind but heartless woman who pays for a desperate man's eyes so she can see for just a few hours (NBC/Photofest).

rich, extremely selfish blind woman who pays a desperate man for his eyes so she can have them surgically implanted in her so she can have, if only for a few hours, the ability to see. Unfortunately, though, the brief time she has sight unexpectedly coincides with the massive New York City blackout that occurred on November 9, 1965. After a brief moment, when she sees the sun rise that morning and rejoices in the miracle of sight, her vision quickly fails. The experience unravels her. Enraged, she pounds on the window of her apartment, which overlooks the city. The glass cracks, and she falls to her death. It's a riveting performance, one of her best during her final professional years.

Conclusion

Aftermath and Appreciation

"It's wonderful to be a perfectionist..."
—Joan Crawford[1]

"Perfectionism like [Crawford's] is what made possible her genius onscreen.... You don't become a legend by skimping on the details."
—Sheila O'Malley[2]

By the late 1950s, viewer enthusiasm for noir and noirish films was ebbing. Noirs were still being made, of course, and the noir influence would remain in films, seep increasingly into television, and eventually evolve into what we now call "neo-noir."[3] But, in many respects, the original noir cycle had run its course. The world was moving on, and audience interests and preferences were changing.

For Joan Crawford, something similar was also occurring. Her life had changed in a big way in 1955 when, after a whirlwind courtship, she married Alfred Steele, the CEO of the Pepsi-Cola Company and the man she would refer to in her later years as the love of her life. Increasingly, she accompanied him on business trips and very quickly carved out a new role for herself as a goodwill ambassador for the company. To make time for this new role, she also cut back on her film and television work.

Much more was to happen in her professional life, however. On April 19, 1959, Steele died suddenly of a heart attack, and, soon afterwards, Crawford was elected to Pepsi-Cola's Board of Directors and took on a largely public relations role with the company, a role she would play until the early 1970s. In 1962, after a stretch of five years during which she had not played a lead role in a film,[4] she made the last of her legendary screen comebacks, teaming with long-time rival Bette Davis in Robert Aldrich's psychological horror-thriller *Whatever Happened to Baby*

195

Jane? The film was by far the biggest financial success of Crawford's career, making nearly ten times its production budget at the box office. It also earned five Academy Award nominations and netted Crawford a nomination in the Best Foreign Actress category by the British Academy of Film and Television Arts (BAFTA).

Despite its success, however, *Whatever Happened to Baby Jane?* failed to reignite Crawford's career to anywhere near the extent that *Mildred Pierce* or *Sudden Fear* had done. She did have some fine moments in films such as William Castle's *Straight-Jacket* (1964), an interesting but sometimes implausible low-budget horror thriller, and, of course, in "Eyes" (1969), the episode of Rod Serling's *Night Gallery* television series. For the most part, though, poorly written roles in low-budget films and television shows took their toll, and, although she did do a bit more television, she finished her film career with the embarrassingly bad science fiction horror film *Trog* in 1970.

One footnote to Crawford's *Trog* experience is a *New York Times* review, which, while roundly panning the film, gives her the backhanded compliment of being a "determined lady" who is "working grimly at her craft."[5] Although this clearly indicates a sad end to a long and distinguished career, it also shows a sincere respect for a professional who, no matter how bad a film's story or production values were, never gave anything less than her best to a project. Even in the most absurd and pathetic of situations, she was, to the end, fully committed to summoning the best within herself for a role.

During her final years, Crawford lived in New York, where she died in her sleep on May 10, 1977.

◈ ◈ ◈

Looking at the full arc of Crawford's forty-seven-year acting career, it can be useful to see it as breaking down into three distinct phases, each of which was roughly a decade and a half in length. The first, from the beginning of her career in 1925 to the early 1940s, is her mainly MGM period.[6] The second, from the early 1940s to the late 1950s (and overlapping a bit with her tenure at MGM), is her mainly noir period. And the third, from the late 1950s to 1972, her last acting appearance, can sadly, but accurately, be called her period of decline.

Although the mainly MGM phase can claim its share of hits and other highpoints, the mainly noir phase is the clear centerpiece of Crawford's professional life. This was when she created her indelible screen portrayals of Anna Holm, Mildred Pierce, Helen Wright, Louise Howell, Daisy Kenyon, Lane Bellamy, Ethel Whitehead, Myra Hudson, and Millicent Wetherby. This was also when she asserted herself more fully and forcefully into the entire filmmaking process—occasionally even functioning as a film's de facto producer—to achieve the high-quality results she strove for with an almost fanatical zeal. And this was the period for which her work is, and will continue to be, best remembered and most highly respected.

In the process of pursuing this high level of quality, Crawford also accomplished something else that is quite impressive: she helped extend the boundaries of film noir and, by doing so, helped expand the possibilities for noir content. Beginning with *A Woman's Face* and *Mildred Pierce* and continuing through to *Sudden Fear* and *Autumn Leaves*, she gave the normally male-dominated noir style a decidedly female slant. Her films focused on women who dealt with the trauma of having a badly scarred face, the challenges of being a single female parent trying to make ends meet in "a man's world," the nightmare of a severe mental illness, the horror of learning that her husband is plotting to kill her, and numerous other topics. In addition, these films treated these subjects in a distinctively Crawford way, usually in melodrama, a form especially well-suited to her own sensibilities and acting style, and usually with great sympathy for her female protagonists. It's intriguing that, unlike Barbara Stanwyck, Gloria Grahame, Claire Trevor, and other actresses more often identified with noir than she usually is, Crawford only rarely played the male-invented femme fatale. Instead, she focused more on conveying a variety of female experiences and perspectives that were drawn mostly from books and stories written by women and/or scripts co-written by women. Rather than sticking with the noir template, she helped to bend and stretch the template in ways that suited her interests and preoccupations as an artist. Like any other true auteur, she made her noir and noirish films her own.

❖ ❖ ❖

On May 22, 1977, just twelve days after Crawford's death, a tribute to her appeared in the *New York Times*. It was written by her old mentor and long-time friend, director George Cukor, and it ended with a very touching sentiment. "I thought Joan Crawford could never die," Cukor wrote. "Come to think of it, as long as celluloid holds together and the word Hollywood means anything to anyone, she never will."[7]

Perhaps more than any other aspect of her professional or personal life, the most compelling proof of this statement's validity are Crawford's finest noir films. As well as being the centerpiece of her career, they represent its crowning achievement, a main reason why her work continues to speak across the decades and will continue to resonate with audiences for a long time to come.

Chapter Notes

Introduction

1. The year of Crawford's birth has long been a subject of contention, with various accounts putting it anywhere between 1904 and 1908. In recent years, however, more widely accepted film information sources, such as the online database IMDb, have identified 1906 as the likely year.

2. Joan Cross, "Name Her and Win $1000," *Movie Weekly*, March 27, 1925.

3. Lawrence J. Quirk and William Schoell, *Joan Crawford: The Essential Biography* (Lexington: The University of Kentucky Press, 2002) p. 29.

4. Donald Spoto, *Possessed: The Life of Joan Crawford* (New York: HarperCollins, 2010) p. 47.

5. Quirk and Schoell, p. 29.

6. Langdon W. Post, review of *The Unknown, New York Evening World*, June 5, 1927.

7. Bob Thomas, *Joan Crawford* (New York: Simon and Schuster, 1978.)

8. Harry Brandt, "WAKE UP! Hollywood Producers," *The Hollywood Reporter*, May 4, 1938.

9. Joan Crawford (with Jane Kesner Ardmore), *A Portrait of Joan: An Autobiography* (Los Angeles: Graymalkin Media, 2017) p. 131.

10. "Screwball Comedy" is a kind of romantic comedy most popular in mid-1930s to early 1940s Hollywood movies that blends the wacky with the sophisticated. These films are usually characterized by social satire; comedic relief through zany, fast-paced and unusual events; sight gags; sarcasm; screwy plot twists or identity reversals; and precisely timed, fast-paced verbal dueling that features witty, sarcastic dialogue.

11. The term "film noir" was first used by Italian-French film critic Nino Frank in an article he had written for the socialist-leaning French film magazine *L'écran Français*, which was published in August 1946.

12. The term "hard-boiled" is often used to identify a tough, unsentimental style of American crime writing that brought a new tone of earthy realism or naturalism to the field of detective fiction. Hard-boiled fiction used graphic sex and violence, vivid but often sordid urban backgrounds, and fast-paced and slangy dialogue.

13. After first appearing in the visual arts and poetry at the beginning of the twentieth century and then in German silent films of the 1920s, expressionism has since become a staple in film noir and other film styles.

14. This subject will be discussed in more detail in Chapter 1 of this book.

15. "Anthology Series" is a term used to describe a kind of U.S. television series especially popular in the 1950s and 1960s, in which each episode consists of an individual, self-contained story and usually stars different actors. This differs from the more conventional television series, in which a regular cast of actors play the same characters in episode after episode.

16. Beginning in the 1920s, women were systematically shut out of many filmmaking professions in Hollywood,

especially film directing and cinematography. During the 1930s, for example, only one woman, Dorothy Arzner, worked regularly as a director. After her retirement in 1943, no woman directed until actress Ida Lupino began directing independent films in 1949.

17. Phillip Lopate, ed., *American Movie Critics: An Anthology from the Silents Until Now* (New York: The Library of America, 2006) p. 432.

18. Eddie Muller, "Introduction to presentation of *Possessed* (1947)," *Noir Alley*, Turner Classic Movies channel, June 6, 2021.

19. Spoto, p. 202.

20. Bob Thomas, Lawrence Quirk, and William Schoell.

Chapter 1

1. Donald Spoto, *Possessed: The Life of Joan Crawford* (New York: HarperCollins, 2010) p. 154.

2. Joan Crawford (with Jane Kesner Ardmore), *A Portrait of Joan: An Autobiography* (Los Angeles: Graymalkin Media, 2017) p. 128.

3. *Ibid.* p. 129.

4. *Ibid.*

5. Karli Lukas, "*A Woman's Face* (1941)," *Senses of Cinema*, Issue 8, July 2000. The term "mise-en-scene" is used to describe the setting of a scene in a play or a film. It refers to everything placed on the stage or in front of the camera, including people.

6. *Ibid.*

7. Sheila O'Malley, "*A Woman's Face* (1941)," *The Sheila Variations*, May 20, 2008, https://www.sheilaomalley.com/?p=8077.

8. *Ibid.*

Chapter 2

1. While the happy ending of *A Woman's Face* is not ideal in the noir universe, it doesn't, at least in this case, detract from the integrity of the story. Anna Holm sincerely wants to change and lead a more normal life, and, with the help of a few good people, she does. In many ways, she is like Jim Wilson, the

troubled cop Robert Ryan plays in Nicholas Ray's excellent 1951 noir *On Dangerous Ground*, who finds peace and perhaps love at the end of the film. Redemption is possible in noir; it just doesn't happen as often as it does in other kinds of stories.

2. Lawrence J. Quirk and William Schoell, *Joan Crawford: The Essential Biography* (Lexington: The University Press of Kentucky, 2002) p. 118.

3. Donald Spoto, *Possessed: The Life of Joan Crawford* (New York: Harper Collins, 2010) p. 171.

4. Rob Nixon and Stephanie Thames, "*Mildred Pierce* (1945)," Turner Classic Movies website.

5. *Ibid.*

6. *Ibid.*

7. *Ibid.*

8. *Ibid.*

9. Crawford's only previous appearance in a Warner Brothers film after signing her 1943 contract was a ninety-second cameo as herself in 1944's *Hollywood Canteen*.

10. Promotional poster for Mildred Pierce.

11. The Motion Picture Association of America (MPAA), or "Hays Office," was the film industry's self-censorship body and administered its much-despised Production Code, which determined what was morally appropriate for audiences to see. After several scandals had rocked the film industry in the 1920s, the MPAA tightened up its censorship. Later, the office relaxed its restrictions somewhat, leading to a relatively brief period between 1929 and 1934 when films openly tested the boundaries of propriety, breaking new ground in the depiction of sex, violence, and other controversial subject matter. This, in turn, led to a conservative backlash and, beginning on July 1, 1934, the strict enforcement of a restrictive code of morality for the next thirty years.

12. Rob Nixon, "*Mildred Pierce* (1945)," Turner Classic Movies website.

13. *Ibid.*

14. Message inscribed in a copy of the novel *Mildred Pierce* by James M. Cain on March 7, 1946, and sent to Crawford. (Mentioned in memo in the Warner Brothers Archives, University of Southern California.)

15. Joan Crawford (with Jane Kesner Ardmore), *A Portrait of Joan: An Autobiography* (Los Angeles: Graymalkin Media, 2017) p. 144.

Chapter 3

1. Anon. "The Music of *Humoresque*," Warner Brothers Entertainment, Inc., 2005 (Produced in association with Creative Domain.)

2. The 1946 film version of *Humoresque* differs from the original story in many ways. Among them: the violinist's family is not Jewish but vaguely ethnic, the action is updated from pre-World War I to the period between the early 1920s to the mid-1940s, the violinist goes on to have a very successful career, the character of the neurotic patroness and the ill-fated love affair are both added, and the violinist ultimately rejects his childhood girlfriend Gina for the patroness.

3. Joan Crawford (with Jane Kesner Ardmore), *A Portrait of Joan: An Autobiography*. (Los Angeles: Graymalkin Media, 2017.)

4. Frank Miller, "*Humoresque*," Turner Classic Movies website, January 17, 2003.

5. *Ibid.*

6. Mark A. Vieira, *Into the Dark: The Hidden World of Film Noir, 1941–1950* (Philadelphia: Running Press, 2016) p. 150.

7. *Variety* Staff, "*Humoresque*," *Variety*, December 31, 1945.

8. Bosley Crowther, "*Humoresque* at the Hollywood," *New York Times*, December 26, 1946.

9. Lawrence J. Quirk, *The Complete Films of Joan Crawford* (Secaucus, NJ: The Citadel Press, 1988) p. 163.

10. Anon, "The Music of *Humoresque*."

11. *Ibid.*

12. *Ibid.*

13. *Ibid.*

Chapter 4

1. To avoid confusion with the film she made in 1931 titled *Possessed*, Crawford asked Warner Brothers to change the title of the 1947 film to *The Secret*, but studio executives rejected the suggestion.

2. Lawrence J. Quirk and William Schoell, *Joan Crawford: The Essential Biography*. (Lexington: The University Press of Kentucky, 2002) p. 139.

3. Massey received his only Academy Award nomination for his work in *Abe Lincoln in Illinois*.

4. Quirk and Schoell, p. 146.

5. *Ibid.*

6. *Ibid.*

7. Lawrence Quirk, *The Complete Films of Joan Crawford* (Secaucus NJ: The Citadel Press, 1968) p. 166.

8. Herman Schoenfeld, "Film Reviews: *Possessed*," *Variety*, June 4, 1947, p. 14. The word "thesping" in the review is Schoenfeld's cute play on words, combining "thespian" and "acting."

9. Gwen Ihnat, "Joan Crawford Elevated Noir Into a Moving Portrait of Mental Illness," *AV Club*, August 20, 2020.

10. David Krauss, "*Possessed* (1947)," *Highdefdigest.com*, November 6, 2014.

11. *Ibid.*

12. Stephanie Thames, "*Possessed* (1947)," TCM website, July 28, 2003.

13. Ihnat.

Chapter 5

1. Charlotte Chandler, *Not the Girl Next Door: Joan Crawford, a Personal Biography* (New York: Simon & Schuster, 2008) p. 181.

2. *Ibid.*

3. *Ibid.*, p. 182.

4. T.M.P., "At the Roxy," *New York Times*, December 25, 1947.

5. Lawrence J. Quirk and William Schoell, *Joan Crawford: The Essential Biography* (Lexington: The University Press of Kentucky, 2002) p. 143.

6. Molly Haskell, "The Woman's Film," *American Movie Critics: An Anthology from the Silents Until Now*, Phillip Lopate, ed. (New York: The Library of America, 2006.)

7. Donald Spoto, *Possessed: The Life of Joan Crawford* (New York: Harper Collins, 2010) p. 191.

8. Dan Callahan, "Review: *Daisy Kenyon*," *Slant*, March 11, 2008.

9. Octavia Randolph, Review of the novel *Daisy Kenyon*, *Goodreads*, February 7, 2015.

10. Although he never practiced law, Preminger reportedly received a law degree from the University of Vienna.

11. Preminger's various battles with the enforcers of the film industry's Production Code in the 1940s and 1950s have become the stuff of Hollywood legend.

12. Zach Campbell, *DAISY KENYON* SYMPOSIUM, Panix.com, February 2004.

Chapter 6

1. Donald Spoto, *Possessed: The Life of Joan Crawford* (New York: Harper Collins, 2010) p. 200.

2. museumofdave, "It's Ted McCord's Movie," *This Woman Is Dangerous*, IMDb, February 17, 2004.

3. The name of the fictional Florida town of Truro in the novel was changed to Boldon for the film. Also, while the novel is set in Florida, the film is set in a fictional Southern state.

4. Herm., "*Flamingo Road*," *Variety*, April 6, 1949.

5. *Ibid.*

6. Bosley Crowther, "*Flamingo Road*, Starring Joan Crawford, Zachary Scott, New Bill at the Strand," *New York Times*, May 7, 1949.

7. James Quandt, "10 Great Films That Inspired Rainer Werner Fassbinder," British Film Institute website, April 6, 2017.

8. *Ibid.*

9. Dave Kehr, "*Flamingo Road*," *Chicago Reader*, October 26, 1985.

10. Alan Bacchus, "*Flamingo Road*," dailyfilmdose.com, Monday, 13 August 2007.

11. Anon. "The Crooked Road to Success: *Flamingo Road* (1949)," palewriter2.home.blog, October 23, 2020.

12. Donna Marie Nowak, *Just Joan: A Joan Crawford Appreciation* (Albany, Georgia: Bear Manor Media, April 25, 2015.)

13. Lawrence J. Quirk and William Schoell, *Joan Crawford: The Essential Biography* (Lexington: The University Press of Kentucky, 2002) p. 148.

14. Quandt.

Chapter 7

1. Lawrence J. Quirk, *The Complete Films of Joan Crawford* (Secaucus, NJ: The Citadel Press, 1988) p. 175.

2. Frank Miller, "*The Damned Don't Cry*," TCM, April 8, 2010.

3. Jeremiah Kipp, "Review: *The Damned Don't Cry*," *Slant Magazine*, June 12, 2005.

4. Eddie Muller, "Introduction to *The Damned Don't Cry*," *Noir Alley*, Turner Classic Movies Channel, October 14, 2018.

5. Donald Spoto, *Possessed: The Life of Joan Crawford* (New York: HarperCollins, 2010) p. 202.

6. *Ibid.*, p. 204.

7. *Ibid.*, p. 202.

8. *Ibid.*

9. Miller.

10. James Ellroy and Otto Penzler, editors, *The Best American Noir of the Century* (Boston and New York: Mariner Books, Houghton Mifflin Harcourt, 2011) p. xiii.

Chapter 8

1. Glenn Erickson, "*This Woman Is Dangerous*," *DVD Savant*, June 22, 2009.

Chapter 9

1. Joan Crawford (with Jane Kesner Ardmore), *A Portrait of Joan: An Autobiography* (Los Angeles: Graymalkin Media, 2017) p. 161.

2. Jim Bawden, "David Miller Remembered," thecolumnists.com, August 15, 2012.

3. Myrna Oliver, "Charles Lang: Won Oscar for *A Farewell to Arms*," *Los Angeles Times*, April 21, 1998.

4. Lawrence J. Quirk and William Schoell, *Joan Crawford: The Essential Biography* (Lexington: The University Press of Kentucky, 2002) p. 162. Crawford, incidentally, was not alone in her criticism of Palance's looks. The gossip columnist Hedda Hopper once remarked that the actor could play Frankenstein's monster "without make-up."

5. Bawden.

6. *Ibid.*

7. *Ibid.*

8. *Ibid.*

9. A.H.Weiler, *"Sudden Fear,* Cleverly Turned Melodrama, Is New Bill at Loew's State," *New York Times,* August 8, 1952.

10. Lawrence J. Quirk, *The Films of Joan Crawford* (Secaucus, NJ: The Citadel Press, 1968) p. 184.

11. Farran Smith Nehme, *"Sudden Fear* (1952)," *filmcomment.com,* August 11, 2016.

12. Sheila O'Malley, "World-Class Acting: On Joan Crawford and *Sudden Fear,"* *rogerebert.com,* March 27, 2017.

13. *Ibid.*

14. Nehme.

15. Martin Scorsese, "The Martin Scorsese Presentation of *Johnny Guitar,"* Republic Pictures (video), September 29, 2012.

16. Donald Spoto, *Possessed: The Life of Joan Crawford* (New York: HarperCollins, 2010) pp. 223–224.

17. For more information on the noir western, I would recommend a previous book of mine, *The Noir Western: Darkness on the Range, 1943–1962* (McFarland, 2015). I know this seems like shameless self-promotion, but this book is one of the very few in-depth explorations into this subject.

18. Eddie Muller, "Noir or Not?— *Johnny Guitar"* (1954), *Noir Alley,* Turner Classic Movies channel, January 11, 2023.

Chapter 10

1. Angelica Jade Bastien, "The Feminine Grotesque: On the Warped Legacy of Joan Crawford," *rogerebert.com,* May 14, 2016.

2. Donald Spoto, *Possessed: The Life of Joan Crawford* (New York: HarperCollins, 2010) p. 227.

3. Bosley Crowther, "Screen: Mild Mystery, *Female on the Beach,* Bows at the Palace" *New York Times,* August 20, 1955, p. 20.

4. Spoto, p. 229.

5. Bosley Crowther, "The Screen: *Queen Bee,* New Film at Loew's State Drones Along," *New York Times,* November 23, 1955.

6. Shane Estes, *"Female on the Beach* (1955)," *oldmoviesaregreat.wordpress. com,* March 26, 2017.

7. David Krauss, "From Silents to the Seventies: *Female on the Beach,"* *High-Def Digest,* February 19, 2019.

8. Spoto, p. 227.

9. Ken Anderson, *"QUEEN BEE* 1955," *lecinemadreams.blogspot.com,* March 31, 2013.

Chapter 11

1. Other directors who could be counted as important mentors for Crawford are Clarence Brown and Frank Borzage at MGM, Vincent Sherman at Warner Brothers, Otto Preminger, and David Miller.

2. Jacques Prevert (original lyrics), Johnny Mercer (English translation), Lyrics to "Autumn Leaves."

3. Edward T. Arnold and Eugene L. Miller, *The Films and Career of Robert Aldrich* (Knoxville: University of Tennessee Press, 1986), pp. 6–9.

4. Nathanael Hood, "The Promise of Recovery: Close-Up on Robert Aldrich's *Autumn Leaves,"* *MUBI.com,* October 24, 2017.

5. "Soap Opera" is a term originally given to ongoing radio and then television dramas that are often melodramatic in nature. This particular term was coined because these programs were often sponsored by soap companies. Eventually, soap opera also became a term to describe any kind of overwrought drama.

6. Jeff Stafford, *"Autumn Leaves,"* Turner Classic Movies website, April 13, 2007.

7. The U.S. House of Representatives Un-American Activities Committee (HUAC) hearings, which investigated allegations of Communist infiltration into the military, government, film industry, and other U.S. institutions, were at their height during the late 1940s and early 1950s. Because movies were considered to have such a pervasive influence on U.S. audiences, the film industry was a major target. Several film-industry figures, most notably a group of writers called "the Hollywood 10," served jail

time for refusing to answer questions meant to incriminate them or colleagues. Numerous others were "blacklisted," or basically denied work, from the late 1940s until the 1960s. To make money, many writers worked with "fronts," sympathetic but not blacklisted colleagues, who sold their scripts and then split the fee with the actual writers. Numerous books and articles have been written about this subject.

8. Jean Rouverol, *Refugees from Hollywood: A Journal of the Blacklist Years* (Albuquerque: University of New Mexico Press, 2000.)

9. Lawrence J. Quirk and William Schoell, *Joan Crawford: The Essential Biography* (Lexington: The University Press of Kentucky, 2002) p. 194.

10. Gene Feldman and Suzette Winter (directors/writers), *Joan Crawford: Always the Star, Biography*, Arts & Entertainment Channel, 1996.

11. Stafford.

12. *Ibid.*

13. Lawrence J. Quirk, *The Complete Films of Joan Crawford.* (Secaucus, NJ: The Citadel Press, 1988) p. 202.

14. *Ibid.*

15. Dan Callahan, "Review: *Autumn Leaves*," *Slant Magazine*, June 16, 2004.

16. *Ibid.*

17. Hood.

18. *Ibid.*

19. Callahan.

20. *Ibid.*

21. Hood.

22. Stafford.

23. After filming several scenes of *Hush, Hush, Sweet Charlotte*, Crawford cited health problems and left the production. Actress Olivia de Havilland stepped in to play Crawford's role.

24. "Psycho-biddy" and "hagsploitation" are nicknames given to describe both *Baby Jane* and numerous horror films it spawned that were popular in the 1960s and 1970s. Like *Baby Jane*, these films exploited the star name recognition of aging Hollywood actresses. Other than Crawford and Davis, those who starred in them included (among others) Olivia de Havilland, Barbara Stanwyck, Ruth Gordon, Geraldine Page, and Shelly Winters.

25. David Thomson, "Iconoclasts/

Robert Aldrich: Going for Broke," *DGA Quarterly*, Spring 2010.

26. Donald Spoto, *Possessed: The Life of Joan Crawford* (New York: HarperCollins, 2010) p. 240.

Chapter 12

1. The numbers here are quite compelling. According to research firm Statista, by 1960, ninety percent of U.S. households, a total of about 145 million people, had daily access to television. According to the U.S. Census Bureau, that same year, weekly moviegoing attendance was about forty million people, down from about ninety million in 1946.

2. Bryan Johnson, "Professional Television Appearances (1952–1959)" *The Concluding Chapter of Crawford*, theconcludingchapterofcrawford.com. (This is a website Johnson administers, which has done considerable research on Crawford's life and work from the 1950s to the 1970s, often calling out and correcting longstanding misinformation.)

3. *Allan Glover, TV Noir: Dark Drama on the Small Screen* (New York: Abrams, 2019) p. 106.

4. These words are part of one of what would ultimately be several introductions, all fairly similar and all read by Serling, over the course of *The Twilight Zone's* five-year run.

Conclusion

1. Joan Crawford, Interview for the British Broadcasting Corporation, December 1966.

2. Sheila O'Malley, "World-Class Acting: On Joan Crawford and *Sudden Fear*," *rogerebert.com*, March 27, 2017.

3. The term "neo-noir" can be defined as noir with a more contemporary sensibility, which may include story elements such as more graphic depictions of violence and a more naturalistic dialogue.

4. In 1959, Crawford did play a relatively small supporting role in the film drama, *The Best of Everything*, which was produced and directed by two of her film

noir collaborators, Jerry Wald and Jean Negulesco.

5. Anon., "*Trog* and *Taste Blood of Dracula*," *New York Times*, October 29, 1970.

6. During this time, MGM also "loaned" Crawford to other studios to work on three films.

7. George Cukor, "She Was Consistently Joan Crawford, Star," *New York Times*, May 22, 1977.

Bibliography

Anderson, Ken. "*QUEEN BEE*, 1955." lecinemadreams.blogspot.com. March 31, 2013.

Anderson, Melissa. "Noir-Inflected *Sudden Fear* Is an Underseen Classic Waiting to Be Rediscovered." *The Village Voice.* August 10, 2016.

Anon. "The Crooked Road to Success: *Flamingo Road* (1949)." palewriter2.home.blog. October 23, 2020.

_____. "Film Reviews: *Johnny Guitar*," *Variety,* May 5, 1954.

_____. "*Flamingo Road* (1949)." IMDb.

_____. "*Humoresque* and the Apotheosis of Joan Crawford." Grand Old Movies. January 11, 2011.

_____. "Joan Crawford Wins Best Actress for *Mildred Pierce* 1946." *Be Kind Rewind.* YouTube. November 19, 2018.

_____. "The Music of *Humoresque*," Warner Brothers Entertainment, Inc. 2005. (Produced in association with Creative Domain.)

Bacchus, Alan. "*Flamingo Road.*" dailyfilmdose.com. August 13, 2007.

Bastien, Angelica Jade. "The Feminine Grotesque: On the Warped Legacy of Joan Crawford." *rogerebert.com.* May 14, 2016.

Bawden, Jim. "David Miller Remembered." thecolumnists.com. August 15, 2012.

Bitel, Anton. "Why *Johnny Guitar* Remains a Superior Subversive Western." *Little White Lies.* September 20, 2021.

Brody, Richard. "The Front Row: *Autumn Leaves.*" *The New Yorker.* March 22, 2017.

_____. "*Johnny Guitar*: One of the Greatest Westerns and the Furthest Extreme of the Hollywood System." *The New Yorker.* August 30, 2022.

Cahall, Gary. "*Female on the Beach* (1955): Life's a Beach, and So Is Joan." *Movie Fan-Fare.* June 9, 2015.

Cain, James M. *Mildred Pierce.* New York: Vintage Books, 1941, 1989.

Callahan, Dan. "Review: *Autumn Leaves.*" *Slant Magazine.* June 16, 2004.

_____. "Review: *Daisy Kenyon.*" *Slant Magazine.* March 11, 2008.

_____. "Review: *Humoresque.*" *Slant Magazine.* June 14, 2005.

Campbell, Zach. *DAISY KENYON* SYMPOSIUM. Panix.com. February 2004.

Chandler, Charlotte. *Not the Girl Next Door: Joan Crawford, a Personal Biography.* New York: Simon & Schuster. 2008.

Crawford, Joan (with Jane Kesner Ardmore). *My Way of Life.* Los Angeles: Graymalkin Media. 2017.

_____. *A Portrait of Joan: An Autobiography.* Los Angeles: Graymalkin Media. 2017.

Crowther, Bosley. "Screen: *Flamingo Road*, Starring Joan Crawford, Zachary Scott, New Bill at the Strand." *New York Times.* May 7, 1949.

_____. "Screen: A New Agonizer; Joan Crawford Stars in *Autumn Leaves.*" *New York Times.* August 2, 1956.

_____. "Screen: *Johnny Guitar* Opens at the Mayfair." *New York Times.* May 28, 1954.

_____. "Screen: Mild Mystery. *Female on the Beach,* Bows at the Palace." *New York Times.* August 20, 1955, p. 20.

_____. "Screen: *Queen Bee,* New Film at Loew's State Drones Along," *New York Times.* November 23, 1955.

Custen, George F. *Twentieth Century's Fox: Darryl F. Zanuck and the Culture of Hollywood.* New York: Basic Books. 1997.

Ebert, Roger. "I Never Met a Woman Who Was More Man." rogerebert.com. May 8, 2008.

Edwards, Richard. "Seven Decades of TV Noir: A Short Introduction." remixhumanities.wordpress.com. May 10, 2013.

Erickson, Glenn. "*This Woman Is Dangerous.*" *DVD Savant.* June 22, 2009.

Estes, Shane. "*Female on the Beach* (1955)." oldmoviesaregreat.wordpress.com. March 26, 2017.

Feldman, Gene, and Winter, Suzette (directors/writers). *Joan Crawford: Always the Star* (Film biography). Arts & Entertainment Channel. 1996.

Fitzgerald, Peter. *Joan Crawford: The Ultimate Movie Star.* Turner Classic Movies. 2002.

Glover, Allen. *TV Noir: Dark Drama on the Small Screen.* New York: Harry N. Abrams, Publisher. 2019.

Herm. "*Flamingo Road.*" *Variety.* April 6, 1949.

Hood, Nathanael. "The Promise of Recovery: Close-Up on Robert Aldrich's *Autumn Leaves.*" MUBI.com. October 24, 2017.

Ihnat, Gwen. "Joan Crawford Elevated Noir Into a Moving Portrait of Mental Illness." AV Club. August 20, 2020.

Johnson, Bryan. "Professional Television Appearances (1952–1959)." The Concluding Chapter of Crawford website.

Kehr, Dave. "*Flamingo Road.*" *Chicago Reader.* October 26, 1985.

Krauss, David. "From Silents to the Seventies: *Female on the Beach.*" *High-Def Digest.* February 19, 2019.

_____. "*Possessed* (1947)." *High-Def-Digest.* November 6, 2014.

Lloyd, Christopher. "Reeling Backward: *Sudden Fear* (1952)." *Film Yap.* January 27, 2021.

LoBianco, Lorraine. "*Sudden Fear.*" Turner Classic Movies website. November 14, 2016.

Lopate, Phillip ed. *American Movie Critics: An Anthology from the Silents Until Now.* New York: The Library of America. 2006.

Loughrey, Clarisse. "Joan Crawford: A Master of Reinvention." *The Independent (UK).* August 17, 2018.

Lukas, Karli. "*A Woman's Face* (1941)." *Senses of Cinema,* Issue 8. July 2000.

Lyons, Arthur. *Death on the Cheap: The Lost B Movies of Film Noir!* Boston: Da Capo Press. 2000.

McGilligan, Patrick. *Nicholas Ray: The Glorious Failure of an American Director.* New York: HarperCollins. 2011.

_____. "Philip Yordan: The Ghosts and the Screenwriter." *Los Angeles Times.* June 26, 1988.

Miller, Frank. "*Humoresque.*" Turner Classic Movies website. January 17, 2003.

Muller, Eddie. "Introduction to Presentation of *Possessed* (1947)." *Noir Alley,* Turner Classic Movies channel. June 6, 2021.

_____. "Noir or Not? - *Johnny Guitar*" (1954). *Noir Alley,* Turner Classic Movies channel. January 11, 2023.

museumofdave. "It's Ted McCord's Movie." IMDb. *This Woman Is Dangerous.* February 17, 2004.

Nehme, Farran Smith. "*Sudden Fear* (1952)." filmcomment.com. August 11, 2016.

Nixon, Rob and Thames, Stephanie. "*Mildred Pierce* (1945)." Turner Classic Movies website.

Oliver, Myrna. "Charles Lang: Won Oscar for *A Farewell to Arms.*" *Los Angeles Times.* April 21, 1998.

O'Malley, Sheila. "*A Woman's Face* (1941)." *The Sheila Variations.* May 20, 2008.

_____. "World-Class Acting: On Joan Crawford and *Sudden Fear*." rogerebert.com. March 27, 2017.

Pronovost, Virginie. "Celebrating Joan Crawford with *Autumn Leaves*." thewonderful-worldofcinema.wordpress.com. July 30, 2016.

Quandt, James. "10 Great Films That Inspired Rainer Werner Fassbinder." British Film Institute website. April 6, 2017.

Quirk, Lawrence J. *The Complete Films of Joan Crawford*. Secaucus, NJ: The Citadel Press. 1988.

Quirk, Lawrence J., and Schoell, William. *Joan Crawford: The Essential Biography*. Lexington: The University Press of Kentucky. 2002.

Rouverol, Jean. *Refugees from Hollywood: A Journal of the Blacklist Years*. Albuquerque: University of New Mexico Press. 2000.

Sanjek, David. "*Johnny Guitar*." *Senses of Cinema*. June 2011.

Schlesinger, Michael. "*Johnny Guitar*." U.S. Library of Congress website. Undated.

Schoenfeld, Herman. "Film Reviews: *Possessed*." *Variety*. June 4, 1947.

Scorsese, Martin. "The Martin Scorsese Presentation of *Johnny Guitar*." Republic Pictures video. September 29, 2012.

Shelby, Spencer. *Dark City: The Film Noir*. Jefferson, NC: McFarland. 1984.

Smith, Imogen Sara. "*Mildred Pierce*: A Woman's Work," Criterion, February 20, 2017.

Solem-Pfeifer, Chance. "*Johnny Guitar* (1954)." *Willamette Week*. April 18, 2023.

Soltes, John. "*Sudden Fear* Features Joan Crawford, Jack Palance in Noir Classic." *Hollywood Soapbox*. August 17, 2016.

Somer, Eric. "*Possessed* (1947)." Filmnoirboard.blogspot.com. April 19, 2015.

Spoto, Donald. *Possessed: The Life of Joan Crawford*. New York: HarperCollins. 2010.

Stafford, Jeff. "*Autumn Leaves*." Turner Classic Movies website. April 13, 2007.

Thames, Stephanie. "*Possessed* (1947)." Turner Classic Movies website. July 28, 2003.

Thomas, Bob. *Joan Crawford: An Autobiography*. New York: Simon & Schuster. 1978.

Thomson, David. "Iconoclasts/Robert Aldrich: Going for Broke." *DGA Quarterly*. Spring 2010.

T.M.P. "At the Roxy." *New York Times*. December 25, 1947.

Variety Staff. "*Humoresque*." *Variety*. Dec 31, 1945.

Vieira, Mark A. *Into the Dark: The Hidden World of Film Noir, 1941–1950*. Philadelphia: Running Press. 2016.

Weiler, A.H. "*Sudden Fear*, Cleverly Turned Melodrama, Is New Bill at Loew's State." *New York Times*. August 8, 1952.

Index

Numbers in **bold italics** refer to pages with illustrations.